The Story of My]

Georg Ebers

Alpha Editions

This edition published in 2024

ISBN : 9789362920157

Design and Setting By
Alpha Editions
www.alphaedis.com
Email - info@alphaedis.com

As per information held with us this book is in Public Domain.
This book is a reproduction of an important historical work. Alpha Editions uses the best technology to reproduce historical work in the same manner it was first published to preserve its original nature. Any marks or number seen are left intentionally to preserve its true form.

Contents

INTRODUCTION. ....- 1 -

CHAPTER I. GLANCING BACKWARD. ....- 3 -

CHAPTER II. MY EARLIEST CHILDHOOD..- 8 -

CHAPTER III. ON FESTAL DAYS ....- 16 -

CHAPTER IV. THE JOURNEY TO HOLLAND TO ATTEND THE GOLDEN WEDDING. ....- 22 -

CHAPTER V. LENNESTRASSE.— LENNE.—EARLY IMPRESSIONS. ....- 26 -

CHAPTER VI. MY INTRODUCTION TO ART, AND ACQUAINTANCES GREAT AND SMALL IN THE LENNESTRASSE. ....- 35 -

CHAPTER VII. WHAT A BERLIN CHILD ENJOYED ON THE SPREE AND AT HIS GRANDMOTHER'S IN DRESDEN. ....- 44 -

CHAPTER VIII. THE REVOLUTIONARY PERIOD BEFORE THE REVOLUTION ....- 51 -

CHAPTER IX. THE EIGHTEENTH OF MARCH. ....- 61 -

CHAPTER X. AFTER THE NIGHT OF REVOLUTION...- 65 -

CHAPTER XI. IN KEILHAU ....- 72 -

CHAPTER XII. FRIEDRICH FROEBEL'S IDEAL OF EDUCATION. ....- 83 -

CHAPTER XIII. THE FOUNDERS OF THE KEILHAU INSTITUTE, AND A GLIMPSE AT THE HISTORY OF THE SCHOOL..- 93 -

CHAPTER XIV. RUDOLSTADT..- 109 -

CHAPTER XV. SUMMER PLEASURES AND RAMBLES ....- 114 -

CHAPTER XVI. AUTUMN, WINTER, EASTER AND DEPARTURE ....- 121 -

CHAPTER XVII. THE GYMNASIUM AND THE FIRST PERIOD OF UNIVERSITY LIFE. ....- 130 -

CHAPTER XVIII. THE TIME OF EFFERVESCENCE, AND MY SCHOOL MATES. ....- 135 -

CHAPTER XIX. A ROMANCE WHICH REALLY HAPPENED. ....- 142 -

CHAPTER XX. AT THE QUEDLINBURG GYMNASIUM ....- 152 -

CHAPTER XXI. AT THE UNIVERSITY. ....- 156 -

CHAPTER XXII. THE SHIPWRECK ....- 166 -

CHAPTER XXIII. THE HARDEST TIME
IN THE SCHOOL OF LIFE. ....- 173 -

CHAPTER XXIV. THE
APPRENTICESHIP..- 177 -

CHAPTER XXV. THE SUMMERS OF
MY CONVALESCENCE..- 187 -

CHAPTER XXVI. CONTINUANCE OF
CONVALESCENCE AND THE FIRST
NOVEL. ....- 198 -

INTRODUCTION.

In this volume, which has all the literary charm and deftness of character drawing that distinguish his novels, Dr. Ebers has told the story of his growth from childhood to maturity, when the loss of his health forced the turbulent student to lead a quieter life, and inclination led him to begin his Egyptian studies, which resulted, first of all, in the writing of An Egyptian Princess, then in his travels in the land of the Pharaohs and the discovery of the Ebers Papyrus (the treatise on medicine dating from the second century B.C.), and finally in the series of brilliant historical novels that has borne his name to the corners of the earth and promises to keep it green forever.

This autobiography carries the reader from 1837, the year of Dr. Ebers's birth in Berlin, to 1863, when An Egyptian Princess was finished. The subsequent events of his life were outwardly calm, as befits the existence of a great scientist and busy romancer, whose fecund fancy was based upon a groundwork of minute historical research.

Dr. Ebers attracted the attention of the learned world by his treatise on Egypt and the Book of Moses, which brought him a professorship at his university, Gottingen, in 1864, the year following the close of this autobiography. His marriage to the daughter of a burgomaster of Riga took place soon afterward. During the long years of their union Mrs. Ebers was his active helpmate, many of the business details relating to his works and their American and English editions being transacted by her.

After his first visit to Egypt, Ebers was called to the University of Leipsic to fill the chair of Egyptology. He went again to Egypt in 1872, and in the course of his excavations at Thebes unearthed the Ebers Papyrus already referred to, which established his name among the leaders of what was then still a new science, whose foundations had been laid by Champollion in 1821.

Ebers continued to occupy his chair at the Leipsic University, but, while fulfilling admirably the many duties of a German professorship, he found time to write several of his novels. Uarda was published in 1876, twelve years after the appearance of An Egyptian Princess, to be followed in quick succession by Homo Sum, The Sisters, The Emperor, and all that long line of brilliant pictures of antiquity. He began his series of tales of the middle ages and the dawn of the modern era in 1881 with The Burgomaster's Wife. In 1889 the precarious state of his health forced him to resign his chair at the university.

Notwithstanding his sufferings and the obstacles they placed in his path, he continued his wonderful intellectual activity until the end. His last novel,

Arachne, was issued but a short time before his death, which took place on August 7, 1898, at the Villa Ebers, in Tutzing, on the Starenberg Lake, near Munich, where most of his later life was spent. The monument erected to his memory by his own indefatigable activity consists of sixteen novels, all of them of perennial value to historical students, as well as of ever-fresh charm to lovers of fiction, many treatises on his chosen branch of learning, two great works of reference on Egypt and Palestine, and short stories, fairy tales, and biographies.

The Story of my Life is characterized by a captivating freshness. Ebers was born under a lucky star, and the pictures of his early home life, his restless student days at that romantic old seat of learning, Gottingen, are bright, vivacious, and full of colour. The biographer, historian, and educator shows himself in places, especially in the sketches of the brothers Grimm, and of Froebel, at whose institute, Keilhau, Ebers received the foundation of his education. His discussion of Froebel's method and of that of his predecessor, Pestalozzi, is full of interest, because written with enthusiasm and understanding. He was a good German, in the largest sense of the word, and this trait, too, is brought forward in his reminiscences of the turbulent days of 1848 in Berlin.

The story of Dr. Ebers's early life was worth the telling, and he has told it himself, as no one else could tell it, with all the consummate skill of his perfected craftsmanship, with all the reverent love of an admiring son, and with all the happy exuberance of a careless youth remembered in all its brightness in the years of his maturity. Finally, the book teaches a beautiful lesson of fortitude in adversity, of suffering patiently borne and valiantly overcome by a spirit that, greatly gifted by Nature, exercised its strength until the thin silver lining illuminated the apparently impenetrable blackness of the cloud that overhung Georg Moritz Ebers's useful and successful life.

CHAPTER I.
GLANCING BACKWARD.

Though I was born in Berlin, it was also in the country. True, it was fifty-five years ago; for my birthday was March 1, 1837, and at that time the house—[No. 4 Thiergartenstrasse]—where I slept and played during the first years of my childhood possessed, besides a field and a meadow, an orchard and dense shrubbery, even a hill and a pond. Three big horses, the property of the owner of our residence, stood in the stable, and the lowing of a cow, usually an unfamiliar sound to Berlin children, blended with my earliest recollections.

The Thiergartenstrasse—along which in those days on sunny mornings, a throng of people on foot, on horseback, and in carriages constantly moved to and fro—ran past the front of these spacious grounds, whose rear was bounded by a piece of water then called the "Schafgraben," and which, spite of the duckweed that covered it with a dark-green network of leafage, was used for boating in light skiffs.

Now a strongly built wall of masonry lines the banks of this ditch, which has been transformed into a deep canal bordered by the handsome houses of the Konigin Augustastrasse, and along which pass countless heavily laden barges called by the Berliners "Zillen."

The land where I played in my childhood has long been occupied by the Matthaikirche, the pretty street which bears the same name, and a portion of Konigin Augustastrasse, but the house which we occupied and its larger neighbour are still surrounded by a fine garden.

This was an Eden for city children, and my mother had chosen it because she beheld it in imagination flowing with the true Garden of Paradise rivers of health and freedom for her little ones.

My father died on the 14th of February, 1837, and on the 1st of March of the same year I was born, a fortnight after the death of the man in whom my mother was bereft of both husband and lover. So I am what is termed a "posthumous" child. This is certainly a sorrowful fate; but though there were many hours, especially in the later years of my life, in which I longed for a father, it often seemed to me a noble destiny and one worthy of the deepest gratitude to have been appointed, from the first moment of my existence, to one of the happiest tasks, that of consolation and cheer.

It was to soothe a mother's heartbreak that I came in the saddest hours of her life, and, though my locks are now grey, I have not forgotten the joyful moments in which that dear mother hugged her fatherless little one, and among other pet names called him her "comfort child."

She told me also that posthumous children were always Fortune's favorites, and in her wise, loving way strove to make me early familiar with the thought that God always held in his special keeping those children whose fathers he had taken before their birth. This confidence accompanied me through all my after life.

As I have said, it was long before I became aware that I lacked anything, especially any blessing so great as a father's faithful love and care; and when life showed to me also a stern face and imposed heavy burdens, my courage was strengthened by my happy confidence that I was one of Fortune's favorites, as others are buoyed up by their firm faith in their "star."

When the time at last came that I longed to express the emotions of my soul in verse, I embodied my mother's prediction in the lines:

> The child who first beholds the light of day
>
> After his father's eyes are closed for aye,
>
> Fortune will guard from every threatening ill,
>
> For God himself a father's place will fill.

People often told me that as the youngest, the nestling, I was my mother's "spoiled child"; but if anything spoiled me it certainly was not that. No child ever yet received too many tokens of love from a sensible mother; and, thank Heaven, the word applied to mine. Fate had summoned her to be both father and mother to me and my four brothers and sisters-one little brother, her second child, had died in infancy—and she proved equal to the task. Everything good which was and is ours we owe to her, and her influence over us all, and especially over me, who was afterward permitted to live longest in close relations with her, was so great and so decisive, that strangers would only half understand these stories of my childhood unless I gave a fuller description of her.

These details are intended particularly for my children, my brothers and sisters, and the dear ones connected with our family by ties of blood and friendship, but I see no reason for not making them also accessible to wider circles. There has been no lack of requests from friends that I should write them, and many of those who listen willingly when I tell romances will doubtless also be glad to learn something concerning the life of the fabulist, who, however, in these records intends to silence imagination and adhere rigidly to the motto of his later life, "To be truthful in love."

My mother's likeness as a young woman accompanies these pages, and must spare me the task of describing her appearance. It was copied from the life-size portrait completed for the young husband by Schadow just prior to his appointment as head of the Dusseldorf Academy of Art, and now in the possession of my brother, Dr. Martin Ebers of Berlin. Unfortunately, our copy lacks the colouring; and the dress of the original, which shows the whole figure, confirms the experience of the error committed in faithfully reproducing the fashion of the day in portraits intended for future generations. It never fully satisfied me; for it very inadequately reproduces what was especially precious to us in our mother and lent her so great a charm—her feminine grace, and the tenderness of heart so winningly expressed in her soft blue eyes.

No one could help pronouncing her beautiful; but to me she was at once the fairest and the best of women, and if I make the suffering Stephanus in Homo Sum say, "For every child his own mother is the best mother," mine certainly was to me. My heart rejoiced when I perceived that every one shared this appreciation. At the time of my birth she was thirty-five, and, as I have heard from many old acquaintances, in the full glow of her beauty.

My father had been one of the Berlin gentlemen to whose spirit of self-sacrifice and taste for art the Konigstadt Theater owed its prosperity, and was thus brought into intimate relations with Carl von Holtei, who worked for its stage both as dramatist and actor. When, as a young professor, I told the grey-haired author in my mother's name something which could not fail to afford him pleasure, I received the most eager assent to my query whether he still remembered her. "How I thank your admirable mother for inducing you to write!" ran the letter. "Only I must enter a protest against your first lines, suggesting that I might have forgotten her. I forget the beautiful, gentle, clever, steadfast woman who (to quote Shakespeare's words) 'came adorned hither like sweet May,' and, stricken by the hardest blows so soon after her entrance into her new life, gloriously endured every trial of fate to become the fairest bride, the noblest wife, most admirable widow, and most faithful mother! No, my young unknown friend, I have far too much with which to reproach myself, have brought from the conflicts of a changeful life a lacerated heart, but I have never reached the point where that heart ceased to cherish Fanny Ebers among the most sacred memories of my chequered career. How often her loved image appears before me when, in lonely twilight hours, I recall the past!"

Yes, Fate early afforded my mother an opportunity to test her character. The city where shortly before my birth she became a widow was not her native place. My father had met her in Holland, when he was scarcely more than a beardless youth. The letter informing his relatives that he had determined not to give up the girl his heart had chosen was not regarded seriously in Berlin; but when the lover, with rare pertinacity, clung to his resolve, they began to feel anxious. The eldest son of one of the richest families in the city, a youth of nineteen, wished to bind himself for life—and to a foreigner—a total stranger.

My mother often told us that her father, too, refused to listen to the young suitor, and how, during that time of conflict, while she was with her family at Scheveningen, a travelling carriage drawn by four horses stopped one day before her parents' unpretending house. From this coach descended the future mother-in-law. She had come to see the paragon of whom her son had written so enthusiastically, and to learn whether it would be possible to yield to the youth's urgent desire to establish a household of his own. And she did find it possible; for the girl's rare beauty and grace speedily won the heart of the anxious woman who had really come to separate the lovers. True, they were required to wait a few years to test the sincerity of their affection. But it withstood the proof, and the young man, who had been sent to Bordeaux to acquire in a commercial house the ability to manage his father's banking business, did not hesitate an instant when his beautiful fiancee caught the smallpox and wrote that her smooth face would probably be disfigured by the malignant disease, but answered that what he loved was not only her beauty but the purity and goodness of her tender heart.

This had been a severe test, and it was to be rewarded: not the smallest scar remained to recall the illness. When my father at last made my mother his wife, the burgomaster of her native city told him that he gave to his keeping the pearl of Rotterdam. Post-horses took the young couple in the most magnificent weather to the distant Prussian capital. It must have been a delightful journey, but when the horses were changed in Potsdam the bride and groom received news that the latter's father was dead.

So my parents entered a house of mourning. My mother at that time had only the slight mastery of German acquired during hours of industrious study for her future husband's sake. She did not possess in all Berlin a single friend or relative of her own family, yet she soon felt at home in the capital. She loved my father. Heaven gave her children, and her rare beauty, her winning charm, and the receptivity of her mind quickly opened all hearts to her in circles even wider than her husband's large family connection. The latter included many households whose guests numbered every one whose achievements in science or art, or possession of large wealth, had rendered them prominent in Berlin, and the "beautiful Hollander," as my mother was then called, became one of the most courted women in society.

Holtei had made her acquaintance at this time, and it was a delight to hear her speak of those gay, brilliant days. How often Baron von Humboldt, Rauch, or Schleiermacher had escorted her to dinner! Hegel had kept a blackened coin won from her at whist. Whenever he sat down to play cards with her he liked to draw it out, and, showing it to his partner, say, "My thaler, fair lady."

My mother, admired and petted, had thoroughly enjoyed the happy period of my father's lifetime, entertaining as a hospitable hostess or visiting friends, and she gladly recalled it. But this brilliant life, filled to overflowing with all sorts of amusements, had been interrupted just before my birth.

The beloved husband had died, and the great wealth of our family, though enough remained for comfortable maintenance, had been much diminished.

Such changes of outward circumstances are termed reverses of fortune, and the phrase is fitting, for by them life gains a new form. Yet real happiness is more frequently increased than lessened, if only they do not entail anxiety concerning daily bread. My mother's position was far removed from this point; but she possessed qualities which would have undoubtedly enabled her, even in far more modest circumstances, to retain her cheerfulness and fight her way bravely with her children through life.

The widow resolved that her sons should make their way by their own industry, like her brothers, who had almost all become able officials in the Dutch colonial service. Besides, the change in her circumstances brought her into closer relations with persons with whom by inclination and choice she became even more intimately associated than with the members of my father's family—I mean the clique of scholars and government officials amid whose circle her children grew up, and whom I shall mention later.

Our relatives, however, even after my father's death, showed the same regard for my mother—who on her side was sincerely attached to many of them—and urged her to accept the hospitality of their homes. I, too, when a child, still more in later years, owe to the Beer family many a happy hour. My father's cousin, Moritz von Oppenfeld, whose wife was an Ebers, was also warmly attached to us. He lived in a house which he owned on the Pariser Platz, now occupied by the French embassy, and in whose spacious apartments and elsewhere his kind heart and tender love prepared countless pleasures for our young lives.

CHAPTER II.
MY EARLIEST CHILDHOOD

My father died in Leipzigerstrasse, where, two weeks after, I was born. It is reported that I was an unusually sturdy, merry little fellow. One of my father's relatives, Frau Mosson, said that I actually laughed on the third day of my life, and several other proofs of my precocious cheerfulness were related by this lady.

So I must believe that—less wise than Lessing's son, who looked at life and thought it would be more prudent to turn his back upon it—I greeted with a laugh the existence which, amid beautiful days of sunshine, was to bring me so many hours of suffering.

Spring was close at hand; the house in noisy Leipzigerstrasse was distasteful to my mother, her soul longed for rest, and at that time she formed the resolutions according to which she afterward strove to train her boys to be able men. Her first object was to obtain pure air for the little children, and room for the larger ones to exercise. So she looked for a residence outside the gate, and succeeded in renting for a term of years No. 4 Thiergartenstrasse, which I have already mentioned.

The owner, Frau Kommissionsrath Reichert, had also lost her husband a short time before, and had determined to let the house, which stood near her own, stand empty rather than rent it to a large family of children.

Alone herself, she shrank from the noise of growing boys and girls. But she had a warm, kind heart, and—she told me this herself—the sight of the beautiful young mother in her deep mourning made her quickly forget her prejudice. "If she had brought ten bawlers instead of five," she remarked, "I would not have refused the house to that angel face."

We all cherish a kindly memory of the vigorous, alert woman, with her round, bright countenance and laughing eyes. She soon became very intimate with my mother, and my second sister, Paula, was her special favorite, on whom she lavished every indulgence. Her horses were the first ones on which I was lifted, and she often took us with her in the carriage or sent us to ride in it.

I still remember distinctly some parts of our garden, especially the shady avenue leading from our balcony on the ground floor to the Schafgraben, the pond, the beautiful flower-beds in front of Frau Reichert's stately house, and the field of potatoes where I—the gardener was the huntsman—saw my first partridge shot. This was probably on the very spot where for many years the notes of the organ have pealed through the Matthaikirche, and the Word of God has been expounded to a congregation whose residences stand on the playground of my childhood.

The house which sheltered us was only two stories high, but pretty and spacious. We needed abundant room, for, besides my mother, the five children, and the female servants, accommodation was required for the governess, and a man who held a position midway between porter and butler and deserved the title of factotum if any one ever did. His name was Kurschner; he was a big-boned, square-built fellow about thirty years old, who always wore in his buttonhole the little ribbon of the order he had gained as a soldier at the siege of Antwerp, and who had been taken into the house by our mother for our protection, for in winter our home, surrounded by its spacious grounds, was very lonely.

As for us five children, first came my oldest sister Martha—now, alas! dead—the wife of Lieutenant-Colonel Baron Curt von Brandenstein, and my brother Martin, who were seven and five years older than I. They were, of course, treated differently from us younger ones.

Paula was my senior by three years; Ludwig, or Ludo—he was called by his nickname all his life—by a year and a half.

Paula, a fresh, pretty, bright, daring child, was often the leader in our games and undertakings. Ludo, who afterward became a soldier and as a Prussian officer did good service in the war, was a gentle boy, somewhat delicate in health—the broad-shouldered man shows no trace of it—and the best of playfellows. We were always together, and were frequently mistaken for twins. We shared everything, and on my birthday, gifts were bestowed on him too; on his, upon me.

Each had forgotten the first person singular of the personal pronoun, and not until comparatively late in life did I learn to use "I" and "me" in the place of "we" and "us."

The sequence of events in this quiet country home has, of course, vanished from my mind, and perhaps many which I mention here occurred in Lennestrasse, where we moved later, but the memories of the time we spent in the Thiergarten overlooked by our second home—are among the brightest of my life. How often the lofty trees and dense shrubbery of our own grounds and the beautiful Berlin Thiergarten rise before my mental vision, when my thoughts turn backward and I see merry children playing among them, and hear their joyous laughter!

FAIRY TALES AND FACT.

What happened in the holy of holies, my mother's chamber, has remained, down to the smallest details, permanently engraved upon my soul.

A mother's heart is like the sun—no matter how much light it diffuses, its warmth and brilliancy never lessen; and though so lavish a flood of tenderness was poured forth on me, the other children were no losers. But I was the youngest, the comforter, the nestling; and never was the fact of so much benefit to me as at that time.

My parents' bed stood in the green room with the bright carpet. It had been brought from Holland, and was far larger and wider than bedsteads of the present day. My mother had kept it. A quilted silk coverlet was spread over it, which felt exquisitely soft, and beneath which one could rest delightfully. When the time for rising came, my mother called me. I climbed joyfully into her warm bed, and she drew her darling into her arms, played all sorts of pranks with him, and never did I listen to more beautiful fairy tales than at those hours. They became instinct with life to me, and have always remained so; for my mother gave them the form of dramas, in which I was permitted to be an actor.

The best one of all was Little Red Riding Hood. I played the little girl who goes into the wood, and she was the wolf. When the wicked beast had disguised itself in the grandmother's cap I not only asked the regulation questions: "Grandmother, what makes you have such big eyes? Grandmother, why is your skin so rough?" etc., but invented new ones to defer the grand final effect, which followed the words, "Grandmother, why do you have such big, sharp teeth?" and the answer, "So that I can eat you," whereupon the wolf sprang on me and devoured me—with kisses.

Another time I was Snow-White and she the wicked step-mother, and also the hunter, the dwarf, and the handsome prince who married her.

How real this merry sport made the distress of persecuted innocence, the terrors and charm of the forest, the joys and splendours of the fairy realm! If the flowers in the garden had raised their voices in song, if the birds on the boughs had called and spoken to me—nay, if a tree had changed into a beautiful fairy, or the toad in the damp path of our shaded avenue into a witch—it would have seemed only natural.

It is a singular thing that actual events which happened in those early days have largely vanished from my memory; but the fairy tales I heard and secretly experienced became firmly impressed on my mind. Education and life provided for my familiarity with reality in all its harshness and angles, its strains and hurts; but who in later years could have flung wide the gates of the kingdom where everything is beautiful and good, and where ugliness is as surely doomed to destruction as evil to punishment? Even poesy in our times turns from the Castalian fount whose crystal-clear water becomes an unclean pool and, though reluctantly, obeys the impulse to make its abode in the dust of reality. Therefore I plead with voice and pen in behalf of fairy tales; therefore I tell them to my children and grandchildren, and have even written a volume of them myself.

How perverse and unjust it is to banish the fairy tale from the life of the child, because devotion to its charm might prove detrimental to the grown person! Has not the former the same claim to consideration as the latter?

Every child is entitled to expect a different treatment and judgment, and to receive what is his due undiminished. Therefore it is unjust to injure and rob the child for the benefit of the man. Are we even sure that the boy is destined to attain the second and third stages—youth and manhood?

True, there are some apostles of caution who deny themselves every joy of existence while in their prime, in order, when their locks are grey, to possess wealth which frequently benefits only their heirs.

All sensible mothers will doubtless, like ours, take care that their children do not believe the stories which they tell them to be true. I do not remember any time when, if my mind had been called upon to decide, I should have thought that anything I invented myself had really happened; but I know that we were often unable to distinguish whether the plausible tale related by some one else belonged to the realm of fact or fiction. On such occasions we appealed to my mother, and her answer instantly set all doubts at rest; for we thought she could never be mistaken, and knew that she always told the truth.

As to the stories invented by myself, I fared like other imaginative children. I could imagine the most marvellous things about every member of the household, and while telling them—but only during that time—I often fancied that they were true; yet the moment I was asked whether these things had actually occurred, it seemed as if I woke from a dream. I at once separated what I had imagined from what I had actually experienced, and it would never have occurred to me to persist against my better knowledge. So the vividly awakened power of imagination led neither me, my brothers and sisters, nor my children and grandchildren into falsehood.

In after years I abhorred it, not only because my mother would rather have permitted any other offence to pass unpunished, but because I had an opportunity of perceiving its ugliness very early in life. When only seven or eight years old I heard a boy—I still remember his name—tell his mother a shameless lie about some prank in which I had shared. I did not interrupt him to vindicate the truth, but I shrank in horror with the feeling of having witnessed a crime.

If Ludo and I, even in the most critical situations, adhered to the truth more rigidly than other boys, we "little ones" owe it especially to our sister Paula, who was always a fanatic in its cause, and even now endures many an annoyance because she scorns the trivial "necessary fibs" deemed allowable by society.

True, the interesting question of how far necessary fibs are justifiable among children, is yet to be considered; but what did we know of such necessity in our sports in the Thiergarten? From what could a lie have saved us except a blow from a beloved mother's little hand, which, it is true, when any special misdeed was punished by a box on the ear, could inflict a tolerable amount of pain by means of the rings which adorned it.

There is a tradition that once when she had slapped Paula's pretty face, the odd child rubbed her cheek and said, with the droll calmness that rarely deserted her, "When you want to strike me again, mother, please take off your rings first."

THE GOVERNESS—THE CEMETERY.

During the time we lived in the Thiergarten my mother's hand scarcely ever touched my face except in a caress. Every memory of her is bright and beautiful. I distinctly remember how merrily she jested and played with us, and from my earliest recollections her beloved face always greets me cheerily. Yet she had moved to the Thiergarten with a heart oppressed by the deepest sorrow.

I know from the woman who accompanied her there as the governess of the two eldest children, and became a faithful friend, how deeply she needed consolation, how completely her feelings harmonized with the widow's weeds she wore, and in which she is said to have been so beautiful.

The name of this rare woman was Bernhardine Kron. A native of Mecklenburg, she united to rich and wide culture the sterling character, warmth of feeling, and fidelity of this sturdy and sympathetic branch of the German nation. She soon became deeply attached to the young widow, to whose children she was to devote her best powers, and, in after years, her eyes often grew dim when she spoke of the time during which she shared our mother's grief and helped her in her work of education.

Both liked to recall in later days the quiet evenings when, after the rest of the household had retired, they read alone or discussed what stirred their hearts. Each gave the other what she could. The German governess went through our classic authors with her employer, and my mother read to her the works of Racine and Corneille, and urged her to speak French and English with her; for, like many natives of Holland, her mastery of both languages was as thorough as if she had grown up in Paris or London. The necessity of studying and sharing her own rich intellectual possessions continued to be a marked trait in my mother's character until late in life, and how much cause for gratitude we all have for the share she gave us of her own knowledge and experience!

Fraulein Kron always deeply appreciated the intellectual development she owed to her employer, while the latter never forgot the comfort and support bestowed by the faithful governess in the most sorrowful days of her life. When I first became conscious of my surroundings, these days were over; but in saying that my first recollections of my mother were bright and cheerful, I forgot the hours devoted to my father's memory. She rarely brought them to our notice; a certain chaste reserve, even later in life, prevented her showing her deepest grief to others. She always strove to cope with her sorest trials alone. Her sunny nature shrank from diffusing shadow and darkness around her.

On the 14th of February, the anniversary of my father's death, wherever she might be, she always withdrew from the members of the household, and even her own children. A second occasion of sharing her sorrowful emotion was repeated several times every summer. This was the visit to the cemetery, which she rarely made alone.

The visits impressed us all strongly, and the one I first remember could not have occurred later than my fifth year, for I distinctly recollect that Frau Rapp's horses took us to the churchyard. My father was buried in the Dreifaltigkeitskirchhof,—[Trinity churchyard]—just outside the Halle Gate. I found it so little changed when I entered it again, two years ago, that I could walk without a guide directly to the Ebers family vault. But what a transformation had taken place in the way!

When we visited it with my mother, which was always in carriages, for it was a long distance from our home, we drove quickly through the city, the gate, and as far as the spot where I found the stately pile of the brick Kreuzkirche; then we turned to the right, and if we had come in cabs we children got out, it was so hard for the horses to drag the vehicles over the sandy road which led to the cemetery.

During this walk we gathered blue cornflowers and scarlet poppies from the fields, bluebells, daisies, ranunculus, and snapdragon from the narrow border of turf along the roadside, and tied them into bouquets for the graves. My mother moved silently with us between the rows of grassy mounds, tombstones, and crosses, while we carried the pots of flowers and wreaths, which, to afford every one the pleasure of helping, she had distributed among us at the gravedigger's house, just back of the cemetery.

Our family burial place—my mother's stone cross now stands there beside my father's—was one of those bounded in the rear by the church yard wall; a marble slab set in the masonry bears the owner's name. It is large enough for us all, and lies at the right of the path between Count Kalckreuth's and the stately mausoleum which contains the earthly remains of Moritz von Oppenfeld—who was by far the dearest of our father's relatives—and his family.

My mother led the way into the small enclosure, which was surrounded by an iron railing, and prayed or thought silently of the beloved dead who rested there.

Is there any way for us Protestants, when love for the dead longs to find expression in action, except to adorn with flowers the places which contain their earthly remains? Their bright hues and a child's beaming face are the only cheerful things which a mourner whose wounds are still bleeding freshly beside a coffin can endure to see, and I might compare flowers to the sound of bells. Both are in place and welcome in the supreme moments of life.

Therefore my mother, besides a heart full of love, always brought to my father's grave children and flowers. When she had satisfied the needs of her own soul, she turned to us, and with cheerful composure directed the decoration of the mound. Then she spoke of our father, and if any of us had recently incurred punishment—one instance of this kind is indelibly impressed on my memory—she passed her arms around the child, and in whispered words, which no one else could hear, entreated the son or daughter not to grieve her so again, but to remember the dead. Such an admonition on this spot could not fail to produce its effect, and brought forgiveness with it.

On our return our hands and hearts were free again, and we were at liberty to use our tongues. During these visits my interest in Schleiermacher was awakened, for his grave—he died in 1834, three years before I was born—lay near our lot, and we often stopped before the stone erected by his friends, grateful pupils, and admirers. It was adorned with his likeness in marble; and my mother, who had frequently met him, pausing in front of it, told us about the keen-sighted theologian, philosopher, and pulpit orator, whose teachings, as I was to learn later, had exerted the most powerful influence upon my principal instructors at Keilhau. She also knew his best enigmas; and the following one, whose terse brevity is unsurpassed:

> "Parted I am sacred,
>
> United abominable"—

she had heard him propound himself. The answer, "Mein eid" (my oath), and "Meineid" (perjury), every one knows.

Nothing was further from my mother's intention than to make these visits to the cemetery special memorial days; on the contrary, they were interwoven into our lives, not set at regular intervals or on certain dates, but when her heart prompted and the weather was favourable for out-of-door excursions. Therefore they became associated in our minds with happy and sacred memories.

CHAPTER III.
ON FESTAL DAYS

The celebration of a memorial day by outward forms was one of my mother's customs; for, spite of her sincerity of feeling, she favoured external ceremonies, and tried when we were very young to awaken a sense of their meaning in our minds.

On all festal occasions we children were freshly dressed from top to toe, and all of us, including the servants, had cakes at breakfast, and the older ones wine at dinner.

On the birthdays these cakes were surrounded by as many candles as we numbered years, and provision was always made for a dainty arrangement of gifts. While we were young, my mother distinguished the "birthday child"—probably in accordance with some custom of her native country—by a silk scarf. She liked to celebrate her own birthday, too, and ever since I can remember—it was on the 25th of July—we had a picnic at that time.

We knew that it was a pleasure to her to see us at her table on that day, and, up to the last years of her life, all whose vocations permitted met at her house on the anniversary.

She went to church on Sunday, and on Good Friday she insisted that my sisters as well as her self should wear black, not only during the service, but throughout the rest of the day.

Few children enjoyed a more beautiful Christmas than ours, for under the tree adorned with special love each found the desire of his or her heart gratified, while behind the family gift-table there always stood another, on which several poorer people whom I might call "clients" of the household, discovered presents which suited their needs. Among them, up to the time I went as a boy of eleven to Keilhau, I never failed to see my oldest sister's nurse with her worthy husband, the shoemaker Grossman, and their well-behaved children. She gladly permitted us to share in the distribution of the alms liberally bestowed on the needy. The seeming paradox, "No one ever grew poor by giving," I first heard from her lips, and she more than once found an opportunity to repeat it.

We, however, never valued her gifts of money so highly as the trouble and inconveniences she cheerfully encountered to aid or add to the happiness of others by means of the numerous relations formed in her social life and the influence gained mainly by her own gracious nature. Many who are now occupying influential positions owe their first start or have had the path smoothed for them by her kindness.

As in many Berlin families, the Christmas Man came to us—an old man disguised by a big beard and provided with a bag filled with nuts and bonbons and sometimes trifling gifts. He addressed us in a feigned voice, saying that the Christ Child had sent him, but the dainties he had were intended only for the good children who could recite some thing for him. Of course, provision for doing this had been made. Everybody pressed forward, but the Christmas Man kept order, and only when each had repeated a little verse did he open the bag and distribute its contents among us.

Usually the Christmas Man brought a companion, who followed him in the guise of Knecht Ruprecht with his own bag of presents, and mingled with his jests threats against naughty children.

The carp served on Christmas eve in every Berlin family, after the distribution of gifts, and which were never absent from my mother's table, I have always had on my own in Jena, Leipsic, and Munich, or wherever the evening of December 24th might find us. On the whole, we remain faithful to the Christmas customs of my own home, which vary little from those of the Germans in Riga, where my wife's family belong; nay, it is so hard for me to relinquish such childish habits, that, when unable to procure a Christmas tree for the two "Eves" I spent on the Nile, I decked a young palm and fastened candles on it. My mother's permission that Knecht Ruprecht should visit us was contrary to her principle never to allow us to be frightened by images of horror. Nay, if she heard that the servants threatened us with the Black Man and other hobgoblins of Berlin nursery tales, she was always very angry. The arguments by which my wife induced me to banish the Christmas Man and Knecht Ruprecht seem still more cogent, now that I think I understand the hearts of children. It is certainly far more beautiful and just as easy-if we desire to utilize Christmas gifts for educational purposes—to stimulate children to goodness by telling them of the pleasure it will give the little Christ Child, rather than by filling them with dread of Knecht Ruprecht.

True, my mother did not fail to endeavor to inspire us with love for the Christ Child and the Saviour, and to draw us near to him. She saw in him, above all else, the embodiment of love, and loved him because her loving heart understood his. In after years my own investigation and thought brought me to the same conviction which she had reached through the relation of her feminine nature to the person and teachings of her Saviour. I perceived that the world as Jesus Christ found it owes him nothing grander, more beautiful, loftier, or more pregnant with importance than that he widened the circle of love which embraced only the individual, the family, the city, or, at the utmost, the country of which a person was a citizen, till it included all mankind, and this human love, of which my mother's life gave us practical proof, is the banner under which all the genuine progress of mankind in later years has been made.

Nineteen centuries have passed since the one that gave us Him who died on the cross, and how far we are still from a perfect realization of this noblest of all the emotions of the heart and spirit! And yet, on the day when this human love has full sway, the social problems which now disturb so many minds and will permit the brains of our best citizens to take no rest, will be solved.

OTHER OBLIGATIONS TO MY MOTHER, AND A SUMMARY OF THE NEW

AND GREAT EVENTS WHICH BEFELL THE GERMANS DURING MY LIFE.

I omit saying more of my mother's religious feelings and relations to God, because I know that it would be contrary to her wishes to inform strangers of the glimpse she afterward afforded me of the inmost depths of her soul.

That, like every other mother, she clasped our little hands in prayer is a matter of course. I could not fall asleep until she had done this and given me my good-night kiss. How often I have dreamed of her when, before going to some entertainment, she came in full evening dress to hear me repeat my little prayer and bid us good-bye!

But she also provided most carefully for the outward life; nay, perhaps she laid a little too much stress upon our manners in greeting strangers, at table, and elsewhere.

Among these forms I might number the fluent use of the French language, which my mother early bestowed upon us as if its acquisition was mere sport-bestowed; for, unhappily, I know of no German grammar school where pupils can learn to speak French with facility; and how many never-to-be-forgotten memories of travel, what great benefits during my period of study in Paris I owe to this capacity! We obtained it by the help of bonnes, who found it easier to speak French to us because our mother always did the same in their presence.

My mother considered it of the first importance to make us familiar with French at a very early age, because, when she reached Berlin with a scanty knowledge of German, her mastery of French secured numerous pleasant things. She often told us how highly French was valued in the capital, and we must believe that the language possesses an imperishable charm for

Germans when we remember that this was the case so shortly after the glorious uprising against the terrible despotism of France. True, French, in addition to its melody and ambiguity, possesses more subtle turns and apt phrases than most other languages; and even the most German of Germans, our Bismarck, must recognize the fitness of its phrases, because he likes to avail himself of them. He has a perfect knowledge of French, and I have noticed that, whenever he mingles it with German, the former has some sentence which enables him to communicate in better and briefer language whatever he may desire to express. What German form of speech, for instance, can convey the idea of fulness which will permit no addition so well as the French popular saying, "Full as an egg," which pleased me in its native land, and which first greeted me in Germany as an expression used by the great chancellor?

My mother's solicitude concerning good manners and perfection in speaking French, which so easily renders children mere dolls, fortunately could not deprive us of our natural freshness and freedom from constraint. But if any peril to the character does lurk in being unduly mindful of external forms, we three brothers were destined to spend a large portion of our boyhood amid surroundings which, as it were, led us back to Nature. Besides, even in Berlin we were not forbidden to play like genuine boys. We had no lack of playmates of both sexes, and with them we certainly talked and shouted no French, but sturdy Berlin German.

In winter, too, we were permitted to enjoy ourselves out of doors, and few boys made handsomer snow-men than those our worthy Kurschner—always with the order in his buttonhole—helped us build in Thiergartenstrasse.

In the house we were obliged to behave courteously, and when I recall the appearance of things there I become vividly aware that no series of years witnessed more decisive changes in every department of life in Germany than those of my boyhood. The furnishing of the rooms differed little from that of the present day, except that the chairs and tables were somewhat more angular and the cushions less comfortable. Instead of the little knobs of the electric bells, a so-called "bell-rope," about the width of one's hand, provided with a brass or metal handle, hung beside the doors.

The first introduction of gas into the city was made by an English company about ten years before my birth; but how many oil lamps I still saw burning, and in my school days the manufacturing city of Kottbus, which at that time contained about ten thousand inhabitants, was lighted by them! In my childhood gas was not used in the houses and theatres of Berlin, and kerosene had not found its way to Germany. The rooms were lighted by oil lamps and candles, while the servants burned tallow-dips. The latter were also used in our nursery, and during the years which I spent at school in Keilhau all our studying was done by them.

Matches were not known. I still remember the tinder box in the kitchen, the steel, the flint, and the threads dipped in sulphur. The sparks made by striking fell on the tinder and caught it on fire here and there. Soon after the long, rough lucifer matches appeared, which were dipped into a little bottle filled, I believe, with asbestos wet with sulphuric acid.

We never saw the gardener light his pipe except with flint, steel, and tinder. The gun he used had a firelock, and when he had put first powder, then a wad, then shot, and lastly another wad into the barrel, he was obliged to shake some powder into the pan, which was lighted by the sparks from the flint striking the steel, if the rain did not make it too damp.

For writing we used exclusively goose-quills, for though steel pens were invented soon after I was born, they were probably very imperfect; and, moreover, had to combat a violent prejudice, for at the first school we attended we were strictly forbidden to use them. So the penknife played an important part on every writing-desk, and it was impossible to imagine a good penman who did not possess skill in the art of shaping the quills.

What has been accomplished between 1837 and the present date in the way of means of communication I need not recapitulate. I only know how long a time was required for a letter from my mother's brothers—one was a resident of Java and the other lived as "Opperhoofd" in Japan—to reach Berlin, and how often an opportunity was used, generally through the courtesy of the Netherland embassy, for sending letters or little gifts to Holland. A letter forwarded by express was the swiftest way of receiving or giving news; but there was the signal telegraph, whose arms we often saw moving up and down, but exclusively in the service of the Government. When, a few years ago, my mother was ill in Holland, a reply to a telegram marked "urgent" was received in Leipsic in eighteen minutes. What would our grandparents have said to such a miracle?

We were soon to learn by experience the number of days required to reach my mother's home from Berlin, for there was then no railroad to Holland.

The remarkable changes wrought during my lifetime in the political affairs of Germany I can merely indicate here. I was born in despotic Prussia, which was united to Austria and the German states and small countries by a loosely formed league. As guardians of this wretched unity the various courts sent diplomats to Frankfort, who interrupted their careless mode of life only to sharpen distrust of other courts or suppress some democratic movement.

The Prussian nation first obtained in 1848 the liberties which had been secured at an earlier date by the other German states, and nothing gives me more cause for gratitude than the boon of being permitted to see the realization and fulfilment of the dream of so many former generations, and my dismembered native land united into one grand, beautiful whole. I deem it a great happiness to have been a contemporary of Emperor William I, Bismarck, and Von Moltke, witnessed their great deeds as a man of mature years, and shared the enthusiasm they evoked and which enabled these men to make our German Fatherland the powerful, united empire it is to-day.

The journey to Holland closes the first part of my childhood. I look back upon it as a beautiful, unshadowed dream out of doors or in a pleasant house where everybody loved me. But I could not single out the years, months, or days of this retrospect. It is only a smooth stream which bears us easily along. There is no series of events, only disconnected images—a faithful dog, a picture on the wall, above all the love and caresses of the mother lavished specially on me as the youngest, and the most blissful of all sounds in the life of a German child, the ringing of the little bell announcing that the Christmas tree is ready.

Only in after days, when the world of fairyland and legend is left behind, does the child have any idea of consecutive events and human destinies. The stories told by mother and grandmother about Snow-White, the Sleeping Beauty, the giants and the dwarfs, Cinderella, the stable at Bethlehem where the Christ-Child lay in the manger beside the oxen and asses, the angels who appeared to the shepherds singing "Glory to God in the Highest," the three kings and the star which led them to the Christ-Child, are firmly impressed on his memory. I don't know how young I was when I saw the first picture of the kings in their purple robes kneeling before the babe in its mother's lap, but its forms and hues were indelibly stamped upon my mental vision, and I never forgot its meaning. True, I had no special thoughts concerning it; nay, I scarcely wondered to see kings in the dust before a child, and now, when I hear the summons of the purest and noblest of Beings, "Suffer little children to come unto me," and understand the sacred simplicity of a child's heart, it no longer awakens surprise.

CHAPTER IV.
THE JOURNEY TO HOLLAND TO ATTEND THE GOLDEN WEDDING.

The rattle of wheels and the blast of the postilion's horn closed the first period of my childhood. When I was four years old we went to my mother's home to attend my grandparents' golden wedding. If I wished to describe the journey in its regular order I should be forced to depend upon the statements of others. So little of all which grown people deem worth seeing and noting in Belgium, Holland, and on the Rhine has remained in my memory, that I cannot help smiling when I hear people say that they intend to take children travelling for their amusement and instruction. In our case we were put in the carriage because my mother would not leave us behind, and wanted to give our grandparents pleasure by our presence. She was right, but in spite of my inborn love of travel the month we spent on the journey seemed a period of very uncomfortable restlessness. A child realizes only a single detail of beauty—a flower, a radiant star, a human face. Any individual recollection of the journey to Holland, aside from what has been told me, is getting into the travelling carriage, a little green leather Bajazzo dressed in red and white given to me by a relative, and the box of candies bestowed to take on the trip by a friend of my mother.

Of our reception in the Belgian capital at the house of Adolphe Jones, the husband of my aunt Henriette, a sister of my mother, I retain many recollections.

Our pleasant host was a painter of animals, whom I afterward saw sharing his friend Verboeckhoven's studio, and whose flocks of sheep were very highly praised. At that time his studio was in his own house, and it seems as if I could still hear the call in my aunt's shrill voice, repeated countless times a day, "Adolphe!" and the answer, following promptly in the deepest bass tones, "Henriette!" This singular freak, which greatly amused us, was due, as I learned afterward, to my aunt's jealousy, which almost bordered on insanity.

In later years I learned to know him as a jovial artist, who in the days of his youth very possibly might have given the strait-laced lady cause for anxiety. Even when his locks were white he was ready for any pleasure; but he devoted himself earnestly to art, and I am under obligation to him for being the means of my mother's possessing the friendship of the animal painter, Verboeckhoven, and that greatest of more modern Belgian artists, Louis

Gallait and his family, in whose society and home I have passed many delightful hours.

In recalling our arrival at the Jones house I first see the merry, smiling face—somewhat faunlike in its expression—of my six-foot uncle, and the plump figure of his wonderfully good and when undisturbed by jealousy—no less cheery wife. There was something specially winning and lovable about her, and I have heard that this lady, my mother's oldest sister, possessed in her youth the same dazzling beauty. At the famous ball in Brussels this so captivated the Duke of Wellington that he offered her his arm to escort her back to her seat. My mother also remembered the Napoleonic days, and I thought she had been specially favoured in seeing this great man when he entered Rotterdam, and also Goethe.

I remember my grandfather as a stately old gentleman. He, as well as the other members of the family, called me Georg Krullebol, which means curly-head, to distinguish me from a cousin called Georg von Gent. I also remember that when, on the morning of December 5th, St. Nicholas day, we children took our shoes to put on, we found them, to our delight, stuffed with gifts; and lastly that on Christmas Eve the tree which had been prepared for us in a room on the ground floor attracted such a crowd of curious spectators in front of the Jones house that we were obliged to close the shutters. Of my grandparents' day of honor I remember nothing except a large room filled with people, and the minutes during which I repeated my little verse. I can still see myself in a short pink skirt, with a wreath of roses on my fair curls, wings on my shoulders, a quiver on my back, and a bow in my hand, standing before the mirror very much pleased with my appearance. Our governess had composed little Cupid's speech, my mother had drilled me thoroughly in it, so I do not remember a moment of anxiety and embarrassment, but merely that it afforded me the purest, deepest pleasure to be permitted to do something.

I must have behaved with the utmost ease before the spectators, many of whom I knew, for I can still hear the loud applause which greeted me, and see myself passed from one to another till I fled from the kisses and pet names of grandparents, aunts, and cousins to my mother's lap. Of the bride and groom of this golden wedding I remember only that my grandfather wore short trousers called 'escarpins' and stockings reaching to the knee. My grandmother, spite of her sixty-six years—she married before she was seventeen—was said to look remarkably pretty. Later I often saw the heavy white silk dress strewn with tiny bouquets which she wore as a bride and again remodelled at her silver wedding; for after her death it was left to my mother. Modern wedding gowns are not treasured so long. I have often wondered why I recollect my grandfather so distinctly and my grandmother so dimly. I have a clear idea of her personal appearance, but this I believe I owe much more to her portrait which hung in my mother's room beside her husband's, and is now one of my own most cherished possessions. Bradley, one of the best English portrait painters, executed it, and all connoisseurs pronounce it a masterpiece.

This festival lives in my memory like the fresh spring morning of a day whose noon is darkened by clouds, and which ends in a heavy thunderstorm.

Black clouds had gathered over the house adorned with garlands and flowers, echoing for days with the gay conversations, jests, and congratulations of the relatives united after long separation and the mirth of children and grandchildren. Not a loud word was permitted to be uttered. We felt that something terrible was impending, and people called it grandfather's illness. Never had I seen my mother's sunny face so anxious and sad. She rarely came to us, and when she did for a short time her thoughts were far away, for she was nursing her father.

Then the day which had been dreaded came. Wherever we looked the women were weeping and the eyes of the men were reddened by tears. My mother, pale and sorrowful, told us that our dear grandfather was dead.

Children cannot understand the terrible solemnity of death. This is a gift bestowed by their guardian angels, that no gloomy shadows may darken the sunny brightness of their souls.

I saw only that cheerful faces were changed to sad ones, that the figures about us moved silently in sable robes and scarcely noticed us. On the tables in the nursery, where our holiday garments were made, black clothes were being cut for us also, and I remember having my mourning dress fitted. I was pleased because it was a new one. I tried to manufacture a suit for my Berlin Jack-in-the-box from the scraps that fell from the dressmaker's table. Nothing amuses a child so much as to imitate what older people are doing. We were forbidden to laugh, but after a few days our mother no longer checked our mirth. Of our stay at Scheveningen I recollect nothing except that the paths in the little garden of the house we occupied were strewn with shells. We dug a big hole in the sand on the downs, but I retained no remembrance of the sea and its majesty, and when I beheld it in later years it seemed as if I were greeting for the first time the eternal Thalassa which was to become so dear and familiar to me.

My grandmother, I learned, passed away scarcely a year after the death of her faithful companion, at the home of her son, a lawyer in The Hague.

Two incidents of the journey back are vividly impressed on my mind. We went by steamer up the Rhine, and stopped at Ehrenbreitstein to visit old Frau Mendelssohn, our guardian's mother, at her estate of Horchheim. The carriage had been sent for us, and on the drive the spirited horses ran away and would have dashed into the Rhine had not my brother Martin, at that time eleven years old, who was sitting on the box by the coachman, saved us.

The other incident is of a less serious nature. I had seen many a salmon in the kitchen, and resolved to fish for one from the steamer; so I tied a bit of candy to a string and dropped it from the deck. The fish were so wanting in taste as to disdain the sweet bait, but my early awakened love of sport kept me patiently a long time in the same spot, which was undoubtedly more agreeable to my mother than the bait was to the salmon. As, protected by the guards, and probably watched by the governess and my brothers and sisters, I devoted myself to this amusement, my mother went down into the cabin to rest. Suddenly there was a loud uproar on the ship. People shouted and screamed, everybody rushed on deck and looked into the river. Whether I, too, heard the fall and saw the life-boat manned I don't remember; but I recollect all the more clearly my mother's rushing frantically from the cabin and clasping me tenderly to her heart as her rescued child. So the drama ended happily, but there had been a terrible scene. Among the steamer's passengers was a crazy Englishman who was being taken, under the charge of a keeper, to an insane asylum. While my mother was asleep the lunatic succeeded in eluding this man's vigilance and plunged into the river. Of course, there was a tumult on board, and my mother heard cries of "Fallen into the river!"

"Save!" "He'll drown!" Maternal anxiety instantly applied them to the child-angler, and she darted up the cabin stairs. I need not describe the state of mind in which she reached the deck, and her emotion when she found her nestling in his place, still holding the line in his hand. As the luckless son of Albion was rescued unharmed, we could look back upon the incident gaily, but neither of us forgot this anxiety—the first I was to cause my mother.

I have forgotten everything else that happened on our way home; but when I think of this first journey, a long one for so young a child, and the many little trips—usually to Dresden, where my grandmother Ebers lived—which I was permitted to take, I wonder whether they inspired the love of travel which moved me so strongly later, or whether it was an inborn instinct. If a popular superstition is correct, I was predestined to journey. No less a personage than Friedrich Froebel, the founder of the kindergarten system, called my attention to it; for when I met him for the first time in the Institute at Keilhau, he seized my curly hair, bent my head back, gazed at me with his kind yet penetrating eyes, and said: "You will wander far through the world, my boy; your teeth are wide apart."

CHAPTER V.
LENNESTRASSE.—LENNE.—EARLY IMPRESSIONS.

Lennestrasse is the scene of the period of my life which began with my return from Holland. If, coming from the Brandenburg Gate, you follow the Thiergarten and pass the superb statue of Goethe, you will reach a corner formed by two blocks of houses. The one on the left, opposite to the city wall, now called Koniggratz, was then known as Schulgartenstrasse. The other, on the right, whose windows overlooked the Thiergarten, bore the name in my childhood of Lennestrasse, which it owed to Lenne, the park superintendent, a man of great talent, but who lives in my memory only as a particularly jovial old gentleman. He occupied No. 1, and was one of my mother's friends. Next to Prince Packler, he may certainly be regarded as one of the most inventive and tasteful landscape gardeners of his time. He transformed the gardens of Sans-Souci and the Pfaueninsel at Potsdam, and laid out the magnificent park on Babelsberg for Emperor William I, when he was only "Prince of Prussia." The magnificent Zoological Garden in Berlin is also his work; but he prided himself most on rendering the Thiergarten a "lung" for the people, and, spite of many obstacles, materially enlarging it. Every moment of the tireless man's time was claimed, and besides King Frederick William IV, who himself uttered many a tolerably good joke, found much pleasure in the society of the gay, clever Rhinelander, whom he often summoned to dine with him at Potsdam. Lenne undoubtedly appreciated this honour, yet I remember the doleful tone in which he sometimes greeted my mother with, "Called to court again!"

Like every one who loves Nature and flowers, he was fond of children. We called him "Uncle Lenne," and often walked down our street hand in hand with him.

It is well known that the part of the city on the other side of the Potsdam Gate was called the "Geheimerath-Quarter." Our street, it is true, lay nearer to the Brandenburg Gate, yet it really belonged to that section; for there was not a single house without at least one Geheimerath (Privy Councillor).

Yet this superabundance of men in "secret" positions lent no touch of mystery to our cheerful street, shaded by the green of the forest. Franker, gayer, sometimes noisier children than its residents could not be found in Berlin. I was only a little fellow when we lived there, and merely tolerated in the "big boys'" sports, but it was a festival when, with Ludo, I could carry their provisions for them or even help them make fireworks. The old Rechnungsrath, who lived in the house owned by Geheimerath Crede, the father of my Leipsic colleague, was their instructor in this art, which was to prove disastrous to my oldest brother and bright Paul Seiffart; for—may they pardon me the treachery—they took one of the fireworks to school, where—I hope accidentally—it went off. At first this caused much amusement, but strict judgment followed, and led to my mother's resolution to send her oldest son away from home to some educational institution.

The well-known teacher, Adolph Diesterweg, whose acquaintance she had made at the house of a friend, recommended Keilhau, and so our little band was deprived of the leader to whom Ludo and I had looked up with a certain degree of reverence on account of his superior strength, his bold spirit of enterprise, and his kindly condescension to us younger ones.

After his departure the house was much quieter, but we did not forget him; his letters from Keilhau were read aloud to us, and his descriptions of the merry school days, the pedestrian tours, and sleigh-rides awakened an ardent longing in Ludo and myself to follow him.

Yet it was so delightful with my mother, the sun around which our little lives revolved! I had no thought, performed no act, without wondering what would be her opinion of it; and this intimate relation, though in an altered form, continued until her death. In looking backward I may regard it as a law of my whole development that my conduct was regulated according to the more or less close mental and outward connection in which I stood with her. The storm and stress period, during which my effervescent youthful spirits led me into all sorts of follies, was the only time in my life in which this close connection threatened to be loosened. Yet Fate provided that it should soon be welded more firmly than ever. When she died, a beloved wife stood by my side, but she was part of myself; and in my mother Fate seemed to have robbed me of the supreme arbitrator, the high court of justice, which alone could judge my acts.

In Lennestrasse it was still she who waked me, prepared us to go to school, took us to walk, and—how could I ever forget it?—gathered us around her "when the lamps were lighted," to read aloud or tell us some story. But nobody was allowed to be perfectly idle. While my sisters sewed, I sketched; and, as Ludo found no pleasure in that, she sometimes had him cut figures out; sometimes—an odd fancy—execute a masterpiece of crocheting, which usually shared the fate of Penelope's web.

We listened with glowing cheeks to Robinson Crusoe and the Arabian Nights, Gulliver's Travels and Don Quixote, both arranged for children, the pretty, stories of Nieritz and others, descriptions of Nature and travel, and Grimm's fairy tales.

On other winter evenings my mother—this will surprise many in the case of so sensible a woman—took us to the theatre. Two of our relatives, Frau Amalie Beer and our beloved Moritz von Oppenfeld, subscribed for boxes in the opera-house, and when they did not use them, which often happened, sent us the key.

So as a boy I heard most of the operas produced at that time, and I saw the ballets, of which Frederick William IV was especially fond, and which Taglioni understood how to arrange so admirably.

Of course, to us children the comic "Robert and Bertram," by Ludwig Schneider, and similar plays, were far more delightful than the grand operas; yet even now I wonder that Don Giovanni's scene with the statue and the conspiracy in the Huguenots stirred me, when a boy of nine or ten, so deeply, and that, though possessing barely the average amount of musical talent, Orpheus's yearning cry, "Eurydice!" rang in my ears so long.

That these frequently repeated pleasures were harmful to us children I willingly admit. And yet—when in after years I was told that I succeeded admirably in describing large bodies of men seized by some strong excitement, and that my novels did not lack dramatic movement or their scenes vividness, and, where it was requisite, splendour—I perhaps owe this to the superb pictures, interwoven with thrilling bursts of melody, which impressed themselves upon my soul when a child.

Fortunately, the outdoor life at Keilhau counteracted the perils which might have arisen from attending theatrical performances too young. What I beheld there, in field and forest, enabled me in after life, when I desired a background for my stories, not to paint stage scenes, but take Nature herself for a model.

I must also record another influence which had its share in my creative toil—my early intercourse with artists and the opportunity of seeing their work.

The statement has been made often enough, but I should like to repeat it here from my own experience, that the most numerous and best impulses which urge the author to artistic development come from his childhood. This law, which results from observing the life and works of the greatest writers, has shown itself very distinctly in a minor one like myself.

There was certainly no lack of varied stimulus during this early period of my existence; but when I look back upon it, I become vividly aware of the serious perils which threaten not only the external but the internal development of the children who grow up in large cities.

Careful watching can guard them from the transgressions to which there are many temptations, but not from the strong and varying impressions which life is constantly forcing upon them. They are thrust too early from the paradise of childhood into the arena of life. There are many things to be seen which enrich the imagination, but where could the young heart find the calmness it needs? The sighing of the wind sweeping over the cornfields and stirring the tree-tops in the forest, the singing of the birds in the boughs, the chirping of the cricket, the vesper-bells summoning the world to rest, all the voices which, in the country, invite to meditation and finally to the formation of a world of one's own, are silenced by the noise of the capital. So it happens that the latter produces active, practical men, and, under favorable circumstances, great scholars, but few artists and poets. If, nevertheless, the capitals are the centers where the poets, artists, sculptors, and architects of the country gather, there is a good reason for it. But I can make no further digression. The sapling requires different soil and care from the tree. I am grateful to my mother for removing us in time from the unrest of Berlin life.

FIRST STUDIES.—MY SISTERS AND THEIR FRIENDS.

My mother told me I was never really taught to read. Ludo, who was a year and a half older, was instructed in the art. I sat by playing, and one day took up Speckter's Fables and read a few words. Trial was then made of my capability, and, finding that I only needed practice to be able to read things I did not know already by heart, my brother and I were thenceforth taught together.

At first the governess had charge of us, afterward we were sent to a little school kept by Herr Liebe in the neighbouring Schulgarten (now Koniggratz) Strasse. It was attended almost entirely by children belonging to the circle of our acquaintances, and the master was a pleasant little man of middle age, who let us do more digging in his garden and playing or singing than actual study.

His only child, a pretty little girl named Clara, was taught with us, and I believe I have Herr Liebe to thank for learning to write. In summer he took us on long walks, frequently to the country seat of Herr Korte, who stood high in the estimation of farmers.

From such excursions, which were followed by others made with the son and tutor of a family among our circle of friends, we always brought our mother great bunches of flowers, and often beautiful stories, too; for the tutor, Candidate Woltmann, was an excellent story-teller, and I early felt a desire to share with those whom I loved whatever charmed me.

It was from this man, who was as fond of the beautiful as he was of children, that I first heard the names of the Greek heroes; and I remember that, after returning from one of these walks, I begged my mother to give us Schwab's Tales of Classic Antiquity, which was owned by one of our companions. We received it on Ludo's birthday, in September, and how we listened when it was read to us—how often we ourselves devoured its delightful contents!

I think the story of the Trojan War made a deeper impression upon me than even the Arabian Nights. Homer's heroes seemed like giant oaks, which far overtopped the little trees of the human wood. They towered like glorious snow mountains above the little hills with which my childish imagination was already filled; and how often we played the Trojan War, and aspired to the honor of acting Hector, Achilles, or Ajax!

Of Herr Liebe, our teacher, I remember only three things. On his daughter's birthday he treated us to cake and wine, and we had to sing a festal song composed by himself, the refrain of which changed every year:

"Clara, with her fair hair thick,

Clara, with her eyes like heaven,

Can no more be called a chick,

For to-day she's really seven."

I remember, too, how when she was eight years old we had to transpose the words a little to make the measure right. Karl von Holtei had a more difficult task when, after the death of the Emperor Francis (Kaiser Franz), he had to fit the name of his successor, Ferdinand, into the beautiful "Gotterhalte Franz den Kaiser," but he got cleverly out of the affair by making it "Gott erhalte Ferdinandum."—[God save the Emperor Francis.]

My second recollection is, that we assisted Herr Liebe, who was a churchwarden and had the honour of taking up the collection, to sort the money, and how it delighted us to hear him scold—with good reason, too—when we found among the silver and copper pieces—as, alas! we almost always did—counters and buttons from various articles of clothing.

In the third place, I must accuse Herr Liebe of having paid very little attention to our behaviour out of school. Had he kept his eyes open, we might have been spared many a bruise and our garments many a rent; for, as often as we could manage it, instead of going directly home from the

Schulgartenstrasse, we passed through the Potsdam Gate to the square beyond. There lurked the enemy, and we sought them out. The enemy were the pupils of a humbler grade of school who called us Privy Councillor's youngsters, which most of us were; and we called them, in return, 'Knoten,' which in its original meaning was anything but an insult, coming as it does by a natural philological process from "Genote," the older form of "Genosse" or comrade.

But to accuse us of arrogance on this account would be doing us wrong. Children don't fight regularly with those whom they despise. Our "Knoten" was only a smart answer to their "Geheimrathsjoren." If they had called us boobies we should probably have called them blockheads, or something of that sort.

This troop, which was not over-well-dressed even before the beginning of the conflict, was led by some boys whose father kept a so-called flower cellar—that is, a basement shop for plants, wreaths, etc.—at the head of Leipzigerstrasse. They often sought us out, but when they did not we enticed them from their cellar by a particular sort of call, and as soon as they appeared we all slipped into some courtyard, where a battle speedily raged, in which our school knapsacks served as weapons of offence and defence. When I got into a passion I was as wild as a fighting cock, and even quiet Ludo could deal hard blows; and I can say the same of most of the "Geheimrathsjoren" and "Knoten." It was not often that any decided success attended the fight, for the janitor or some inhabitant of the house usually interfered and brought it all to an untimely end. I remember still how a fat woman, probably a cook, seized me by the collar and pushed me out into the street, crying: "Fie! fie! such young gentlemen ought to be ashamed of themselves."

Hegel, however, whose influence at that time was still great in the learned circles of Berlin, had called shame "anger against what is natural," and we liked what was natural. So the battles with the "Knoten" were continued until the Berlin revolution called forth more serious struggles, and our mother sent us away to Keilhau.

Our sisters went to school also, a school kept by Fraulein Sollmann in the Dorotheenstrasse. And yet we had a tutor, I do not really know why. Whether our mother had heard of the fights, and recognized the impossibility of following us about everywhere, or whether the candidate was to teach us the rudiments of Latin after we went to the Schmidt school in the Leipziger Platz, at the beginning of my tenth year, I neglected to inquire.

The Easter holidays always brought Brother Martin home. Then he told us about Keilhau, and we longed to accompany him there; and yet we had so many good schoolmates and friends at home, such spacious playgrounds and beautiful toys! I recall with especial pleasure the army of tin soldiers with which we fought battles, and the brass cannon that mowed down their ranks. We could build castles and cathedrals with our blocks, and cooking was a pleasure, too, when our sisters allowed us to act as scullions and waiters in white aprons and caps.

Martha, the eldest, was already a grown young lady, but so sweet and kind that we never feared a rebuff from her; and her friends, too, liked us little ones.

Martha's contemporaries formed a peculiarly charming circle. There was the beautiful Emma Baeyer, the daughter of General Baeyer, who afterward conducted the measuring of the meridian for central Europe; pretty, lively Anna Bisting; and Gretchen Bugler, a handsome, merry girl, who afterward married Paul Heyse and died young; Clara and Agnes Mitscherlich, the daughters of the celebrated chemist, the younger of whom was especially dear to my childish heart. Gustel Grimm, too, the daughter of Wilhelm Grimm, was often at our house. The queen of my heart, however, was the sister of our playmate, Max Geppert, and at this time the most intimate friend of my sister Paula. The two took dancing lessons together, and there was no greater joy than when the lesson was at our house, for then the young ladies occasionally did us the favour of dancing with us, to Herr Guichard's tiny violin.

Warm as was my love for the beautiful Annchen, my adored one came near getting a cold from it, for, rogue that I was, I hid her overshoes during the lesson on one rainy Saturday evening, that I might have the pleasure of taking them to her the next morning.

She looked at that time like the woman with whom I celebrated my silver wedding two years ago, and certainly belonged to the same feminine genre, which I value and place as high above all others as Simonides von Amorgos preferred the beelike woman to every other of her sex: I mean the kind whose womanliness and gentle charm touch the heart before one ever thinks of intellect or beauty.

Our mother smiled at these affairs, and her daughters, as girls, gave her no great trouble in guarding their not too impressionable hearts.

There was only one boy for whom Paula showed a preference, and that was pretty blond Paul, our Martin's friend, comrade, and contemporary, the son of our neighbour, the Privy-Councillor Seiffart; and we lived a good deal together, for his mother and ours were bosom friends, and our house was as open to him as his to us.

Paul was born on the same November day as my sister, though several years earlier, and their common birthday was celebrated, while we were little, by a puppet-show at the neighbour's, conducted by some master in the business, on a pretty little stage in the great hall at the Seiffarts' residence.

I have never forgotten those performances, and laugh now when I think of the knight who shouted to his servant Kasperle, "Fear my thread!" (Zwirn), when what he intended to say was, "Fear my anger!" (Zorn). Or of that same Kasperle, when he gave his wife a tremendous drubbing with a stake, and then inquired, "Want another ounce of unburned wood-ashes, my darling?"

Paula was very fond of these farces. She was, however, from a child rather a singular young creature, who did not by any means enjoy all the amusements of her age. When grown, it was often with difficulty that our mother persuaded her to attend a ball, while Martha's eyes sparkled joyously when there was a dance in prospect; and yet the tall and slender Paula looked extremely pretty in a ball dress.

Gay and active, indeed bold as a boy sometimes, so that she would lead in taking the rather dangerous leap from a balcony of our high ground floor into the garden, clever, and full of droll fancies, she dwelt much in her own thoughts. Several volumes of her journal came to me after our mother's death, and it is odd enough to find the thirteen-year-old girl confessing that she likes no worldly pleasures, and yet, being a very truthful child, she was only expressing a perfectly sincere feeling.

It was touching to read in the same confessions: "I was in a dreamy mood, and they said I must be longing for something—Paul, no doubt. I did not dispute it, for I really was longing for some one, though it was not a boy, but our dead father." And Paula was only three years old when he left us!

No one would have thought, who saw her delight when there were fireworks in the Seiffarts' garden, or when in our own, with her curls and her gown flying, her cheeks glowing, and her eyes flashing, she played with all her heart at "catch" or "robber and princess," or, all animation and interest, conducted a performance of our puppet-show, that she would sometimes shun all noisy pleasure, that she longed with enthusiastic piety for the Sunday churchgoing, and could plunge into meditation on subjects that usually lie far from childish thoughts and feelings.

Yet who would fancy her thoughtless when she wrote in her journal: "Fie, Paula! You have taken no trouble. Mother had a right to expect a better report. However, to be happy, one must forget what cannot be altered."

In reality, she was not in the least "featherheaded." Her life proved that, and it is apparent, too, in the words I found on another page of her journal, at thirteen: "Mother and Martha are at the Drakes; I will learn my hymn, and then read in the Bible about the sufferings of Jesus. Oh, what anguish that must have been! And I? What do I do that is good, in making others happy or consoling their trouble? This must be different, Paula! I will begin a new life. Mother always says we are happy when we deny self in order to do good. Ah, if we always could! But I will try; for He did, though He might have escaped, for our sins and to make us happy."

===

CHAPTER VI.
MY INTRODUCTION TO ART, AND ACQUAINTANCES GREAT AND SMALL IN THE LENNESTRASSE.

The Drakes mentioned in my sister's journal are the family of the sculptor, to whom Berlin and many another German city owe such splendid works of art.

He was also one of our neighbours, and a warm friendship bound him and his young wife to my mother. He was kind to us children, too, and had us in his studio, which was connected with the house like the other and larger one in the Thiergarten. He even gave us a bit of clay to shape. I have often watched him at work for hours, chattering to him, but happier still to listen while he told us of his childhood when he was a poor boy. He exhorted us to be thankful that we were better off, but generally added that he would not exchange for anything in the world those days when he went barefoot. His bright, clear artist's eyes sparkled as he spoke, and it must indeed have been a glorious satisfaction to have conquered the greatest hindrances by his own might, and to have raised himself to the highest pinnacle of life—that of art. I had a dim impression of this when he talked to us, and now I consider every one enviable who has only himself to thank for all he is, like Drake, his friend in art Ritschl, and my dear friend Josef Popf, in Rome, all three laurel-crowned masters in the art of sculpture.

In Drake's studio I saw statues, busts, and reliefs grow out of the rude mass of clay; I saw the plaster cast turned into marble, and the master, with his sure hand, evoking splendid forms from the primary limestone. What I could not understand, the calm, kindly man explained with unfailing patience, and so I got an early insight into the sculptor's creative art.

It was these recollections of my childhood that suggested to me the character of little Pennu in Uarda, of Polykarp in Homo Sum, of Pollux in The Emperor, and the cheery Alexander in Per Aspera.

I often visited also, during my last years in Berlin, the studio of another sculptor. His name was Streichenberg, and his workshop was in our garden in the Linkstrasse.

If a thoughtful earnestness was the rule in Drake's studio, in that of Prof. Streichenberg artistic gaiety reigned. He often whistled or sang at his work, and his young Italian assistant played the guitar. But while I still know exactly what Drake executed in our presence, so that I could draw the separate groups of the charming relief, the Genii of the Thiergarten, I do not remember a single stroke of Streichenberg's work, though I can recall all the better the gay manner of the artist whom we again met in 1848 as a demagogue.

At the Schmidt school Franz and Paul Meyerheim were among our comrades, and how full of admiration I was when one of them—Franz, I think, who was then ten or eleven years old—showed us a hussar he had painted himself in oil on a piece of canvas! The brothers took us to their home, and there I saw at his work their kindly father, the creator of so many charming pictures of country and child life.

There was also a member of the artist family of the Begas, Adalbert, who was one of our contemporaries and playmates, some of whose beautiful portraits I saw afterward, but whom, to my regret, I never met again.

Most memorable of all were our meetings with Peter Cornelius, who also lived in the Lennestrasse. When I think of him it always seems as if he were looking me in the face. Whoever once gazed into his eyes could never forget them. He was a little man, with waxen-pale, and almost harsh, though well-formed features, and smooth, long, coal-black hair. He might scarcely have been noticed save for his eyes, which overpowered all else, as the sunlight puts out starlight. Those eyes would have drawn attention to him anywhere. His peculiar seriousness and his aristocratic reserve of manner were calculated to keep children at a distance, even to repel them, and we avoided the stern little man whom we had heard belonged to the greatest of the great. When he and his amiable wife became acquainted with our mother, however, and he called us to him, it is indescribable how his harsh features softened in the intercourse with us little ones, till they assumed an expression of the utmost benevolence, and with what penetrating, I might say fatherly kindness, he talked and even jested with us in his impressive way. I had the best of it, for my blond curly head struck him as usable in some work of his, and my mother readily consented to my being his model. So I had to keep still several hours day after day, though I confess, to my shame, that I remember nothing about the sittings except having eaten some particularly good candied fruit.

Even now I smile at the recollection of his making an angel or a spirit of peace out of the wild boy who perhaps just before had been scuffling with the enemy from the flower-cellar.

There was another celebrated inhabitant of the Lennestrasse whose connection with us was still closer than that of Peter Cornelius. It was the councillor of consistory and court chaplain Strauss, who lived at No. 3.

Two men more unlike than he and his great artist-neighbour can hardly be imagined, though their cradles were not far apart, for the painter was born in Dusseldorf, and the clergyman at Iserlohn, in Westphalia.

Cornelius appears to me like a peculiarly delicate type of the Latin race, while Strauss might be called a prototype of the sturdy Lower Saxons. Broad-shouldered, stout, ruddy, with small but kindly blue eyes, and a resonant bass voice suited to fill great spaces, he was always at his ease and made others easy. He had a touch of the assured yet fine dignity of a well-placed and well-educated Catholic prelate, though combined with the warlike spirit of a Protestant.

Looking more closely at his healthy face, it revealed not only benevolent amiability but superior sense and plain traces of that cheery elasticity of soul which gave him such power over the hearts of the listening congregation, and the disposition and mind of the king.

His religious views I do not accept, but I believe his strictly orthodox belief was based upon conviction, and cannot be charged to any odious display of piety to ingratiate himself with the king. It was in the time of our boyhood that Alexander von Humboldt, going once with the king to church, in Potsdam, in answer to the sneering question how he, who passed for a freethinker at court, could go to the house of God, made the apt reply, "In order to get on, your Excellency."

When Strauss met us in the street and called to us with a certain unction in his melodious voice, "Good-morning, my dear children in Christ!" our hearts went out to him, and it seemed as if we had received a blessing. He and his son Otto used to call me "Marcus Aurelius," on account of my curly blond head; and how often did he put his strong hand into my thick locks to draw me toward him!

Strauss was in the counsels of the king, Frederick William IV, and at important moments exercised an influence on his political decisions. Yet that somewhat eccentric prince could not resist his inclination to make cheap jokes at Strauss's expense. After creating him court-chaplain, he said to Alexander von Humboldt: "A trick in natural history which you cannot copy! I have turned an ostrich (Strauss) into a bullfinch (Dompfaffer)"—in allusion to Strauss's being a preacher at the cathedral (Dom).

Fritz, the worthy man's eldest son, came to see me in Leipsic. Our studies in the department of biblical geography had led us to different conclusions, but our scientific views were constantly intermingled with recollections of the Lennestrasse.

But better than he, who was much older, do I remember his brother Otto, then a bright, amiable young man, and his mother, who was from the Rhine country, a warm-hearted, kindly woman of aristocratic bearing.

Our mother had a very high opinion of the court chaplain, who had christened us all and afterward confirmed my sisters, and officiated at Martha's marriage. But, much as she appreciated him as a friend and counsellor, she could not accept his strict theology. Though she received the communion at his hands, with my sisters, she preferred the sermons of the regimental chaplain, Bollert, and later those of the excellent Sydow. I well remember her grief when Bollert, whose free interpretation of Scripture had aroused displeasure at court, was sent to Potsdam.

I find an amusing echo of the effect of this measure in Paula's journal, and it would have been almost impossible for a growing girl of active mind to take no note of opinions which she heard everywhere expressed.

Our entire circle was loyal; especially Privy-Councillor Seiffart, one of our most intimate friends, a sarcastic Conservative, who was credited with the expresssion, "The limited intellect of subjects," which, however, belonged to his superior, Minister von Rochow. Still, almost all my mother's acquaintances, and the younger ones without exception, felt a desire for better political conditions and a constitution for the brave, loyal, reflecting, and well-educated Prussian people. In the same house with us lived two men who had suffered for their political convictions—the brothers Grimm. They had been ejected from their chairs among the seven professors of Gottingen, who were sacrificed to the arbitrary humour of King Ernst August of Hanover.

Their dignified figures are among the noblest and most memorable recollections of the Lennestrasse. They were, it might be said, one person, for they were seldom seen apart; yet each had preserved his own distinct individuality.

If ever the external appearance of distinguished men corresponded with the idea formed of them from their deeds and works, it was so in their case. One did not need to know them to perceive at the first glance that they were labourers in the department of intellectual life, though whether as scientists or poets even a practised observer would have found it difficult to determine. Their long, flowing, wavy hair, and an atmosphere of ideality which enveloped them both, might have inclined one to the latter supposition; while the form of their brows, indicating deep thought and severe mental labor, and their slightly stooping shoulders, would have suggested the former. Wilhelm's milder features were really those of a poet, while Jakob's sterner cast of countenance, and his piercing eyes, indicated more naturally a searcher after knowledge.

But just as certainly as that they both belonged to the strongest champions of German science, the Muse had kissed them in their cradle. Not only their manner of restoring our German legends, but almost all their writings, give evidence of a poetical mode of viewing things, and of an intuition peculiar to the spirit of poetry. Many of their writings, too, are full of poetical beauties.

That both were men in the fullest meaning of the word was revealed at the first glance. They proved it when, to stand by their convictions, they put themselves and their families at the mercy of a problematical future; and when, in advanced years, they undertook the gigantic work of compiling so large and profound a German dictionary. Jakob looked as if nothing could bend him; Wilhelm as if, though equally strong, he might yield out of love.

And what a fascinating, I might almost say childlike, amiability was united to manliness in both characters! Yes, theirs was indeed that sublime simplicity which genius has in common with the children whom the Saviour called to him. It spoke from the eyes whose gaze was so searching, and echoed in their language which so easily mastered difficult things, though when they condescended to play with their children and with us, and jested so naively, we were half tempted to think ourselves the wiser.

But we knew with what intellectual giants we had to do; no one had needed to tell us that, at least; and when they called me to them I felt as if the king himself had honoured me.

Only Wilhelm was married, and his wife had hardly her equal for sunny and simple kindness of heart. A pleasanter, more motherly, sweeter matron I never met.

Hermann, who won good rank as a poet, and was one of the very foremost of our aesthetics, was much older than we. The tall young man, who often walked as if he were absorbed in thought, seemed to us a peculiar and unapproachable person. His younger brother, Rudolf, on the other hand, was a cheery fellow, whose beauty and brightness charmed me unspeakably. When he came along with elastic tread as if he were challenging life to a conflict, and I saw him spring up the stairs three steps at a time, I was delighted, and I knew that my mother was very fond of him. It was just the same with "Gustel," his sister, who was as amiable and kindly as her mother.

I can still see the torchlight procession with which the Berlin students honoured the beloved and respected brothers, and which we watched from the Grimms' windows because they were higher than ours. But there is a yet brighter light of fire in my memory. It was shed by the burning opera house. Our mother, who liked to have us participate in anything remarkable which might be a recollection for life, took us out of our beds to the next house, where the Seiffarts lived, and which had a little tower on it. Thence we gazed in admiration at the ever-deepening glow of the sky, toward which great tongues of flame kept streaming up, while across the dusk shot formless masses like radiant spark-showering birds. Pillars of smoke mingled with the clouds, and the metallic note of the fire-bells calling for help accompanied the grand spectacle. I was only six years old, but I remember distinctly that when Ludo and I were taken to the Lutz swimming-baths next day, we found first on the drill-ground, then on the bank of the Spree, and in the water, charred pieces, large and small, of the side-scenes of the theatre. They were the glowing birds whose flight I had watched from the tower of the Crede house.

This remark reminds me how early our mother provided for our physical development, for I clearly remember that the tutor who took us little fellows to the bath called our attention to these bits of decoration while we were swimming. When I went to Keilhau, at eleven years old, I had mastered the art completely.

I did, in fact, many things at an earlier age than is customary, because I was always associated with my brother, who was a year and a half older.

We were early taught to skate, too, and how many happy hours we passed, frequently with our sisters, on the ice by the Louisa and Rousseau Islands in the Thiergarten! The first ladies who at that time distinguished themselves as skaters were the wife and daughter of the celebrated surgeon Dieffenbach—two fine, supple figures, who moved gracefully over the ice, and in their fur-bordered jackets and Polish caps trimmed with sable excited universal admiration.

On the whole, we had time enough for such things, though we lost many a free hour in music lessons. Ludo was learning to play on the piano, but I had chosen another instrument. Among our best friends, the three fine sons of Privy-Councillor Oesterreich and others, there was a pleasant boy named Victor Rubens, whose parents were likewise friends of my mother. In the hospitable house of this agreeable family I had heard the composer Vieuxtemps play the violin when I was nine years old. I went home fairly enraptured, and begged my mother to let me take lessons. My wish was fulfilled, and for many years I exerted myself zealously, without any result, to accomplish something on the violin. I did, indeed, attain to a certain degree of skill, but I was so little satisfied with my own performances that I one day renounced the hope of becoming a practical musician, and presented my handsome violin—a gift from my grandmother—to a talented young virtuoso, the son of my sisters' French teacher.

The actress Crelinger, when she came to see my mother, made a great impression on me, at this time, by her majestic appearance and her deep, musical voice. She, and her daughter, Clara Stich, afterward Frau Liedtcke, the splendid singer, Frau Jachmann-Wagner, and the charming Frau Schlegel-Koster, were the only members of the theatrical profession who were included among the Gepperts' friends, and whose acquaintance we made in consequence.

Frau Crelinger's husband was a highly respected jurist and councillor of justice, but among all the councillors' wives by whom she was surrounded I never heard her make use of her husband's title. She was simply "Frau" in society, and for the public Crelinger. She knew her name had an importance of its own. Even though posterity twines no wreaths for actors, it is done in the grateful memory of survivors. I shall never forget the ennobling and elevating hours I afterward owed to that great and noble interpreter of character.

I am also indebted to Frau Jachmann-Wagner for much enjoyment both in opera and the drama. She now renders meritorious service by fitting on the soundest artistic principles—younger singers for the stage.

Among my mother's papers was a humorous note announcing the arrival of a friend from Oranienburg, and signed:

"Your faithful old dog, Runge,

Who was born in a quiet way

At Neustadt, I've heard say."

He came not once, but several times. He bore the title of professor, was a chemist, and I learned from friends versed in that science that it was indebted to him for interesting discoveries.

He had been an acquaintance of my father, and no one who met him, bubbling over with animation and lively wit, could easily forget him. He had a full face and long, straight, dark hair hanging on his short neck, while intellect and kindness beamed from his twinkling eyes. When he tossed me up and laughed, I laughed too, and it seemed as if all Nature must laugh with us.

I have not met so strong and original a character for many a long year, and I was very glad to read in the autobiography of Wackernagel that when it went ill with him in Berlin, Hoffman von Fallersleben and this same Runge invited him to Breslau to share their poverty, which was so great that they often did not know at night where they should get the next day's bread.

How many other names with and without the title of privy-councillor occur to me, but I must not allow myself to think of them.

Fraulein Lamperi, however, must have a place here. She used to dine with us at least once a week, and was among the most faithful adherents of our family. She had been governess to my father and his only sister, and later was in the service of the Princess of Prussia, afterward the Empress Augusta, as waiting-woman.

She, too, was one of those original characters whom we never find now.

She was so clever that, incredible as it sounds, she made herself a wig and some false teeth, and yet she came of a race whose women were not accustomed to serve themselves with their own hands; for the blood of the venerable and aristocratic Altoviti family of Florence flowed in her veins. Her father came into the world as a marquis of that name, but was disinherited when, against the will of his family, he married the dancer Lamperi. With her he went first to Warsaw, and then to Berlin, where he supported himself and his children by giving lessons in the languages. One daughter was a prominent member of the Berlin ballet, the other was prepared by a most careful education to be a governess. She gave various lessons to my sisters, and criticised our proceedings sharply, as she did those of her fellow-creatures in general. "I can't help it—I Must say what I think," was the palliating remark which followed every severe censure; and I owe to her the conviction that it is much easier to express disapproval, when it can be done with impunity, than to keep it to one's self, as I am also indebted to her for the subject of my fairy tale, The Elixir.

I shall return to Fraulein Lamperi, for her connection with our family did not cease until her death, and she lived to be ninety. Her aristocratic connections in Florence—be it said to their honour—never repudiated her, but visited her when they came to Berlin, and the equipage of the Italian ambassador followed at her funeral, for he, too, belonged to her father's kindred. The extreme kindness extended to her by Emperor William I and his sovereign spouse solaced her old age in various ways.

One of the dearest friends of my sister Paula and of our family knew more of me, unfortunately, at this time than I of her. Her name was Babette Meyer, now Countess Palckreuth. She lived in our neighbourhood, and was a charming, graceful child, but not one of our acquaintances.

When she was grown up—we were good friends then—she told me she was coming from school one winter day, and some boys threw snowballs at her. Then Ludo and I appeared—"the Ebers boys" and she thought that would be the end of her; but instead of attacking her we fell upon the boys, who turned upon us, and drove them away, she escaping betwixt Scylla and Charybdis.

Before this praiseworthy deed we had, however, thrown snow at a young lady in wanton mischief. I forgive our heedlessness as we were forgiven, but it is really a painful thought to me that we should have snowballed a poor insane man, well known in the Thiergarten and Lennestrasse, and who seriously imagined that he was made of glass.

I began to relate this, thinking of our uproarious laughter when the poor fellow cried out: "Let me alone! I shall break! Don't you hear me clink?" Then I stopped, for my heart aches when I reflect what terrible distress our thoughtlessness caused the unfortunate creature. We were not bad-hearted children, and yet it occurred to none of us to put ourselves in the place of the whimpering man and think what he suffered. But we could not do it. A child is naturally egotistical, and unable in such a case to distinguish between what is amusing and what is sad. Had the cry, "It hurts me!" once fallen from the trembling lips of the "glass man," I think we should have thrown nothing more at him.

But our young hearts did not, under all circumstances, allow what amused us to cast kinder feelings into the shade. The "man of glass" had a feminine 'pendant' in the "crazy Frau Councillor with the velvet envelope." This was a name she herself had given to a threadbare little velvet cloak, when some naughty boys—were we among them?—were snowballing her, and she besought us not to injure her velvet envelope. But when there was ice on the ground and one of the boys was trying to get her on to a slide, Ludo and I interfered and prevented it. Naturally, there was a good fight in consequence, but I am glad of it to this day.

CHAPTER VII.
WHAT A BERLIN CHILD ENJOYED ON THE SPREE AND AT HIS GRANDMOTHER'S IN DRESDEN.

In the summer we were all frequently taken to the new Zoological Garden, where we were especially delighted with the drollery of the monkeys. Even then I felt a certain pity for the deer and does in confinement, and for the wild beasts in their cages, and this so grew upon me that many a visit to a zoological garden has been spoiled by it. Once in Keilhau I caught a fawn in the wood and was delighted with my beautiful prize. I meant to bring it up with our rabbits, and had already carried it quite a distance, when suddenly I began to be sorry for it, and thought how its mother would grieve, upon which I took it back to the spot where I had found it and returned to the institution as fast as I could, but said nothing at first about my "stupidity," for I was ashamed of it.

Excursions into the country were the most delightful pleasures of the summer. The shorter ones took us to the suburbs of the capital, and sometimes to Charlottenburg, where several of our acquaintances lived, and our guardian, Alexander Mendelssohn, had a country house with a beautiful garden, where there was never any lack of the owner's children and grandchildren for playmates. Sometimes we were allowed to go there with other boys. We then had a few Groschen to get something at a restaurant, and were generally brought home in a Kremser carriage. These carriages were to be found in a long row by the wall outside of the Brandenburg Gate or at the Palace in Charlottenburg or by the "Turkish tent"—for at that time there were no omnibuses running to the decidedly rural neighbouring city. Even when the carriages were arranged to carry ten or twelve persons there was but one horse, and it was these Rosinantes which probably gave rise to the following rhyme:

"A Spandau wind,

A child of Berlin,

A Charlottenburg horse,

Are all not worth a pin."

The Berlin children were, on the whole, better than their reputation, but not so the Charlottenburg horses. The Kremser carriages were named from the man who owned most of them. The business was carried on by an association. A single individual rarely hired one; either a family took possession of it, or you got in and waited patiently till enough persons had collected for the driver to think it worth while to take his whip and say, "Well, get up!"

But this same Herr Kremser also had nice carriages for excursions into the country, drawn by two or four horses, as might be required. For the four-horse Kremser chariots there was even a driver in jockey costume, who rode the saddle-horse.

Other excursions took us to the beautiful Humboldt's Tegel, to the Muggel and Schlachten Lakes, to Franzosisch Buchholz, Treptow, and Stralau. We were, unfortunately, never allowed to attend the celebrated fishing festival at Stralau.

But the crowning expedition of all was on our mother's birthday, either to the Pichelsbergen, wooded hills mirrored in ponds where fish abounded, or to the Pfaueninsel at Potsdam.

The country around Berlin is considered hopelessly ugly, but with great injustice. I have convinced myself since that I do not look back as fondly on the Pichelsbergen and the Havelufer at Potsdam, where it was granted us to pass such happy hours in the springtime of life, because the force of imagination has clothed them with fancied charms. No, these places have indeed a singularly peaceful attractiveness, and if I prefer them, as a child of the century, to real mountains, there was a time when the artist's eye would have given them the preference over the grand landscapes of the Alpine world.

At the beginning of the last century the latter were considered repelling. They oppressed the soul by their immensity. No painter then undertook to depict giant mountains with eternal snow upon summits which towered above the clouds. A Salvator Rosa or Poussin, or even the great Ruysdael, would have preferred to set up his easel at the Pichelsbergen or in the country about Potsdam, rather than at the foot of Mont Blanc, the Kunigssee, or the Eibsee, in which the rocks of the Zugspitze—my vis-a-vis at Tutzingen—are magnificently reflected.

There is nothing more beautiful than the moderate, finely rounded heights at these peaceful spots rich in vegetation and in water, when gilded by the fading light of a lovely summer evening or illumined by the rosy tinge of the afterglow. Many of our later German painters have learned to value the charm of such a subject, while of our writers Fontane has seized and very happily rendered all their witchery. At my brother Ludo's manorhouse on the banks of the Dahme, at his place Dolgenbrodt, in Mark Brandenburg, Fontane experienced all the attraction of the plain, which I have never felt more deeply than in that very spot and on a certain evening at Potsdam when the bells of the little church of Sakrow seemed to bid farewell to the sinking sun and invite him to return.

In the East I have seen the day-star set more brilliantly, but never met with a more harmonious and lovely splendour of colour than on summer evenings in the Mark, except in Holland on the shore of the North Sea.

Can I ever forget those festal days when, after saying our little congratulatory verses to our mother, and admiring her birthday table, which her friends always loaded with flowers, we awaited the carriages that were to take us into the country? Besides a great excursion wagon, there were generally some other coaches which conveyed us and the families of our nearest friends on our jaunt.

How the young faces beamed, and how happy the old ones looked, and what big baskets there were full of good things beside the coachman and behind the carriage!

We were soon out of the city, and the birds by the wayside could not have twittered and sung in May more gaily than we during these drives.

Once we let the horses rest, and took luncheon at Stimming near the Wannsee, where Heinrich von Kleist with the beloved of his heart put an end to his sad life. Before we stopped we met a troop of travelling journeymen, and our mother, in the gratitude of her heart, threw them a thaler, and said "Drink to my happiness; to-day is my birthday."

When we had rested and gone on quite a distance we found the journeymen ranged beside the road, and as they threw into the carriage an immense bouquet of field flowers which they had gathered, one of them exclaimed: "Long live the birthday-child! And health and happiness to the beautiful, kind lady!" The others, and we, too, joined with all our might in a "Hurrah!"

We felt like pagan Romans, who on starting out had perceived the happiest omens in earth and sky.

And at the Pfaueninsel!

Frau Friedrich, the wife of the man in charge of the fountains, kept a neat inn, in which, however, she by no means dished up to all persons what they would like. But our mother knew her through Lenne, by whom her husband was employed, and she took good care of us. How attractive to us children was the choice yet large collection she possessed! Most of the members of the royal house had often been her guests, and had increased it to a little museum which contained countless milk and cream jugs of every sort and metal, even the most precious, and of porcelain and glass of every age. Many would have been rare and welcome ornaments to any trades-museum. Our mother had contributed a remarkably handsome Japanese jug which her brother had sent her.

After the banquet we young ones ran races, while the older people rested till coffee and punch were served. Whether dancing was allowed at the Pfaueninsel I no longer remember, but at the Pichelsbergen it certainly was, and there were even three musicians to play.

And how delightful it was in the wood; how pleasant the rowing on the water, during which, when the joy of existence was at its height, the saddest songs were sung! Oh, I could relate a hundred things of those birthdays in the country, but I have completely forgotten how we got home. I only know that we waked the next morning full of happy recollections.

In the summer holidays we often took journeys—generally to Dresden, where our father's mother with her daughter, our aunt Sophie, had gone to live, the latter having married Baron Adolf von Brandenstein, an officer in the Saxon Guard, who, after laying aside the bearskin cap and red coat, the becoming uniform of that time, was at the head of the Dresden post office.

I remember these visits with pleasure, and the days when our grandmother and aunt came to Berlin. I was fond of both of them, especially my lively aunt, who was always ready for a joke, and my affection was returned. But these, our nearest relatives, in early childhood only passed through our lives like brilliant meteors; the visits we exchanged lasted only a few days; and when they came to Berlin, in spite of my mother's pressing invitations, they never stayed at our house, but in a hotel. I cannot imagine, either, that our grandmother would ever have consented to visit any one. There was a peculiar exclusiveness about her, I might almost say a cool reserve, which, although proofs of her cordial love were not wanting, prevented her from caressing us or playing with us as grandmothers do. She belonged to another age, and our mother taught us, when greeting her, to kiss her little white hand, which was always covered up to the fingers with waving lace, and to treat her with the utmost deference. There was an air of aristocratic quiet in her surroundings which caused a feeling of constraint. I can still see the suite of spacious rooms she occupied, where silence reigned except when Coco, the parrot, raised his shrill voice. Her companion, Fraulein Raffius, always lowered her voice in her presence, though when out of it she could play with us very merrily. The elderly servant, who, singularly enough, was of noble family—his real name was Von Wurmkessel—did his duty as noiselessly as a shadow. Then there was a faint perfume of mignonette in most of the rooms, which makes me think of them whenever I see the pretty flower, for, as is well known, smell is the most powerful of all the senses in awakening memory.

I never sat in my grandmother's lap. When we wished to talk with her we had to sit beside her; and if we kept still she would question us searchingly about everything—our play, our friends, our school.

This silence, which always struck us children at first with astonishment, was interrupted very gaily by our aunt, whose liveliness broke in upon it like the sound of a horn amid the stillness of a forest. Her cheerful voice was audible even in the hall, and when she crossed the threshold we flew to her, and the spell was broken. For she, the only daughter, put no restraint on herself in the reserved presence of her mother. She kissed her boisterously, asked how she was, as if she were the mother, the other the child. Indeed, she took the liberty sometimes of calling the old lady "Henrietta"—that was her name—or even "Hetty." Then, when grandmother pointed to us and exclaimed reproachfully, "Why, Sophie!" our aunt could always disarm her with gay jests.

Though the two were generally at a distance, their existence made itself felt again and again either through letters or presents or by their coming to Berlin, which always brought holidays for us.

These journeys were accomplished under difficulties. Our aunt had always used an open carriage, and was really convinced that she would stifle in a closed railway compartment. But as she would not forego the benefit of rapid transit, our grandmother was obliged, even after her daughter's marriage, to hire an open truck for her, on which, with her faithful maid Minna, and one of her dogs, or sometimes with her husband or a friend as a companion, she established herself comfortably in an armchair of her own, with various other conveniences about her. The railway officials knew her, and no doubt shrugged their shoulders, but the warmheartedness shining in her eyes and her unvarying cheerfulness carried everything before them, so that her eccentricity was readily overlooked. And she had plenty of similar caprices. I was visiting her once in the Christmas holidays, when I was a schoolboy in the upper class, and we had retired for the night. At one o'clock my aunt suddenly appeared at my bedside, waked me, and told me to get up. The first snow had fallen, and she had had the horses harnessed for us to go sleighing, which she particularly enjoyed.

Resistance was useless, and the swift flight over the snow by moonlight proved to be very enjoyable. Between four and five o'clock in the morning we were at home again.

Winter brought many other amusements. I remember with particular pleasure the Christmas fair, which now, as I learn to my regret, is no longer held. And yet, what a source of delight it once was to children! What rich food it offered to their minds! The Christmas trees and pyramids at the Stechbahn, the various wares, the gingerbread and toys in the booths, offered by no means the greatest charm. A still stronger attraction were the boys with the humming "baboons," the rattles and flags, for from them purchases had always to be made, with jokes thrown into the bargain—bad ones, which are invariably the most amusing; and what a pleasure it was to twirl the "baboon" with one's own little hand, and, if the hand got cold during the process, one did not feel it, for it seemed like midsummer with a swarm of flies buzzing about one!

But most enjoyable of all was probably the throng of people, great and small, and all there was to hear and see among them and to answer. It seemed as if the Christmas joy of the city was concentrated there, and filled the not over-clear atmosphere like the pungent odour of Christmas trees.

Put there were other things to experience as well as mere gaiety—the pale child in the corner, with its little bare feet, holding in its cold, red hands the six little sheep of snow-white wool on a tiny green board; and that other yonder, with the little man made of prunes spitted on tiny sticks.

How small and pale the child is! And how eloquently the blue eyes invite a purchaser, for it is only with looks that the wares are extolled! I still see them both before me! The threepenny pieces they get are to help their starving mother to heat the attic room in those winter days which, cold though they are, may warm the heart. Looking at them our mother told us how hunger hurts, and how painful want and misery are to bear, and we never left the Christmas fair without buying a few sheep or a prune man, though all we could do with them was to give them away again. When I wrote my fairy-tale, The Nuts, I had the Christmas fair at Berlin in my mind's eye, and I seemed to see the wretched little girl who, among all the happy folk, had found nothing but cold, pain, anguish, and a handful of nuts, and who afterward fared so happily—not, indeed, among men, but with the most beautiful angels in heaven.

Why are the Berlin children defrauded of this bright and innocent pleasure, and their hearts denied the practice of exercising charity?

Turning my thoughts backward, it seems to me as if almost too much beauty and pleasure were crowded together at Christmas, richly provided with presents as we were besides, for over and above the Christmas fair there was Kroll's Christmas exhibition, where clever heads and skilful hands transformed a series of great halls, at one time into the domain of winter, at another into the kingdom of the fairies. There was nothing to do but look.

Imagination came to a standstill, for what could it add to these wonders? Yet the fairyland of which Ludo and I had dreamed was more beautiful and more real than this palpable magnificence of tin and pasteboard; which is, perhaps, one reason why the overexcited imagination of a city child shrinks back and tries to find in reality what a boy brought up in the quiet of the country can conjure up before his mind himself.

Then, too, there were delightful sights in the Gropius panorama and Fuchs's confectioner's shop—in the one place entertaining things, in the other instructive. At the panorama half the world was spread out before us in splendid pictures, so presented and exhibited as to give the most vivid impression of reality.

From the letters of our mother's brothers, who were Dutch officials in Java and Japan, as well as from books of travel which had been read to us, we had already heard much of the wonders of the Orient; and at the Gropius panorama the inner call that I had often seemed to hear—"Away! to the East"—only grew the stronger. It has never been wholly silent since, but at that time I formed the resolution to sail around the world, or—probably from reading some book—to be a noble pirate. Nor should I have been dissatisfied with the fate of Robinson Crusoe. The Christmas exhibition at Fuchs's, Unter den Linden, was merely entertaining—Berlin jokes in pictures mainly of a political or satirical order. Most distinctly of all I remember the sentimental lady of rank who orders her servant to catch a fly on a tea-tray and put it carefully out of the window. The obedient Thomas gets hold of the insect, takes it to the window, and with the remark, "Your ladyship, it is pouring, the poor thing might take cold," brings it back again to the tea-tray.

There was plenty of such entertainment in winter, and we had our part in much of it. Rellstab, the well-known editor of Voss's journal, made a clever collection of such jokes in his Christmas Wanderings. We could read, and whatever was offered by that literary St. Nicholas and highly respected musical critic for cultivated Berlin our mother was quite willing we should enjoy.

CHAPTER VIII.
THE REVOLUTIONARY PERIOD BEFORE THE REVOLUTION

On the 18th of March, the day of the fighting in the streets of Berlin, we had been living for a year in the large suite of apartments at No. 7 Linkstrasse.

Of those who inhabited the same house with us I remember only the sculptor Streichenberg, whose studio was next to our pretty garden, and the Beyers, a married couple. He, later a general and commander of the troops besieging Strasburg in 1870, was at that time a first lieutenant. She was a refined, extremely amiable, and very musical woman, who had met our mother before, and now entered into the friendliest relations with her.

A guest of their quiet household, a little Danish girl, one of Fran Beyer's relatives, shared our play in the garden, and worked with us at the flower beds which had been placed in our charge. I remember how perfectly charming I thought her, and that her name was Detta Lvsenor.

All the details of our intercourse with her and other new acquaintances who played with us in the garden have vanished from my memory, for the occurrences of that time are thrown into shadow by the public events and political excitement around us. Even children could not remain untouched by what was impending, for all that we saw or heard referred to it and, in our household, views violently opposed to each other, with the exception of extreme republicanism, were freely discussed.

The majority of our conservative acquaintances were loud in complaint, and bewailed the king's weakness, and the religious corruption and hypocritical aspirations which were aroused by the honest, but romantic and fanatical religious zeal of Frederick William IV. I must have heard the loudest lamentations concerning this cancer of society at this time, for they are the most deeply imprinted in my memory. Even such men as the Gepperts, Franz Kugler, H. M. Romberg, Drake, Wilcke, and others, with whose moderate political views I became acquainted later, used to join us. Loyal they all were, and our mother was so strongly attached to the house of Hohenzollern that I heard her request one of the younger men, when he sharply declared it was time to force the king to abdicate, either to moderate his speech or cease to visit her house.

Our mother could not prevent, however, similar and worse speeches from coming to our ears.

A particularly deep impression was made upon us by a tall man with a big blond beard, whose name I have forgotten, but whom we generally met at the sculptor Streichenberg's when he took us with him in our play hours into his great workshop. This man appeared to be in very good circumstances, for he always wore patent-leather boots, and a large diamond ring on his finger; but with his vivacious, even passionate temperament, he trampled in the dust the things I had always revered. I hung on his lips when he talked of the rights of the people, and of his own vocation to break the way for freedom, or when he anathematized those who oppressed a noble nation with the odious yoke of slavery.

Catch phrases, like "hanging the last king with the guts of the last priest," I heard for the first time from him, and although such speeches did not please me, they made an impression because they awakened so much surprise, and more than once he called upon us to be true sons of our time and not a tyrant's bondmen. We heard similar remarks elsewhere in a more moderate form, and from our companions at school in boyish language.

There were two parties there also, but besides loyalty another sentiment flourished which would now be called chauvinism, yet which possessed a noble influence, since it fostered in our hearts that most beautiful flower of the young mind, enthusiasm for a great cause.

And during the history lessons on Brandenburg-Prussia our cheeks would glow, for what German state could boast a grander, prouder history than Prussia under the Hohenzollerns, rising by ability, faithfulness to duty, courage, and self-sacrificing love of country from small beginnings to the highest power?

The Liebe school had been attended only by children of good families, while in the Schmidt school a Count Waldersee and Hoym, the son of a capmaker and dealer in eatables, sat together on the same bench. The most diverse tendencies were represented, and all sorts of satirical songs and lampoons found their way to us. Such parodies as this in the Song of Prussia we could understand very well:

"I am a Prussian, my colours you know,

From darkness to light they boldly go;

But that for Freedom my fathers died,

Is a fact which I have not yet descried."

Nor did more delicate allusions escape us; for who had not heard, for instance, of the Friends of Light, who played a part among the Berlin liberals? To whose ears had not come some longing cry for freedom, and especially freedom of the press?

And though that ever-recurring word Pressfreiheit (freedom of the press) was altered by the wags for us boys into Fressfreiheit (liberty to stuff yourself); though, too, it was condemned in conservative circles as a dangerous demand, threatening the peace of the family and opening the door to unbridled license among writers for the papers, still we had heard the other side of the question; that the right freely to express an opinion belonged to every citizen, and that only through the power of free speech could the way be cleared for a better condition of things. In short, there was no catchword of that stormy period which we ten and twelve-year-old boys could not have interpreted at least superficially.

To me it seemed a fine thing to be able to say what one thought right, still I could not understand why such great importance should be attributed to freedom of the press. The father of our friend Bardua was entitled a counsellor of the Supreme Court, but then he had also filled the office of a censor, and what a nice, bright boy his son was!

Among our comrades was also the son of Prof. Hengstenberg, who was the head of the pietists and Protestant zealots, whom we had heard mentioned as the darkest of all obscurants, and his influence over the king execrated. By the central flight of steps at the little terrace in front of the royal palace stood the fine statues of the horse-tamers, and the steps were called Hengstenberg (Hengste, horses, and Berg, mountain). And this name was explained by the circumstance that whoever would approach the king must do so by the way of "Hengstenberg."

We knew that quip, too, and yet the son of this mischievous enemy of progress was a particularly fine, bright boy, whom we all liked, and whose father, when I saw him, astonished me, for he was a kindly man and could laugh as cheerfully as anybody.

It was all very difficult to understand; and, as we had more friends among the conservatives than among the democrats, we played usually with the former, and troubled ourselves very little about the politics of our friends' fathers. There was, however, some looking askance at each other, and cries of "Loyal Legioner!" "Pietist!" "Democrat!" "Friend of Light!" were not wanting.

As often happens in the course of history, uncomprehended or only half-comprehended catchwords serve as a banner around which a great following collects.

The parties did not come to blows, probably for the sole reason that we conservatives were by far the stronger. Yet there was a fermentation among us, and a day came when, young as I was, I felt that those who called the king weak and wished for a change were in the right.

In the spring of 1847 every one felt as if standing on a volcano.

When, in 1844, it was reported that Burgomaster Tschech had fired at the king—I was then seven years old—we children shared the horror and indignation of our mother, although in the face of such a serious event we boys joined in the silly song which was then in everybody's mouth, and which began somewhat in this fashion:

"Was there ever a man so insolent

As Tschech, the mayor, on mischief bent?"

What did we not hear at that time about all the hopes that had been placed on the crown-prince, and how ill he had fulfilled them as king! How often I listened quietly in some corner while my mother discussed such topics with gentlemen, and from the beginning of the year 1847 there was hardly a conversation in Berlin which did not sooner or later touch upon politics and the general discontent or anxiety. But I had no need to listen in order to hear such things. On every walk we took they were forced upon our ears; the air was full of them, the very stones repeated them.

Even we boys had heard of Johann Jacoby's "Four Questions," which declared a constitution a necessity.

I have not forgotten the indignation called forth, even among our acquaintances of moderate views, by Hassenpflug's promotion; and if his name had never come to my ears at home, the comic papers, caricatures, and the talk everywhere would have acquainted me with the feelings awakened among the people of Berlin by the favour he enjoyed. And added to this were a thousand little features, anecdotes, and events which all pointed to the universal discontent.

The wars for freedom lay far behind us. How much had been promised to the people when the foreign foe was to be driven out, and how little had been granted! After the July revolution of 1830, many German states had obtained a constitution, while in Prussia not only did everything remain in the same condition, but the shameful time of the spying by the agitators had begun, when so many young men who had deserved well of their country, like Ernst Moriz, Arndt, and Jahn, distinguished and honourable scholars like Welcker, suffered severely under these odious persecutions. One must have read the biography of the honest and laborious Germanist Wackernagel to be able to credit the fact that that quiet searcher after knowledge was pursued far into middle life by the most bitter persecution and rancorous injuries, because as a schoolboy—whether in the third or fourth class I do not know—he had written a letter in which was set forth some new division, thought out in his childish brain, for the united German Empire of which he dreamed.

Such men as Kamptz and Dambach kept their places by casting suspicion upon others and condemning them, but they little dreamed when they summoned before their execrable tribunal the insignificant student Fritz Reuter, of Mecklenburg, how he would brand their system and their names. Most of these youths who had been plunged into misery by such rascally abuse of office and the shameful way in which a king naturally anything but malignant, was misled and deceived, were either dead and gone, or had been released from prison as mature men. What hatred must have filled their souls for that form of government which had dared thus to punish their pure enthusiasm for a sacred cause—the unity and well-earned freedom of their native land! Ah, there were dangerous forces to subdue among those grey-haired martyrs, for it was their fiery spirit and high hearts which had brought them to ruin.

Those who had been disappointed in the results of the war for liberty, and those who had suffered in the demagogue period, had ventured to hope once more when the much-extolled crown-prince, Frederick William IV, mounted the throne. What disappointment was in store for them; what new suffering was laid upon them when, instead of the rosy dawn of freedom which they fancied they had seen, a deeper darkness and a more reckless oppression set in! What they had taken for larks announcing the breaking of a brighter day turned out to be bats and similar vermin of the night. In the state the exercise of a boundless arbitrary power; in the Church, dark intolerance; and, in its train, slavish submission, favour-seeking, rolling up of the eyes, and hypocrisy as means to unworthy ends, and especially to that of speedy promotion—the deepest corruption of all—that of the soul.

What naturally followed caused the loyalists the keenest pain, for the injury done to the strong monarchical feeling of the Prussian people in the person and the conduct of Frederick William IV was not to be estimated. Only the simple heroic greatness and the paternal dignity of an Emperor William could have repaired it.

In the year preceding the revolution there had been a bad harvest, and frightful stories were told of famine in the weaving districts of Silesia. Even before Virchow, in his free-spoken work on the famine-typhus, had faithfully described the full misery of those wretched sufferers, it had become apparent to the rulers in Berlin that something must be done to relieve the public distress.

The king now began to realize distinctly the universal discontent, and in order to meet it and still further demands he summoned the General Assembly.

I remember distinctly how fine our mother thought the speech with which he opened that precursor of the Prussian Chambers, and the address showed him in fact to be an excellent orator.

To him, believing as he did with the most complete conviction in royalty by the grace of God and in his calling by higher powers, any relinquishing of his prerogative would seem like a betrayal of his divine mission. The expression he uttered in the Assembly in the course of his speech—"I and my people will serve the Lord"—came from the very depths of his heart; and nothing could be more sincerely meant than the remark, "From one weakness I know myself to be absolutely free: I do not strive for vain public favour. My only effort is to do my duty to the best of my knowledge and according to my conscience, and to deserve the gratitude of my people, though it should be denied me."

The last words have a foreboding sound, and prove what is indeed evident from many other expressions—that he had begun to experience in his own person the truth of the remark he had made when full of hope, and hailed with joyful anticipations at his coronation—"The path of a king is full of sorrow, unless his people stand by him with loyal heart and mind."

His people did not do that, and it was well for them; for the path indicated by the royal hand would have led them to darkness and to the indignity of ever-increasing bondage, mental and temporal.

The prince himself is entitled to the deepest sympathy. He wished to do right, and was endowed with great and noble gifts which would have done honour to a private individual, but could not suffice for the ruler of a powerful state in difficult times.

Hardly had the king opened the General Assembly in April, 1848, and, for the relief of distress among the poorer classes in the capital, repealed the town dues on corn, when the first actual evidences of discontent broke out. The town tax was so strictly enforced at that time at all the gates of Berlin that even hacks entering the city were stopped and searched for provisions of meat or bread—a search which was usually conducted in a cursory and courteous manner.

In my sister Paula's journal I have an almost daily account of that period, with frequent reference to political events, but it is not my task to write a history of the Berlin revolution.

Those of my sister's records which refer to the revolutionary period begin with a mention of the so-called potato revolution, which occurred ten days after the opening of the General Assembly, though it had no connection with it.

[Excessive prices had been asked for a peck of potatoes, which enraged the purchasers, who threw them into the gutter and laid hands on some of the market-women. The assembled crowd then plundered some bakers' and butchers' shops, and was finally dispersed by the military. A certain Herr Winckler is said to have lost his life. Many windows were broken, etc.]

This riot took place on the 21st of April, and on the 2d of May Paula alludes to a performance at the opera-house, which Ludo and I attended. It was the last appearance of Fran Viardot Garcia as Iphigenia, but I fear Paula is right in saying that the great singer did her best for an ungrateful public, for the attention of the audience was directed chiefly to the king and queen. The latter appeared in the theatre for the first time since a severe illness, the enthusiasm was great, and there was no end to the cries of "Long live the king and queen!" which were repeated between every act.

I relate the circumstance to show with what a devoted and faithful affection the people of Berlin still clung to the royal pair. On the other hand, their regard for the Prince of Prussia, afterward Emperor William, was already shaken. He who alone remained firm when all about the king were wavering, was regarded as the embodiment of military rule, against which a violent opposition was rising.

Our mother was even then devoted to him with a reverence which bordered upon affection, and we children with her.

We felt more familiar with him, too; than with any other members of the ruling house, for Fraulein Lamperi, who was in a measure like one of our own family, was always relating the most attractive stories about him and his noble spouse, whose waiting-woman she had been.

Of Frederick William IV it was generally jokes that were told, some of them very witty ones. We once came in contact with him in a singular way.

Our old cook, Frau Marx, who called herself "the Marxen," was nearly blind, and wished to enter an institution, for which it was necessary to have his Majesty's consent. Many years before, when she was living in a count's family, she had taught the king, as a young prince, to churn, and on the strength of this a petition was drawn up for her by my family. This she handed into the king's carriage, in the palace court-yard, and to his question who she was, she replied, "Why, I'm old Marxen, and your Majesty is my last retreat." This speech was repeated to my mother by the adjutant who came to inquire about the petitioner, and he assured her that his Majesty had been greatly amused by the old woman's singular choice of words, and had repeated it several times to persons about him. Her wish was fulfilled at once.

The memory of those March days of 1848 is impressed on my soul in ineffaceable characters. More beautiful weather I never knew. It seemed as if May had taken the place of its stormy predecessor. From the 13th the sun shone constantly from a cloudless sky, and on the 18th the fruit-trees in our garden were in full bloom. Whoever was not kept in the house by duty or sickness was eager to be out. The public gardens were filled by afternoon, and whoever wanted to address the people had no need to call an audience together. Whatever rancour, indignation, discontent, and sorrow had lurked under ground now came forth, and the buds of longing and joyful expectation hourly unfolded in greater strength and fuller bloom.

The news of the Paris revolution, whose confirmation had reached Berlin in the last few days of February, had caused all this growth and blossoming like sunshine and warm rain. There was no repressing it, and the authorities felt daily more and more that their old measures of restraint were failing.

The accounts from Paris were accompanied by report after report from the rest of Germany, shaking the old structure of absolutism like the repeated shocks of a battering-ram.

Freedom of the press was not yet granted, but tongues had begun to move freely-indeed, often without any restraint. As early as the 7th of March, and in bad weather, too, meetings began to be held in tents. As soon as the fine spring days came we found great crowds listening to bearded orators, who told them of the revolution in Paris and of the addresses to the king—how they had passed hither and thither, and how they had been received. They had all contained very much the same demands—freedom of the press, representatives of the people to be chosen by free election, all religious confessions to be placed on an equal footing in the exercise of political rights, and representation of the people in the German Confederacy.

These demands were discussed with fiery zeal, and the royal promise, just given, of calling together the Assembly again and issuing a law on the press, after the Confederate Diet should have been moved to a similar measure, was condemned in strong terms as an insufficient and half-way procedure—a payment on account, in order to gain time.

On the 15th the particulars of the Vienna revolution and Metternich's flight reached Berlin; and we, too, learned the news, and heard our mother and her friends asking anxiously, "How will this end?"

Unspeakable excitement had taken possession of young and old—at home, in the street, and at school—for blood had already flowed in the city. On the 13th, cavalry had dispersed a crowd in the vicinity of the palace, and the same thing was repeated on the two following days. Fortunately, few were injured; but rumour, ever ready to increase and enhance the horrible desire of many fanatics to stir up the fire of discontent, had conspired to make wounded men dead ones, and slight injuries severe.

These exaggerations ran through the city, arousing indignation; and the correspondents of foreign papers, knowing that readers often like best what is most incredible, had sent the accounts to the provinces and foreign countries.

But blood had flowed. Hatred of the soldiery, to which, however, some among the insurgents had once been proud to belong, grew with fateful rapidity, and was still further inflamed by those who saw in the military the brazen wall that stood between them and the fulfillment of their most ardent wishes.

A spark might spring the open and overcharged mine into the air; an ill-chosen or misunderstood expression, a thoughtless act, might bring about an explosion.

The greatest danger threatened from fresh conflicts between the army and the people, and it was to the fear of this that various young or elderly gentlemen owed their office of going about wherever a crowd was assembled and urging the populace to keep the peace. They were distinguished by a white band around the arm bearing the words, "Commissioner of Protection," and a white rod a foot and a half long designed to awaken the respect accorded by the English to their constables. We recognized many well-known men; but the Berlin populace, called by Goethe insolent, is not easily impressed, and we saw constables surrounded by street boys like an owl with a train of little birds fluttering teasingly around it. Even grown persons called them nicknames and jeered at their sticks, which they styled "cues" and "tooth-picks."

A large number of students, too, had expressed their readiness to join this protective commission, either as constables or deputies, and had received the wand and band at the City Hall.

How painful the exercise of their vocation was made to them it would be difficult to describe. News from Austria and South Germany, where the people's cause seemed to be advancing with giant strides to the desired goal, hourly increased the offensive strength of the excited populace.

On the afternoon of the 16th the Potsdam Platz, only a few hundred steps from our house, was filled with shouting and listening throngs, crowded around the sculptor Streichenberg, his blond-bearded friend, and other violently gesticulating leaders. This multitude received constant reenforcements from the city and through Bellevuestrasse. On the left, at the end of the beautiful street with its rows of budding chestnut-trees, lay "Kemperhof," a pleasure resort where we had often listened to the music of a band clad in green hunting costume. Many must have come thence, for I find that on the 16th an assemblage was held there from which grew the far more important one on the morning of the 17th, with its decisive conclusion in Kopenickerstrasse.

At this meeting, on the afternoon of the 17th, it was decided to set on foot a peaceful manifestation of the wishes of the people, and a new address to the king was drawn up. It was settled that on the 28th of March, at two o'clock, thousands of citizens with the badges of the protective commission should appear before the palace and send in a deputation to his Majesty with a document which should clearly convey the principal requirements of the people.

What they were to represent to the king as urgently necessary was: The withdrawal of the military force, the organization of an armed citizen guard, the granting of an unconditional freedom of the press, which had been promised for a lifetime, and the calling of the General Assembly. I shall return to the address later.

CHAPTER IX.
THE EIGHTEENTH OF MARCH.

THE 17th passed so quietly that hopes of a peaceable outcome of the fateful conflict began to awake. My own recollections confirm this.

People believed so positively that the difficulty would be adjusted, that in the forenoon of the 18th my mother sent my eldest sister Martha to her drawing-lesson, which was given at General Baeyer's, in the Friedrichstrasse.

Ludo and I went to school, and when it was over the many joyful faces in the street confirmed what we had heard during the school hours.

The king had granted the Constitution and the "freedom of the press."

Crowds were collected in front of the placards which announced this fact, but there was no need to force our way through; their contents were read aloud at every corner and fountain.

One passer-by repeated it to another, and friend shouted to friend across the street. "Have you heard the news?" was the almost invariable question when people accosted one another, and at least one "Thank God!" was contained in every conversation. Two or three older acquaintances whom we met charged us, in all haste, to tell our mother; but she had heard it already, and her joy was so great that she forgot to scold us for staying away so long. Fraulein Lamperi, on the contrary, who dined with us, wept. She was convinced that the unfortunate king had been forced into something which would bring ruin both to him and his subjects. "His poor Majesty!" she sobbed in the midst of our joy.

Our mother loved the king too, but she was a daughter of the free Netherlands; two of her brothers and sisters lived in England; and the friends she most valued, whom she knew to be warmly and faithfully attached to the house of Hohenzollern, thought it high time that the Prussian people attained the majority to which that day had brought them. Moreover, her active mind knew no rest till it had won a clear insight into questions concerning the times and herself. So she had reached the conviction that no peace between king and people could be expected unless a constitution was granted. In Parliament she would have sat on the right, but that her adopted country should have a Parliament filled her with joyful pride.

Ludo and I were very gay. It was Saturday, and towards evening we were going to a children's ball given by Privy-Councillor Romberg—the specialist for nervous diseases—for his daughter Marie, for which new blue jackets had been made.

We were eagerly expecting them, and about three o'clock the tailor came.

Our mother was present when he tried them on, and when she remarked that now all was well, the man shook his head, and declared that the concessions of the forenoon had had no other object than to befool the people; that would appear before long.

While I write, it seems as if I saw again that poor little bearer of the first evil tidings, and heard once more the first shots which interrupted his prophecy with eloquent confirmation.

Our mother turned pale.

The tailor folded up his cloth and hurried away. What did his words mean, and what was the firing outside?

We strained our ears to listen. The noise seemed to grow louder and come nearer; and, just as our mother cried, "For Heaven's sake, Martha!" the cook burst into the room, exclaiming, "The row began in the Schlossplatz!"

Fraulein Lamperi shrieked, seized her bonnet and cloak, and the pompadour which she took with her everywhere, to hurry home as fast as she could.

Our mother could think only of Martha. She had dined at the Baeyers' and was now perhaps on the way home. Somebody must be sent to meet her. But of what use would be the escort of a maid; and Kurschner was gone, and the porter not to be found!

The cook was sent in one direction, the chambermaid in another, to seek a male escort for Martha.

And then there was Frau Lieutenant Beyer, our neighbour in the house, whose husband was on the general staff, asking: "How is it possible? Everything was granted! What can have happened?"

The answer was a rattle of musketry. We leaned out of the window, from which we could see as far as Potsdamstrasse. What a rush there was towards the gate! Three or four men dashed down the middle of the quiet street. The tall, bearded fellow at the head we knew well. It was the upholsterer Specht, who had often put up curtains and done similar work for us, a good and capable workman.

But what a change! Instead of a neat little hammer, he was flourishing an axe, and he and his companions looked as furious as if they were going to revenge some terrible injury.

He caught sight of us, and I remember distinctly the whites of his rolling eyes as he raised his axe higher, and shouted hoarsely, and as if the threat was meant for us:

"They shall get it!"

Our mother and Frau Beyer had seen and heard him too, and the firing in the direction of which the upholsterer and his companions were running was very near.

The fight must already be raging in Leipzigerstrasse.

At last the porter came back and announced that barricades had been built at the corner of Mauer-and Friedrichstrasse, and that a violent conflict had broken out there and in other places between the soldiers and the citizens. And our Martha was in Friedrichstrasse, and did not come. We lived beyond the gate, and it was not to be expected that fighting would break out in our neighbourhood; but back of our gardens, in the vicinity of the Potsdam railway station, the beating of drums was heard. The firing, however, which became more and more violent, was louder than any other noise; and when we saw our mother wild with anxiety, we, too, began to be alarmed for our dear, sweet Martha.

It was already dark, and still we waited in vain.

At last some one rang. Our mother hurried to the door—a thing she never did.

When we, too, ran into the hall, she had her arms around the child who had incurred such danger, and we little ones kissed her also, and Martha looked especially pretty in her happy astonishment at such a reception.

She, too, had been anxious enough while good Heinrich, General Maeyer's servant, who had been his faithful comrade in arms from 1813 to 1815, brought her home through all sorts of by-ways. But they had been obliged in various places to pass near where the fighting was going on, and the tender-hearted seventeen-year-old girl had seen such terrible things that she burst into tears as she described them.

For us the worst anxiety was over, and our mother recovered her composure. It was perhaps advisable for her, a defenceless widow, to leave the city, which might on the morrow be given over to the unbridled will of insurgents or of soldiers intoxicated with victory. So she determined to make all preparations for going with us to our grandmother in Dresden.

Meanwhile the fighting in the streets seemed to have increased in certain places to a battle, for the crash of the artillery grapeshot was constantly intermingled with the crackling of the infantry fire, and through it all the bells were sounding the tocsin, a wailing, warning sound, which stirred the inmost heart.

It was a fearful din, rattling and thundering and ringing, while the sky emulated the bloodsoaked earth and glowed in fiery red. It was said that the royal iron foundry was in flames.

At last the hour of bedtime came, and I still remember how our mother told us to pray for the king and those poor people who, in order to attain something we could not understand, were in such great peril.

CHAPTER X.
AFTER THE NIGHT OF REVOLUTION.

When we rose the next morning the firing was over. It was said that all was quiet, and we had the well-known proclamation, "To my dear people of Berlin." The horrors of the past night appeared, indeed, to have been the result of an unfortunate mistake. The king himself explained that the two shots by the troops, which had been taken for the signal to attack the people, were from muskets which had gone off by some unlucky accident—"thank God, without injuring any one."

He closed with the words: "Listen to the paternal voice of your king, residents of my loyal and beautiful Berlin; forget what has occurred, as I will forget it with all my heart, for the sake of the great future which, by the blessing of God, will dawn for Prussia, and, through Prussia, for Germany. Your affectionate queen and faithful mother, who is very ill, joins her heart-felt and tearful entreaties to mine."

The king also pledged his royal word that the troops would be withdrawn as soon as the Berlin people were ready for peace and removed the barricades.

So peace seemed restored, for there had been no fighting for hours, and we heard that the troops were already withdrawing.

Our departure for Dresden was out of the question—railway communication had ceased. The bells which had sounded the tocsin all night with their brazen tongues seemed, after such furious exertion, to have no strength for summoning worshippers to church. All the houses of God were closed that Sunday.

Our longing to get out of doors grew to impatience, which was destined to be satisfied, for our mother had a violent headache, and we were sent to get her usual medicine. We reached the Ring pharmacy—a little house in the Potsdam Platz occupied by the well-known writer, Max Ring—in a very few minutes. We performed our errand with the utmost care, gave the medicine to the cook on our return, and hurried off into the city.

When we had left the Mauer-and Friedrichstrasse behind, our hearts began to beat faster, and what we saw on the rest of the way through the longest street of Berlin as far as the Linden was of such a nature that the mere thought of it awakens in me to this day an ardent hope that I may never witness such sights again.

Rage, hate, and destruction had celebrated the maddest orgies on our path, and Death, with passionate vehemence, had swung his sharpest scythe. Wild savagery and merciless destruction had blended with the shrewdest deliberation and skillful knowledge in constructing the bars which the German, avoiding his own good familiar word, called barricades. An elderly gentleman who was explaining their construction, pointed out to us the ingenuity with which some of the barricades had been strengthened for defence on the one side, and left comparatively weak on the other. Every trench dug where the paving was torn up had its object, and each heap of stones its particular design.

But the ordinary spectator needed a guide to recognize this. At the first sight, his attention was claimed by the confused medley and the many heart-rending signs of the horrors practised by man on man.

Here was a pool of blood, there a bearded corpse; here a blood-stained weapon, there another blackened with powder. Like a caldron where a witch mixes all manner of strange things for a philter, each barricade consisted of every sort of rubbish, together with objects originally useful. All kinds of overturned vehicles, from an omnibus to a perambulator, from a carriage to a hand-cart, were everywhere to be found. Wardrobes, commodes, chairs, boards, laths, bookshelves, bath tubs and washtubs, iron and wooden pipes, were piled together, and the interstices filled with sacks of straw and rags, mattresses, and carriage cushions. Whence came the planks yonder, if they were not stripped from the floor of some room? Children and promenaders had sat only yesterday on those benches and, the night before that, oil lamps or gas flames had burned on those lamp-posts. The sign-boards on top had invited customers into shop or inn, and the roll of carpet beneath was perhaps to have covered some floor to-morrow. Oleander shrubs, which I was to see later in rocky vales of Greece or Algeria, had possibly been put out here only the day before into the spring sunshine. The warehouses of the capital no doubt contained everything that could be needed, no matter how or when, but Berlin seemed to me too small for all the trash that was dragged out of the houses in that March night.

Bloody and terrible pictures rose before our minds, and perhaps there was no need of Assessor Geppert's calling to us sternly, "Off home with you, boys!" to turn our feet in that direction.

So home we ran, but stopped once, for at a fountain, either in Leipzigstrasse or Potsdamstrasse, a ball from the artillery had struck in the wood-work, and around it a firm hand had written with chalk in a semicircle, "TO MY DEAR PEOPLE OF BERLIN." On the lower part of the fountain the king's proclamation to the citizens, with the same heading, was posted up.

What a criticism upon it!

The address set forth that a band of miscreants, principally foreigners, had by patent falsehood turned the affair in the Schlossplatz to the furtherance of their evil designs, and filled the heated minds of his dear and faithful people of Berlin with thoughts of vengeance for blood which was supposed to have been spilled. Thus they had become the abominable authors of actual bloodshed.

The king really believed in this "band of miscreants," and attributed the revolution, which he called a 'coup monte' (premeditated affair), to those wretches. His letters to Bunsen are proof of it.

Among those who read his address, "To my Dear People of Berlin," there were many who were wiser. There had really been no need of foreign agitators to make them take up arms.

On the morning of the 18th their rejoicing and cheering came from full hearts, but when they saw or learned that the crowd had been fired into on the Schlossplatz, their already heated blood boiled over; the people so long cheated of their rights, who had been put off when half the rest of Germany had their demands fulfilled, could bear it no longer.

I must remind myself again that I am not writing a history of the Berlin revolution. Nor would my own youthful impressions justify me in forming an independent opinion as to the motives of that remarkable and somewhat incomprehensible event; but, with the assistance of friends more intimately acquainted with the circumstances, I have of late obtained a not wholly superficial knowledge of them, which, with my own recollections, leads me to adopt the opinion of Heinrich von Sybel concerning the much discussed and still unanswered question, whether the Berlin revolution was the result of a long-prepared conspiracy or the spontaneous outburst of enthusiasm for liberty among the citizens. He says: "Both these views are equally well founded, for only the united effort of the two forces could insure a possibility of victory."

Here again the great historian has found the true solution. It was for the interest of the Poles, the French, and other revolutionary spirits, to bring about a bloody conflict in Berlin, and there were many of them in the capital that spring, among whom must have been men who knew how to build barricades and organize revolts; and it can hardly be doubted that, at the decisive moment, they tried to enhance the vengefulness and combativeness of the people by strong drink and fiery speeches, perhaps, in regard to the dregs of the populace, by money. There is weighty evidence in support of this. But it is still more certain—and, though I was but eleven years old and brought up in a loyal atmosphere, I, too, felt and experienced it—that before the 18th of March the general discontent was at the highest point. There was no controlling it.

If the chief of police, Von Minutoli, asserts that he knew beforehand the hour when the revolution was to break out, this is no special evidence of foresight; for the first threat the citizens had ventured to utter against the king was in the address drawn up at the sitting of the popular assembly in Kopenickstrasse, and couched in the following terms "If this is granted us, and granted at once, then we will guarantee a genuine peace." To finish the proposition with a statement of what would occur in the opposite case, was left to his Majesty; the assembly had simply decided that the "peaceful demonstration of the wishes of the people" should take place on the 18th, at two o'clock, several thousand citizens taking part in it. While the address was handed in, and until the reply was received, the ambassadors of the people were to remain quietly assembled in the Schlossplatz. What was to happen in case the above-mentioned demands were not granted is nowhere set down, but there is little doubt that many of those present intended to trust to the fortune of arms. The address contained an ultimatum, and Brass is right in calling it, and the meeting in which it originated, the starting point of the revolution. Whoever had considered the matter attentively might easily say, "On the 18th, at two o'clock, it will be decided either so or so." The king had come to his determination earlier than that. Sybel puts it beyond question that he had been forced to it by the situation in Europe, not by threats or the compulsion of a conflict in the streets. Nevertheless it came to a street fight, for the enemies of order were skillful enough to start a fresh conflagration with the charred beams of the house whose fire had been put out. But all their efforts would have been in vain had not the conduct of the Government, and the events of the last few days, paved the way.

Among my mother's conservative friends, and in her own mind, there was a strong belief that the fighting in Berlin had broken out in consequence of long-continued stirring of the people by foreign agitators; but I can affirm that in my later life, before I began to reflect particularly on the subject, it always seemed to me, when I recalled the time which preceded the 18th of March, as if existing circumstances must have led to the expectation of an outbreak at any moment.

It is difficult in these days to form an idea of the sharp divisions which succeeded the night of the revolution in Berlin, just as one can hardly conceive now, even in court circles, of the whole extent and enthusiastic strength of the sentiment of Prussian loyalty at that time. These opposite principles separated friends, estranged families long united in love, and made themselves felt even in the Schmidt school during the short time that we continued to go there.

Our bold excursion over the barricades was unpunished, so far as I remember. Perhaps it was not even noticed, for our mother, in spite of her violent headache, had to make preparations for the illumination of our tolerably long row of windows. Not to have lighted the house would have imperilled the window-panes. To my regret, we were not allowed to see the illumination. I have since thought it a peculiarly amusing trick of fate that the palace of the Russian embassy—the property of the autocrat Nicholas—was obliged to celebrate with a brilliant display of lights the movement for liberty in a sister country.

On Monday, the 20th, we were sent to school, but it was closed, and we took advantage of the circumstance to get into the heart of the city. The appearance of the town-hall peppered with balls I have never forgotten. Most of the barricades were cleared away; instead, there were singular inscriptions in chalk on the doors of various public buildings.

At the beginning of Leipzigstrasse, at the main entrance of the Ministry of War, we read the words, "National Property." Elsewhere, and particularly at the palace of the Prince of Prussia, was "Property of the Citizens" or "Property of the entire Nation."

An excited throng had gathered in front of the plain and simple palace to whose high ground-floor windows troops of loyal and grateful Germans have often looked up with love and admiration to see the beloved countenance of the grey-haired imperial hero. That day we stood among the crowd and listened to the speech of a student, who addressed us from the great balcony amid a storm of applause. Whether it was the same honest fellow who besought the people to desist from their design of burning the prince's palace because the library would be imperilled, I do not know, but the answer, "Leave the poor boys their books," is authentic.

And it is also true, unhappily, that it was difficult to save from destruction the house of the man whose Hohenzollern blood asserted itself justly against the weakness of his royal brother. Through those days of terror he was what he always had been and would remain, an upright man and soldier, in the highest and noblest meaning of the words.

What we saw and heard in the palace and its courts, swarming with citizens and students, was so low and revolting that I dislike to think of it.

Some of the lifeless heroes were just being borne past on litters, greeted by the wine-flushed faces of armed students and citizens. The teachers who had overtaken us on the way recognized among them college friends who praised the delicious vintage supplied by the palace guards.

My brother and I were also fated to see Frederick William IV. ride down the Behrenstrasse and the Unter den Linden with a large black, red, and yellow band around his arm.

The burial of those who had fallen during the night of the revolution was one of the most imposing ceremonies ever witnessed in Berlin. We boys were permitted to look at it only for a short time, yet the whole impression of the procession, which we really ought not to have been allowed to see, has lingered in my memory.

It was wonderful weather, as warm as summer, and the vast escort which accompanied the two hundred coffins of the champions of freedom to their last resting-place seemed endless. We were forbidden to go on the platform in front of the Neuenkirche where they were placed, but the spectacle must have produced a strange yet deeply pathetic impression.

Pastor Sydow, who represented the Protestant clergy as the Prelate Roland did the Catholics, and the Rabbi Dr. Sachs the Jews, afterwards told me that the multitude of coffins, adorned with the rarest flowers and lavishly draped with black, presented an image of mournful splendour never to be forgotten, and I can easily believe it.

This funeral remains in my memory as an endless line of coffins and black-garbed men with banners and hats bound with crape, bearing flowers, emblems of guilds, and trade symbols. Mounted standard bearers, gentlemen in robes—the professors of the university—and students in holiday attire, mingled in the motley yet solemn train.

How many tears were shed over those coffins which contained the earthly remains of many a young life once rich in hopes and glowing with warm enthusiasm, many a quiet heart which had throbbed joyously for man's noblest possession! The interment in the Friedrichshain, where four hundred singers raised their voices, and a band of music composed of the hautboy players of many regiments poured mighty volumes of sound over the open graves of the dead, must have been alike dignified and majestic.

But the opposition between the contending parties was still too great, and the demand upon the king to salute the dead had aroused such anger in my mother's circle, that she kept aloof from these magnificent and in themselves perfectly justifiable funeral obsequies. It seemed almost unendurable that the king had constrained himself to stand on the balcony of the palace with his head bared, holding his helmet in his hand, while the procession passed.

The effect of this act upon the loyal citizens of Berlin can scarcely be described. I have seen men—even our humble Kurschner—weep during the account of it by eye-witnesses.

Whoever knew Frederick William IV. also knew that neither genuine reconciliation nor respect for the fallen champions of liberty induced him to show this outward token of respect, which was to him the deepest humiliation.

The insincerity of the sovereign's agreement with the ideas, events, and men of his day was evident in the reaction which appeared only too soon. His conviction showed itself under different forms, but remained unchanged, both in political and religious affairs.

During the interval life had assumed a new aspect. The minority had become the majority, and many a son of a strictly conservative man was forbidden to oppose the "red." Only no one needed to conceal his loyalty to the king, for at that time the democrats still shared it. A good word for the Prince of Prussia, on the contrary, inevitably led to a brawl, but we did not shrink from it, and, thank Heaven, we were among the strongest boys.

This intrusion of politics into the school-room and the whole tense life of the capital was extremely undesirable, and, if continued, could not fail to have an injurious influence upon immature lads; so my mother hastily decided that, instead of waiting until the next year, we should go to Keilhau at once.

She has often said that this was the most difficult resolve of her life, but it was also one of the best, since it removed us from the motley, confusing impressions of the city, and the petting we received at home, and transferred us to the surroundings most suitable for boys of our age.

The first of the greater divisions of my life closes with the Easter which follows the Berlin revolution of March, 1848.

Not until I attained years of maturity did I perceive that these conflicts, which, long after, I heard execrated in certain quarters as a blot upon Prussian history, rather deserved the warmest gratitude of the nation. During those beautiful spring days, no matter by what hands—among them were the noblest and purest—were sown the seeds of the dignity and freedom of public life which we now enjoy.

The words "March conquests" have been uttered by jeering lips, but I think at the present time there are few among the more far-sighted conservatives who would like to dispense with them. To me and, thank Heaven, to the majority of Germans, life deprived of them would seem unendurable. My mother afterward learned to share this opinion, though, like ourselves, in whose hearts she early implanted it, she retained to her last hour her loyalty to the king.

CHAPTER XI.
IN KEILHAU

Keilhau! How much is comprised in that one short word!

It recalls to my memory the pure happiness of the fairest period of boyhood, a throng of honoured, beloved, and merry figures, and hundreds of stirring, bright, and amusing scenes in a period of life rich in instruction and amusement, as well as the stage so lavishly endowed by Nature on which they were performed. Jean Paul has termed melancholy the blending of joy and pain, and it was doubtless a kindred feeling which filled my heart in the days before my departure, and induced me to be particularly good and obliging to every body in the house. My mother took us once more to my father's grave in the Dreifaltigkeits cemetery, where I made many good resolutions. Only the best reports should reach home from Keilhau, and I had already obtained excellent ones in Berlin.

On the evening of our departure there were numerous kisses and farewell glances at all that was left behind; but when we were seated in the car with my mother, rushing through the landscape adorned with the most luxuriant spring foliage, my heart suddenly expanded, and the pleasure of travel and delight in the many new scenes before me destroyed every other feeling.

The first vineyard I saw at Naumburg—I had long forgotten those on the Rhine—interested me deeply; the Rudelsburg at Kosen, the ruins of a real ancient castle, pleased me no less because I had never heard Franz Kugler's song:

> "Beside the Saale's verdant strand
>
> Once stood full many a castle grand,
>
> But roofless ruins are they all;
>
> The wind sweeps through from hall to hall;
>
> Slow drift the clouds above,"

which refers to this charming part of the Thuringian hill country. We were soon to learn to sing it at Keilhau. Weimar was the first goal of this journey. We had heard much of our classic poets; nay, I knew Schiller's Bell and some of Goethe's poems by heart, and we had heard them mentioned with deep reverence. Now we were to see their home, and a strange emotion took possession of me when we entered it.

Every detail of this first journey has remained stamped on my memory. I even know what we ordered for supper at the hotel where we spent the night. But my mother had a severe headache, so we saw none of the sights of Weimar except the Goethe house in the city and the other one in the park. I cannot tell what my feelings were, they are too strongly blended with later impressions. I only know that the latter especially seemed to me very small. I had imagined the "Goethe House" like the palace of the Prince of Prussia or Prince Radziwill in Wilhelmstrasse. The Grand Duke's palace, on the contrary, appeared aristocratic and stately. We looked at it very closely, because it was the birthplace of the Princess of Prussia, of whom Fraulein Lamperi had told us so much.

The next morning my mother was well again. The railroad connecting Weimar and Rudolstadt, near which Keilhau is located, was built long after, so we continued our journey in an open carriage and reached Rudolstadt about noon.

After we had rested a short time, the carriage which was to take us to Keilhau drove up.

As we were getting in, an old gentleman approached, who instantly made a strong impression upon me. In outward appearance he bore a marked resemblance to Wilhelm Grimm. I should have noticed him among hundreds; for long grey locks, parted in the middle, floated around a nobly formed head, his massive yet refined features bore the stamp of a most kindly nature, and his eyes were the mirror of a pure, childlike soul. The rare charm of their sunny sparkle, when his warm heart expanded to pleasure or his keen intellect had succeeded in solving any problem, comes back vividly to my memory as I write, and they beamed brightly enough when he perceived our companion. They were old acquaintances, for my mother had been to Keilhau several times on Martin's account. She addressed him by the name of Middendorf, and we recognized him as one of the heads of the institute, of whom we had heard many pleasant things.

He had driven to Rudolstadt with the "old bay," but he willingly accepted a seat in our carriage.

We had scarcely left the street with the hotel behind us, when he began to speak of Schiller, and pointed out the mountain which bore his name and to which in his "Walk" he had cried:

"Hail! oh my Mount, with radiant crimson peak."

Then he told us of the Lengefeld sisters, whom the poet had so often met here, and one of whom, Charlotte, afterward became his wife. All this was done in a way which had no touch of pedagogy or of anything specially prepared for children, yet every word was easily understood and interested us. Besides, his voice had a deep, musical tone, to which my ear was susceptible at an early age. He understood children of our disposition and knew what pleased them.

In Schaale, the first village through which we passed, he said, pointing to the stream which flowed into the Saale close by: "Look, boys, now we are coming into our own neighbourhood, the valley of the Schaal. It owes its name to this brook, which rises in our own meadows, and I suppose you would like to know why our village is called Keilhau?"

While speaking, he pointed up the stream and briefly described its course.

We assented.

We had passed the village of Schaale. The one before us, with the church, was called Eichfeld, and at our right was another which we could not see, Lichtstadt. In ancient times, he told us, the mountain sides and the bottom of the whole valley had been clothed with dense oak forests. Then people came who wanted to till the ground. They began to clear (lichten) these woods at Lichtstadt. This was a difficult task, and they had used axes (Keile) for the purpose. At Eichfeld they felled the oaks (Fiche), and carried the trunks to Schaale, where the bark (Schale) was stripped off to make tan for the tanners on the Saale. So the name of Lichtstadt came from the clearing of the forests, Eichfeld from the felling of the oaks, Schaale from stripping off the bark, and Keilhau from the hewing with axes.

This simple tale of ancient times had sprung from the Thuringian soil, so rich in legends, and, little as it might satisfy the etymologist, it delighted me. I believed it, and when afterward I looked down from a height into the valley and saw the Saale, my imagination clothed the bare or pineclad mountain slopes with huge oak forests, and beheld the giant forms of the ancient Thuringians felling the trees with their heavy axes.

The idea of violence which seemed to be connected with the name of Keilhau had suddenly disappeared. It had gained meaning to me, and Herr Middendorf had given us an excellent proof of a fundamental requirement of Friedrich Froebel, the founder of the institution: "The external must be spiritualized and given an inner significance."

The same talented pedagogue had said, "Our education associates instruction with the external world which surrounds the human being as child and youth"; and Middendorf carried out this precept when, at the first meeting, he questioned us about the trees and bushes by the wayside, and when we were obliged to confess our ignorance of most of them, he mentioned their names and described their peculiarities.

At last we reached the Keilhau plain, a bowl whose walls formed tolerably high mountains which surrounded it on all sides except toward Rudolstadt, where an opening permitted the Schaalbach to wind through meadows and fields. So the village lies like an egg in a nest open in one direction, like the beetle in the calyx of a flower which has lost one of its leaves. Nature has girded it on three sides with protecting walls which keep the wind from entering the valley, and to this, and the delicious, crystal-clear water which flows from the mountains into the pumps, its surprising healthfulness is doubtless due. During my residence there of four and a half years there was no epidemic disease among the boys, and on the fiftieth jubilee of the institute, in 1867, which I attended, the statement was made that during the half century of its existence only one pupil had died, and he had had heart disease when his parents sent him to the school.

We must have arrived on Sunday, for we met on the road several peasants in long blue coats, and peasant women in dark cloth cloaks with gold-embroidered borders, and little black caps from which ribbons three or four feet long hung down the wearers' backs. The cloaks descended from mother to daughter. They were very heavy, yet I afterward saw peasant women wear them to church in summer.

At last we drove into the broad village street. At the right, opposite to the first houses, lay a small pond called the village pool, on which ducks and geese floated, and whose dark surface, glittering with many hues, reflected the shepherd's hut. After we had passed some very fine farmhouses, we reached the "Plan," where bright waters plashed into a stone trough, a linden tree shaded the dancing-ground, and a pretty house was pointed out as the schoolhouse of the village children.

A short distance farther away the church rose in the background. But we had no time to look at it, for we were already driving up to the institute itself, which was at the end of the village, and consisted of two rows of houses with an open space closed at the rear by the wide front of a large building.

The bakery, a small dwelling, and the large gymnasium were at our left; on the right, the so-called Lower House, with the residences of the head-masters' families, and the school and sleeping-rooms of the smaller pupils, whom we dubbed the "Panzen," and among whom were boys only eight and nine years old.

The large house before whose central door—to which a flight of stone steps led—we stopped, was the Upper House, our future home.

Almost at the same moment we heard a loud noise inside, and an army of boys came rushing down the steps. These were the "pupils," and my heart began to throb faster.

They gathered around the Rudolstadt carriage boldly enough and stared at us. I noticed that almost all were bareheaded. Many wore their hair falling in long locks down their backs. The few who had any coverings used black velvet caps, such as in Berlin would be seen only at the theatre or in an artist's studio.

Middendorf had stepped quickly among the lads, and as they came running up to take his hand or hang on his arm we saw how they loved him.

But we had little time for observation. Barop, the head-master, was already hastening down the steps, welcoming my mother and ourselves with his deep, musical tones, in a pure Westphalian dialect.

ENTERING THE INSTITUTE.

Barop's voice sounded so sincere and cordial that it banished every thought of fear, otherwise his appearance might have inspired boys of our age with a certain degree of timidity, for he was a broad-shouldered man of gigantic stature, who, like Middendorf, wore his grey hair parted in the middle, though it was cut somewhat shorter. A pair of dark eyes sparkled under heavy, bushy brows, which gave them the aspect of clear springs shaded by dense thickets. They now gazed kindly at us, but later we were to learn their irresistible power. I have said, and I still think, that the eyes of the artist, Peter Cornelius, are the most forceful I have ever seen, for the very genius of art gazed from them. Those of our Barop produced no weaker influence in their way, for they revealed scarcely less impressively the character of a man. To them, especially, was due the implicit obedience that every one rendered him. When they flashed with indignation the defiance of the boldest and most refractory quailed. But they could sparkle cheerily, too, and whoever met his frank, kindly gaze felt honoured and uplifted.

Earnest, thoroughly natural, able, strong, reliable, rigidly just, free from any touch of caprice, he lacked no quality demanded by his arduous profession, and hence he whom even the youngest addressed as "Barop" never failed for an instant to receive the respect which was his due, and, moreover, had from us all the voluntary gift of affection, nay, of love. He was, I repeat, every inch a man.

When very young, the conviction that the education of German boys was his real calling obtained so firm a hold upon his mind that he could not be dissuaded from giving up the study of the law, in which he had made considerable progress at Halle, and devoting himself to pedagogy.

His father, a busy lawyer, had threatened him with disinheritance if he did not relinquish his intention of accepting the by no means brilliant position of a teacher at Keilhau; but he remained loyal to his choice, though his father executed his threat and cast him off. After the old gentleman's death his brothers and sisters voluntarily restored his portion of the property, but, as he himself told me long after, the quarrel with one so dear to him saddened his life for years. For the sake of the "fidelity to one's self" which he required from others he had lost his father's love, but he had obeyed a resistless inner voice, and the genuineness of his vocation was to be brilliantly proved.

Success followed his efforts, though he assumed the management of the Keilhau Institute under the most difficult circumstances.

Beneath its roof he had found in the niece of Friedrich Froebel a beloved wife, peculiarly suited both to him and to her future position. She was as little as he was big, but what energy, what tireless activity this dainty, delicate woman possessed! To each one of us she showed a mother's sympathy, managed the whole great household down to the smallest details, and certainly neglected nothing in the care of her own sons and daughters.

A third master, the archdeacon Langethal, was one of the founders of the institution, but had left it several years before.

As I mention him with the same warmth that I speak of Middendorf and Barop, many readers will suspect that this portion of my reminiscences contains a receipt for favours, and that reverence and gratitude, nay, perhaps the fear of injuring an institution still existing, induces me to show only the lights and cover the shadows with the mantle of love.

I will not deny that a boy from eleven to fifteen years readily overlooks in those who occupy an almost paternal relation to him faults which would be immediately noted by the unclouded eyes of a critical observer; but I consider myself justified in describing what I saw in my youth exactly as it impressed itself on my memory. I have never perceived the smallest flaw or even a trait or act worthy of censure in either Barop, Middendorf, or Langethal. Finally, I may say that, after having learned in later years from abundant data willingly placed at my disposal by Johannes Barop, our teacher's son and the present master of the institute, the most minute details concerning their character and work, none of these images have sustained any material injury.

In Friedrich Froebel, the real founder of the institute, who repeatedly lived among us for months, I have learned to know from his own works and the comprehensive amount of literature devoted to him, a really talented idealist, who on the one hand cannot be absolved from an amazing contempt for or indifference to the material demands of life, and on the other possessed a certain artless selfishness which gave him courage, whenever he wished to promote objects undoubtedly pure and noble, to deal arbitrarily with other lives, even where it could hardly redound to their advantage. I shall have more to say of him later.

The source of Middendorf's greatness in the sphere where life and his own choice had placed him may even be imputed to him as a fault. He, the most enthusiastic of all Froebel's disciples, remained to his life's end a lovable child, in whom the powers of a rich poetic soul surpassed those of the thoughtful, well-trained mind. He would have been ill-adapted for any practical position, but no one could be better suited to enter into the soul-life of young human beings, cherish and ennoble them.

A deeper insight into the lives of Barop and Langethal taught me to prize these men more and more.

They have all rested under the sod for decades, and though their institute, to which I owe so much, has remained dear and precious, and the years I spent in the pleasant Thuringian mountain valley are numbered among the fairest in my life, I must renounce making proselytes for the Keilhau Institute, because, when I saw its present head for the last time, as a very young man, I heard from him, to my sincere regret, that, since the introduction of the law of military service, he found himself compelled to make the course of study at Rudolstadt conform to the system of teaching in a Realschule.—[School in which the arts and sciences as well as the languages are taught.-TR.]—He was forced to do so in order to give his graduates the certificate for the one year's military service.

The classics, formerly held in such high esteem beneath its roof, must now rank below the sciences and modern languages, which are regarded as most important. But love for Germany and the development of German character, which Froebel made the foundation of his method of education, are too deeply rooted there ever to be extirpated. Both are as zealously fostered in Keilhau now as in former years.

After a cordial greeting from Barop, we had desks assigned us in the schoolroom, which were supplied with piles of books, writing materials, and other necessaries. Ludo's bed stood in the same dormitory with mine. Both were hard enough, but this had not damped our gay spirits, and when we were taken to the other boys we were soon playing merrily with the rest.

The first difficulty occurred after supper, and proved to be one of the most serious I encountered during my stay in the school.

My mother had unpacked our trunks and arranged everything in order. Among the articles were some which were new to the boys, and special notice was attracted by several pairs of kid gloves and a box of pomade which belonged in our pretty leather dressing-case, a gift from my grandmother.

Dandified, or, as we should now term them, "dudish" affairs, were not allowed at Keilhau; so various witticisms were made which culminated when a pupil of about our own age from a city on the Weser called us Berlin pomade-pots. This vexed me, but a Berlin boy always has an answer ready, and mine was defiant enough. The matter might have ended here had not the same lad stroked my hair to see how Berlin pomade smelt. From a child nothing has been more unendurable than to feel a stranger's hand touch me, especially on the head, and, before I was aware of it, I had dealt my enemy a resounding slap. Of course, he instantly rushed at me, and there would have been a violent scuffle had not the older pupils interfered. If we wanted to do anything, we must wrestle. This suited my antagonist, and I, too, was not averse to the contest, for I had unusually strong arms, a well-developed chest, and had practised wrestling in the Berlin gymnasium.

The struggle began under the direction of the older pupils, and the grip on which I had relied did not fail. It consisted in clutching the antagonist just above the hips. If the latter were not greatly my superior, and I could exert my whole strength to clasp him to me, he was lost. This time the clever trick did its duty, and my adversary was speedily stretched on the ground. I turned my back on him, but he rose, panting breathlessly. "It's like a bear squeezing one." In reply to every question from the older boys who stood around us laughing, he always made the same answer, "Like a bear."

I had reason to remember this very common incident in boy life, for it gave me the nickname used by old and young till after my departure. Henceforward I was always called "the bear." Last year I had the pleasure of receiving a visit from Dr. Bareuther, a member of the Austrian Senate and a pupil of Keilhau. We had not met for forty years, and his first words were: "Look at me, Bear. Who am I?"

My brother had brought his nickname with him, and everybody called him Ludo instead of Ludwig. The pretty, bright, agile lad, who also never flinched, soon became especially popular, and my companions were also fond of me, as I learned, when, during the last years of my stay at the institute, they elected me captain of the first Bergwart—that is, commander-in-chief of the whole body of pupils.

My first fight secured my position forever. We doubtless owed our initiation on the second day into everything which was done by the pupils, both openly and secretly, to the good impression made by Martin. There was nothing wrong, and even where mischief was concerned I can term it to-day "harmless." The new boys or "foxes" were not neglected or "hazed," as in many other schools. Only every one, even the newly arrived younger teachers, was obliged to submit to the "initiation." This took place in winter, and consisted in being buried in the snow and having pockets, clothing, nay, even shirts, filled with the clean but wet mass. Yet I remember no cold caused by this rude baptism. My mother remained several days with us, and as the weather was fine she accompanied us to the neighbouring heights—the Kirschberg, to which, after the peaceful cemetery of the institute was left behind, a zigzag path led; the Kohn, at whose foot rose the Upper House; and the Steiger, from whose base flowed the Schaalbach, and whose summit afforded a view of a great portion of the Thuringian mountains.

We older pupils afterwards had a tall tower erected there as a monument to Barop, and the prospect from its lofty summit, which is more that a thousand feet high, is magnificent.

Even before the completion of this lookout, the view was one of the most beautiful and widest far or near, and we were treated like most new-comers. During the ascent our eyes were bandaged, and when the handkerchief was removed a marvellous picture appeared before our astonished gaze. In the foreground, toward the left, rose the wooded height crowned by the stately ruins of the Blankenburg. Beyond opened the beautiful leafy bed of the Saale, proudly dominated by the Leuchtenburg. Before us there was scarcely any barrier to the vision; for behind the nearer ranges of hills one chain of the wooded Thuringian Mountains towered beyond another, and where the horizon seemed to close the grand picture, peak after peak blended with the sky and the clouds, and the light veil of mist floating about them seemed to merge all into an indivisible whole.

I have gazed from this spot into the distance at every hour of the day and season of the year. But the fairest time of all on the Steiger was at sunset, on clear autumn days, when the scene close at hand, where the threads of gossamer were floating, was steeped in golden light, the distance in such exquisite tints-from crimson to the deepest violet blue, edged with a line of light-the Saale glimmered with a silvery lustre amid its fringe of alders, and the sun flashed on the glittering panes of the Leuchtenburg.

We were now old enough to enjoy the magnificence of this prospect. My young heart swelled at the sight; and if in after years my eyes could grasp the charm of a beautiful landscape and my pen successfully describe it, I learned the art here.

It was pleasant, too, that my mother saw all this with us, though she must often have gone to rest very much wearied from her rambles. But teachers and pupils vied with each other in attentions to her. She had won all hearts. We noticed and rejoiced in it till the day came when she left us.

She was obliged to start very early in the morning, in order to reach Berlin the same evening. The other boys were not up, but Barop, Middendorf, and several other teachers had risen to take leave of her. A few more kisses, a wave of her handkerchief, and the carriage vanished in the village. Ludo and I were alone, and I vividly remember the moment when we suddenly began to weep and sob as bitterly as if it had been an eternal farewell. How often one human being becomes the sun of another's life! And it is most frequently the mother who plays this beautiful part.

Yet the anguish of parting did not last very long, and whoever had watched the boys playing ball an hour later would have heard our voices among the merriest. Afterwards we rarely had attacks of homesickness, there were so many new things in Keilhau, and even familiar objects seemed changed in form and purpose.

From the city we were in every sense transferred to the woods.

True, we had grown up in the beautiful park of the Thiergarten, but only on its edge; to live in and with Nature, "become one with her," as Middendorf said, we had not learned.

I once read in a novel by Jensen, as a well-attested fact, that during an inquiry made in a charity school in the capital a considerable number of the pupils had never seen a butterfly or a sunset. We were certainly not to be classed among such children. But our intercourse with Nature had been limited to formal visits which we were permitted to pay the august lady at stated intervals. In Keilhau she became a familiar friend, and we therefore were soon initiated into many of her secrets; for none seemed to be withheld from our Middendorf and Barop, whom duty and inclination alike prompted to sharpen our ears also for her language. The Keilhau games and walks usually led up the mountains or into the forest, and here the older pupils acted as teachers, but not in any pedagogical way. Their own interest in whatever was worthy of note in Nature was so keen that they could not help pointing it out to their less experienced companions.

On our "picnics" from Berlin we had taken dainty mugs in order to drink from the wells; now we learned to seek and find the springs themselves, and how delicious the crystal fluid tastes from the hollow of the hand, Diogenes's drinking-cup! Old Councillor Wellmer, in the Crede House, in Berlin, a zealous entomologist, owned a large collection of beetles, and had carefully impaled his pets on long slender pins in neat boxes, which filled numerous glass cases. They lacked nothing but life. In Keilhau we found every variety of insect in central Germany, on the bushes and in the moss, the turf, the bark of trees, or on the flowers and blades of grass, and they were alive and allowed us to watch them. Instead of neatly written labels, living lips told us their names.

We had listened to the notes of the birds in the Thiergarten; but our mother, the tutor, the placards, our nice clothing, prohibited our following the feathered songsters into the thickets. But in Keilhau we were allowed to pursue them to their nests. The woods were open to every one, and nothing could injure our plain jackets and stout boots. Even in my second year at Keilhau I could distinguish all the notes of the numerous birds in the Thuringian forests, and, with Ludo, began the collection of eggs whose increase afforded us so much pleasure. Our teachers' love for all animate creation had made them impose bounds on the zeal of the egg-hunters, who were required always to leave one egg in the nest, and if it contained but one not to molest it. How many trees we climbed, what steep cliffs we scaled, through what crevices we squeezed to add a rare egg to our collection; nay, we even risked our limbs and necks! Life is valued so much less by the young, to whom it is brightest, and before whom it still stretches in a long vista, than by the old, for whom its charms are already beginning to fade, and who are near its end. I shall never forget the afternoon when, supplied with ropes and poles, we went to the Owl Mountain, which originally owed its name to Middendorf, because when he came to Keilhau he noticed that its rocky slope served as a home for several pairs of horned owls. Since then their numbers had increased, and for some time larger night birds had been flying in and out of a certain crevice. It was still the laying season, and their nests must be there. Climbing the steep precipice was no easy task, but we succeeded, and were then lowered from above into the crevice. At that time we set to work with the delight of discoverers, but now I frown when I consider that those who let first the daring Albrecht von Calm, of Brunswick, and then me into the chasm by ropes were boys of thirteen or fourteen at the utmost. Marbod, my companion's brother, was one of the strongest of our number, and we were obliged to force our way like chimney sweeps by pressing our hands and feet against the walls of the narrow rough crevice. Yet it now seems a miracle that the adventure resulted in no injury. Unfortunately, we found the young birds already hatched, and were compelled to return with our errand unperformed. But we afterward obtained such eggs, and their form is more nearly ball-shape than that seen in those of most other birds. We knew how the eggs of all the feathered guests of Germany were coloured and marked, and the chest of drawers containing our collection stood for years in my mother's attic. When I inquired about it a few years ago, it could not be found, and Ludo, who had helped in gathering it, lamented its loss with me.

CHAPTER XII.
FRIEDRICH FROEBEL'S IDEAL OF EDUCATION.

Dangerous enterprises were of course forbidden, but the teachers of the institute neglected no means of training our bodies to endure every exertion and peril; for Froebel was still alive, and the ideal of education, for whose realization he had established the Keilhau school, had become to his assistants and followers strong and healthy realities. But Froebel's purpose did not require the culture of physical strength. His most marked postulates were the preservation and development of the individuality of the boys entrusted to his care, and their training in German character and German nature; for he beheld the sum of all the traits of higher, purer manhood united in those of the true German.

Love for the heart, strength for the character, seemed to him the highest gifts with which he could endow his pupils for life.

He sought to rear the boy to unity with himself, with God, with Nature, and with mankind, and the way led to trust in God through religion, trust in himself by developing the strength of mind and body, and confidence in mankind—that is, in others, by active relations with life and a loving interest in the past and present destinies of our fellow-men. This required an eye and heart open to our surroundings, sociability, and a deeper insight into history. Here Nature seems to be forgotten. But Nature comes into the category of religion, for to him religion means: To know and feel at one with ourselves, with God, and with man; to be loyal to ourselves, to God, and to Nature: and to remain in continual active, living relations with God.

The teacher must lead the pupils to men as well as to God and Nature, and direct them from action to perception and thought. For action he takes special degrees, capacity, skill, trustworthiness; for perception, consciousness, insight, clearness. Only the practical and clear-sighted man can maintain himself as a thinker, opening out as a teacher new trains of thought, and comprehending the basis of what is already acquired and the laws which govern it.

Froebel wishes to have the child regarded as a bud on the great tree of life, and therefore each pupil needs to be considered individually, developed mentally and physically, fostered and trained as a bud on the huge tree of the human race. Even as a system of instruction, education ought not to be a rigid plan, incapable of modification, it should be adapted to the individuality of the child, the period in which it is growing to maturity, and its environment. The child should be led to feel, work, and act by its own experiences in the present and in its home, not by the opinions of others or by fixed, prescribed rules. From independent, carefully directed acts and knowledge, perceptions, and thoughts, the product of this education must come forth—a man, or, as it is elsewhere stated, a thorough German. At Keilhau he is to be perfected, converted into a finished production without a flaw. If the institute has fulfilled its duty to the individual, he will be:

To his native land, a brave son in the hour of peril, in the spirit of self-sacrifice and sturdy strength.

To the family, a faithful child and a father who will secure prosperity.

To the state, an upright, honest, industrious citizen.

To the army, a clear-sighted, strong, healthy, brave soldier and leader.

To the trades, arts, and sciences, a skilled helper, an active promoter, a worker accustomed to thorough investigation, who has grown to maturity in close intercourse with Nature.

To Jesus Christ, a faithful disciple and brother; a loving, obedient child of God.

To mankind, a human being according to the image of God, and not according to that of a fashion journal.

No one is reared for the drawing-room; but where there is a drawing-room in which mental gifts are fostered and truth finds an abode, a true graduate of Keilhau will be an ornament. "No instruction in bowing and tying cravats is necessary; people learn that only too quickly," said Froebel.

The right education must be a harmonious one, and must be thoroughly in unison with the necessary phenomena and demands of human life.

Thus the Keilhau system of education must claim the whole man, his inner as well as his outer existence. Its purpose is to watch the nature of each individual boy, his peculiarities, traits, talents, above all, his character, and afford to all the necessary development and culture. It follows step by step the development of the human being, from the almost instinctive impulse to feeling, consciousness, and will. At each one of these steps each child is permitted to have only what he can bear, understand, and assimilate, while at the same time it serves as a ladder to the next higher step of development and culture. In this way Froebel, whose own notes, collected from different sources, we are here following, hopes to guard against a defective or misdirected education; for what the pupil knows and can do has sprung, as it were, from his own brain. Nothing has been learned, but developed from within. Therefore the boy who is sent into the world will understand how to use it, and possess the means for his own further development and perfection from step to step.

Every human being has a talent for some calling or vocation, and strength for its development. It is the task of the institute to cultivate the powers which are especially requisite for the future fulfilment of the calling appointed by Nature herself. Here, too, the advance must be step by step. Where talent or inclination lead, every individual will be prepared to deal with even the greatest obstacles, and must possess even the capacity to represent externally what has been perceived and thought—that is, to speak and write clearly and accurately—for in this way the intellectual power of the individual will first be made active and visible to others. We perceive that Froebel strongly antagonizes the Roman postulate that knowledge should be imparted to boys according to a thoroughly tested method and succession approved by the mature human intellect, and which seem most useful to it for later life.

The systematic method which, up to the time of Pestalozzi, prevailed in Germany, and is again embodied in our present mode of education, seemed to him objectionable. The Swiss reformer pointed out that the mother's heart had instinctively found the only correct system of instruction, and set before the pedagogue the task of watching and cultivating the child's talents with maternal love and care. He utterly rejected the old system, and Froebel stationed himself as a fellow-combatant at his side, but went still further. This stand required a high degree of courage at the time of the founding of Keilhau, when Hegel's influence was omnipotent in educational circles, for Hegel set before the school the task of imparting culture, and forgot that it lacked the most essential conditions; for the school can give only knowledge, while true education demands a close relation between the person to be educated and the world from which the school, as Hegel conceived it, is widely sundered.

Froebel recognized that the extent of the knowledge imparted to each pupil was of less importance, and that the school could not be expected to bestow on each individual a thoroughly completed education, but an intellect so well trained that when the time came for him to enter into relations with the world and higher instructors he would have at his disposal the means to draw from both that form of culture which the school is unable to impart. He therefore turned his back abruptly on the old system, denied that the main object of education was to meet the needs of afterlife, and opposed having the interests of the child sacrificed to those of the man; for the child in his eyes is sacred, an independent blessing bestowed upon him by God, towards whom he has the one duty of restoring to those who confided it to him in a higher degree of perfection, with unfolded mind and soul, and a body and character steeled against every peril. "A child," he says, "who knows how to do right in his own childish sphere, will grow naturally into an upright manhood."

With regard to instruction, his view, briefly stated, is as follows: The boy whose special talents are carefully developed, to whom we give the power of absorbing and reproducing everything which is connected with his talent, will know how to assimilate, by his own work in the world and wider educational advantages, everything which will render him a perfect and thoroughly educated man. With half the amount of preliminary knowledge in the province of his specialty, the boy or youth dismissed by us as a harmoniously developed man, to whom we have given the methods requisite for the acquisition of all desirable branches of knowledge, will accomplish more than his intellectual twin who has been trained according to the ideas of the Romans (and, let us add, Hegel).

I think Froebel is right. If his educational principles were the common property of mankind, we might hope for a realization of Jean Paul's prediction that the world would end with a child's paradise. We enjoyed a foretaste of this paradise in Keilhau. But when I survey our modern gymnasia, I am forced to believe that if they should succeed in equipping their pupils with still greater numbers of rules for the future, the happiness of the child would be wholly sacrificed to the interests of the man, and the life of this world would close with the birth of overwise greybeards. I might well be tempted to devote still more time to the educational principles of the man who, from the depths of his full, warm heart, addressed to parents the appeal, "Come, let us live for our children," but it would lead me beyond the allotted limits.

Many of Froebel's pedagogical principles undoubtedly appear at first sight a pallid theorem, partly a matter of course, partly impracticable. During our stay in Keilhau we never heard of these claims, concerning which we pupils were the subject of experiment. Far less did we feel that we were being educated according to any fixed method. We perceived very little of any form of government. The relation between us and our teachers was so natural and affectionate that it seemed as if no other was possible.

Yet, when I compared our life at Keilhau with the principles previously mentioned, I found that Barop, Middendorf, and old Langethal, as well as the sub-teachers Bagge, Budstedt, and Schaffner, had followed them in our education, and succeeded in applying many of those which seemed the most difficult to carry into execution. This filled me with sincere admiration, though I soon perceived that it could have been done only by men in whom Froebel had transplanted his ideal, men who were no less enthusiastic concerning their profession than he, and whose personality predestined them to solve successfully tasks which presented difficulties almost unconquerable by others.

Every boy was to be educated according to his peculiar temperament, with special regard to his disposition, talents, and character. Although there were sixty of us, this was actually done in the case of each individual.

Thus the teachers perceived that the endowments of my brother, with whom I had hitherto shared everything, required a totally different system of education from mine. While I was set to studying Greek, he was released from it and assigned to modern languages and the arts and sciences. They considered me better suited for a life of study, him qualified for some practical calling or a military career.

Even in the tasks allotted to each, and the opinions passed upon our physical and mental achievements, there never was any fixed standard. These teachers always kept in view the whole individual, and especially his character. Thereby the parents of a Keilhau pupil were far better informed in many respects than those of our gymnasiasts, who so often yield to the temptation of estimating their sons' work by the greater or less number of errors in their Latin exercises.

It afforded me genuine pleasure to look through the Keilhau reports. Each contained a description of character, with a criticism of the work accomplished, partly with reference to the pupil's capacity, partly to the demands of the school. Some are little masterpieces of psychological penetration.

Many of those who have followed these statements will ask how the German nature and German character can be developed in the boys.

It was thoroughly done in Keilhau.

But the solution of the problem required men like Langethal and Middendorf, who, even in their personal appearance models of German strength and dignity, had fought for their native land, and who were surpassed in depth and warmth of feeling by no man.

I repeat that what Froebel termed German was really the higher traits of human character; but nothing was more deeply imprinted on our souls than love for our native land. Here the young voices not only extolled the warlike deeds of the brave Prussians, but recited with equal fervor all the songs with which true patriotism has inspired German poets. Perhaps this delight in Germanism went too far in many respects; it fostered hatred and scorn of everything "foreign," and was the cause of the long hair and cap, pike and broad shirt collar worn by many a pupil. Yet their number was not very large, and Ludo, our most intimate friends, and I never joined them.

Barop himself smiled at their "Teutonism" but indulged it, and it was stimulated by some of the teachers, especially the magnificent Zeller, so full of vigour and joy in existence. I can still see the gigantic young Swiss, as he made the pines tremble with his "Odin, Odin, death to the Romans!"

One of the pupils, Count zur Lippe, whose name was Hermann, was called "Arminius," in memory of the conqueror of Varus. But these were external things.

On the other hand, how vividly, during the history lesson, Langethal, the old warrior of 1813, described the course of the conflict for liberty!

Friedrich Froebel had also pronounced esteem for manual labour to be genuinely and originally German, and therefore each pupil was assigned a place where he could wield spades and pickaxes, roll stones, sow, and reap.

These occupations were intended to strengthen the body, according to Froebel's rules, and absorbed the greater part of the hours not devoted to instruction.

Midway up the Dissauberg was the spacious wrestling-ground with the shooting-stand, and in the court-yard of the institute the gymnasium for every spare moment of the winter. There fencing was practised with fleurets (thrusting swords), not rapiers, which Barop rightly believed had less effect upon developing the agility of youthful bodies. Even when boys of twelve, Ludo and I, like most of the other pupils, had our own excellent rifles, a Christmas gift from our mother, and how quickly our keen young eyes learned to hit the bull's-eye! There was good swimming in the pond of the institute, and skating was practised there on the frozen surface of the neighbouring meadow; then we had our coasting parties at the "Upper House" and down the long slope of the Dissau, the climbing and rambling, the wrestling and jumping over the backs of comrades, the ditches, hedges, and fences, the games of prisoner's base which no Keilhau pupil will ever forget, the ball-playing and the various games of running for which there was always time, although at the end of the year we had acquired a sufficient amount of knowledge. The stiffest boy who came to Keilhau grew nimble, the biceps of the veriest weakling enlarged, the most timid nature was roused to courage. Indeed, here, if anywhere, it required courage to be cowardly.

If Froebel and Langethal had seen in the principle of comradeship the best furtherance of discipline, it was proved here; for we formed one large family, and if any act really worthy of punishment, no mere ebullition of youthful spirits, was committed by any of the pupils, Barop summoned us all, formed us into a court of justice, and we examined into the affair and fixed the penalty ourselves. For dishonourable acts, expulsion from the institute; for grave offences, confinement to the room—a punishment which pledged even us, who imposed it, to avoid all intercourse with the culprit for a certain length of time. For lighter misdemeanours the offender was confined to the house or the court-yard. If trivial matters were to be censured this Areopagus was not convened.

And we, the judges, were rigid executors of the punishment. Barop afterwards told me that he was frequently compelled to urge us to be more gentle. Old Froebel regarded these meetings as means for coming into unity with life. The same purpose was served by the form of our intercourse with one another, the pedestrian excursions, and the many incidents related by our teachers of their own lives, especially the historical instruction which was connected with the history of civilization and so arranged as to seek to make us familiar not only with the deeds of nations and bloody battles, but with the life of the human race.

In spite of, or on account of, the court of justice I have just mentioned, there could be no informers among us, for Barop only half listened to the accuser, and often sent him harshly from the room without summoning the school-mate whom he accused. Besides, we ourselves knew how to punish the sycophant so that he took good care not to act as tale-bearer a second time.

MANNERS, AND FROEBEL'S KINDERGARTEN

The wives of the teachers had even more to do with our deportment than the dancing-master, especially Frau Barop and her husband's sister Frau von Born, who had settled in Keilhau on account of having her sons educated there.

The fact that the head-master's daughters and several girls, who were friends or relatives of his family, shared many of our lessons, also contributed essentially to soften the manners of the young German savages.

I mention our "manners" especially because, as I afterwards learned, they had been the subject of sharp differences of opinion between Friedrich Froebel and Langethal, and because the arguments of the former are so characteristic that I deem them worthy of record.

There could be no lack of delicacy of feeling on the part of the founder of the kindergarten system, who had said, "If you are talking with any one, and your child comes to ask you about anything which interests him, break off your conversation, no matter what may be the rank of the person who is speaking to you," and who also directed that the child should receive not only love but respect. The first postulate shows that he valued the demands of the soul far above social forms. Thus it happened that during the first years of the institute, which he then governed himself, he was reproached with paying too little attention to the outward forms, the "behaviour," the manners of the boys entrusted to his care. His characteristic answer was: "I place no value on these forms unless they depend upon and express the inner self. Where that is thoroughly trained for life and work, externals may be left to themselves, and will supplement the other." The opponent admits this, but declares that the Keilhau method, which made no account of outward form, may defer this "supplement" in a way disastrous to certain pupils. Froebel's answer is: "Certainly, a wax pear can be made much more quickly and is just as beautiful as those on the tree, which require a much longer time to ripen. But the wax pear is only to look at, can barely be touched, far less could it afford refreshment to the thirsty and the sick. It is empty—a mere nothing! The child's nature, it is said, resembles wax. Very well, we don't grudge wax fruits to any one who likes them. But nothing must be expected from them if we are ill and thirsty; and what is to become of them when temptations and trials come, and to whom do they not come? Our educational products must mature slowly, but thoroughly, to genuine human beings whose inner selves will be deficient in no respect. Let the tailor provide for the clothes."

Froebel himself was certainly very careless in the choice of his. The long cloth coat in which I always saw him was fashioned by the village tailor, and the old gentleman probably liked the garment because half a dozen children hung by the tails when he crossed the court-yard. It needed to be durable; but the well-fitting coats worn by Barop and Langethal were equally so, and both men believed that the good gardener should also care for the form of the fruit he cultivates, because, when ripe, it is more valuable if it looks well. They, too, cared nothing for wax fruits; nay, did not even consider them because they did not recognize them as fruit at all.

Froebel's conversion was delayed, but after his marriage it was all the more thorough. The choice of this intellectual and kindly natured man, who set no value on the external forms of life, was, I might say, "naturally" a very elegant woman, a native of Berlin, the widow of the Kriegsrath Hofmeister. She speedily opened Froebel's eyes to the aesthetic and artistic element in the lives of the boys entrusted to his care—the element to which Langethal, from the time of his entrance into the institution, had directed his attention.

So in Keilhau, too, woman was to pave the way to greater refinement.

This had occurred long before our entrance into the institution. Froebel did not allude to wax pears now when he saw the pupils well dressed and courteous in manner; nay, afterwards, in establishing the kindergarten, he praised and sought to utilize the comprehensive influence upon humanity of "woman," the guardian of lofty morality. Wives and mothers owe him as great a debt of gratitude as children, and should never forget the saying,

"The mother's heart alone is the true source of the welfare of the child, and the salvation of humanity." The fundamental necessity of the hour is to prepare this soil for the noble human blossom, and render it fit for its mission.

To meet the need mentioned in this sentence the whole labour of the evening of his life was devoted. Amid many cares and in defiance of strong opposition he exerted his best powers for the realization of his ideal, finding courage to do so in the conviction uttered in the saying, "Only through the pure hands and full hearts of wives and mothers can the kingdom of God become a reality."

Unfortunately, I cannot enter more comprehensively here into the details of the kindergarten system—it is connected with Keilhau only in so far that both were founded by the same man. Old Froebel was often visited there by female kindergarten teachers and pedagogues who wished to learn something of this new institute. We called the former "Schakelinen"; the latter, according to a popular etymology, "Schakale." The odd name bestowed upon the female kindergarten teachers was derived, as I learned afterwards, from no beast of prey, but from a figure in Jean Paul's "Levana," endowed with beautiful gifts. Her name is Madame Jacqueline, and she was used by the author to give expression to his own opinions of female education. Froebel has adopted many suggestions of Jean Paul, but the idea of the kindergarten arose from his own unhappy childhood. He wished to make the first five years of life, which to him had been a chain of sorrows, happy and fruitful to children—especially to those who, like him, were motherless.

Sullen tempers, the rod, and the strictest, almost cruel, constraint had overshadowed his childhood, and now his effort was directed towards having the whole world of little people join joyously in his favourite cry, "Friede, Freude, Freiheit!" (Peace, Pleasure, Liberty), which corresponds with the motto of the Jahn gymnasium, "Frisch, fromm, frohlich, frei."

He also desired to utilize for public instruction the educational talents which woman undoubtedly possesses.

As in his youth, shoulder to shoulder with Pestalozzi, he had striven to rear growing boys in a motherly fashion to be worthy men, he now wished to turn to account, for the benefit of the whole wide circle of younger children, the trait of maternal solicitude which exists in every woman. Women were to be trained for teachers, and the places where children received their first instruction were to resemble nurseries as closely as possible. He also desired to see the maternal tone prevail in this instruction.

He, through whose whole life had run the echo of the Saviour's words, "Suffer little children to come unto me," understood the child's nature, and knew that its impulse to play must be used, in order to afford it suitable future nourishment for the mind and soul.

The instruction, the activity, and the movements of the child should be associated with the things which most interest him, and meanwhile it should be constantly employed in some creative occupation adapted to its intelligence.

If, for instance, butter was spoken of, by the help of suitable motions the cow was milked, the milk was poured into a pan and skimmed, the cream was churned, the butter was made into pats and finally sent to market. Then came the payment, which required little accounts. When the game was over, a different one followed, perhaps something which rendered the little hands skilful by preparing fine weaving from strips of paper; for Froebel had perceived that change brought rest.

Every kindergarten should have a small garden, to afford an opportunity to watch the development of the plants, though only one at a time—for instance, the bean. By watching the clouds in the sky he directed the childish intelligence to the rivers, seas, and circulation of moisture. In the autumn the observation of the chrysalis state of insects was connected with that of the various stages of their existence.

In this way the child can be guided in its play to a certain creative activity, rendered familiar with the life of Nature, the claims of the household, the toil of the peasants, mechanics, etc., and at the same time increase its dexterity in using its fingers and the suppleness of its body. It learns to play, to obey, and to submit to the rules of the school, and is protected from the contradictory orders of unreasonable mothers and nurses.

Women and girls, too, were benefitted by the kindergarten.

Mothers, whose time, inclination, or talents, forbade them to devote sufficient time to the child, were relieved by the kindergarten. Girls learned, as if in a preparatory school of future wife and motherhood, how to give the little one what it needed, and, as Froebel expresses it, to become the mediators between Nature and mind.

Yet even this enterprise, the outcome of pure love for the most innocent and harmless creatures, was prohibited and persecuted as perilous to the state under Frederick William IV, during the period of the reaction which followed the insurrection of 1848.

CHAPTER XIII.
THE FOUNDERS OF THE KEILHAU INSTITUTE, AND A GLIMPSE AT THE HISTORY OF THE SCHOOL.

I was well acquainted with the three founders of our institute—Fredrich Froebel, Middendorf, and Langethal—and the two latter were my teachers. Froebel was decidedly "the master who planned it."

When we came to Keilhau he was already sixty-six years old, a man of lofty stature, with a face which seemed to be carved with a dull knife out of brown wood.

His long nose, strong chin, and large ears, behind which the long locks, parted in the middle, were smoothly brushed, would have rendered him positively ugly, had not his "Come, let us live for our children," beamed so invitingly in his clear eyes. People did not think whether he was handsome or not; his features bore the impress of his intellectual power so distinctly that the first glance revealed the presence of a remarkable man.

Yet I must confess—and his portrait agrees with my memory—that his face by no means suggested the idealist and man of feeling; it seemed rather expressive of shrewdness, and to have been lined and worn by severe conflicts concerning the most diverse interests. But his voice and his glance were unusually winning, and his power over the heart of the child was limitless. A few words were sufficient to win completely the shyest boy whom he desired to attract; and thus it happened that, even when he had been with us only a few weeks, he was never seen crossing the court-yard without a group of the younger pupils hanging to his coattails and clasping his hands and arms.

Usually they were persuading him to tell stories, and when he condescended to do so, older ones flocked around him too, and they were never disappointed. What fire, what animation the old man had retained! We never called him anything but "Oheim." The word "Onkel" he detested as foreign, because it was derived from "avunculus" and "oncle." With the high appreciation he had of "Tante"—whom he termed, next to the mother, the most important factor of education in the family—our "Oheim" was probably specially agreeable to him.

He was thoroughly a self-made man. The son of a pastor in Oberweissbach, in Thuringia, he had had a dreary childhood; for his mother died young, and he soon had a step-mother, who treated him with the utmost tenderness until her own children were born. Then an indescribably sad time began for the neglected boy, whose dreamy temperament vexed even his own father. Yet in this solitude his love for Nature awoke. He studied plants, animals, minerals; and while his young heart vainly longed for love, he would have gladly displayed affection himself, if his timidity would have permitted him to do so. His family, seeing him prefer to dissect the bones of some animal rather than to talk with his parents, probably considered him a very unlovable child when they sent him, in his tenth year, to school in the city of Ilm.

He was received into the home of the pastor, his uncle Hoffman, whose mother-in-law, who kept the house, treated him in the most cordial manner, and helped him to conquer the diffidence acquired during the solitude of the first years of his childhood. This excellent woman first made him familiar with the maternal feminine solicitude, closer observation of which afterwards led him, as well as Pestalozzi, to a reform of the system of educating youth.

In his sixteenth year he went to a forester for instruction, but did not remain long. Meantime he had gained some mathematical knowledge, and devoted himself to surveying. By this and similar work he earned a living, until, at the end of seven years, he went to Frankfort-on-the-Main to learn the rudiments of building. There Fate brought him into contact with the pedagogue Gruner, a follower of Pestalozzi's method, and this experienced man, after their first conversation, exclaimed: "You must become a schoolmaster!"

I have often noticed in life that a word at the right time and place has sufficed to give the destiny of a human being a different turn, and the remark of the Frankfort educator fell into Froebel's soul like a spark. He now saw his real profession clearly and distinctly before him.

The restless years of wandering, during which, unloved and scarcely heeded, he had been thrust from one place to another, had awakened in his warm heart a longing to keep others from the same fate. He, who had been guided by no kind hand and felt miserable and at variance with himself, had long been ceaselessly troubled by the problem of how the young human plant could be trained to harmony with itself and to sturdy industry. Gruner showed him that others were already devoting their best powers to solve it, and offered him an opportunity to try his ability in his model school.

Froebel joyfully accepted this offer, cast aside every other thought, and, with the enthusiasm peculiar to him, threw himself into the new calling in a manner which led Gruner to praise the "fire and life" he understood how to awaken in his pupils. He also left it to Froebel to arrange the plan of instruction which the Frankfort Senate wanted for the "model school," and succeeded in keeping him two years in his institution.

When a certain Frau von Holzhausen was looking for a man who would have the ability to lead her spoiled sons into the right path, and Froebel had been recommended, he separated from Gruner and performed his task with rare fidelity and a skill bordering upon genius. The children, who were physically puny, recovered under his care, and the grateful mother made him their private tutor from 1807 till 1810. He chose Verdun, where Pestalozzi was then living, as his place of residence, and made himself thoroughly familiar with his method of education. As a whole, he could agree with him; but, as has already been mentioned, in some respects he went further than the Swiss reformer. He himself called these years his "university course as a pedagogue," but they also furnished him with the means to continue the studies in natural history which he had commenced in Jena. He had laid aside for this purpose part of his salary as tutor, and was permitted, from 1810 to 1812, to complete in Gottingen his astronomical and mineralogical studies. Yet the wish to try his powers as a pedagogue never deserted him; and when, in 1812, the position of teacher in the Plamann Institute in Berlin was offered him, he accepted it. During his leisure hours he devoted himself to gymnastic exercises, and even late in life his eyes sparkled when he spoke of his friend, old Jahn, and the political elevation of Prussia.

When the summons "To my People" called the German youth to war, Froebel had already entered his thirty-first year, but this did not prevent his resigning his office and being one of the first to take up arms. He went to the field with the Lutzow Jagers, and soon after made the acquaintance among his comrades of the theological students Langethal and Middendorf. When, after the Peace of Paris, the young friends parted, they vowed eternal fidelity, and each solemnly promised to obey the other's summons, should it ever come. As soon as Froebel took off the dark uniform of the black Jagers he received a position as curator of the museum of mineralogy in the Berlin University, which he filled so admirably that the position of Professor of Mineralogy was offered to him from Sweden. But he declined, for another vocation summoned him which duty and inclination forbade him to refuse.

His brother, a pastor in the Thuringian village of Griesheim on the Ilm, died, leaving three sons who needed an instructor. The widow wished her brother-in-law Friedrich to fill this office, and another brother, a farmer in Osterode, wanted his two boys to join the trio. When Froebel, in the spring of 1817, resigned his position, his friend Langethal begged him to take his brother Eduard as another pupil, and thus Pestalozzi's enthusiastic disciple and comrade found his dearest wish fulfilled. He was now the head of his own school for boys, and these first six pupils—as he hoped with the confidence in the star of success peculiar to so many men of genius—must soon increase to twenty. Some of these boys were specially gifted: one became the scholar and politician Julius Froebel, who belonged to the Frankfort Parliament of 1848, and another the Jena Professor of Botany, Eduard Langethal.

The new principal of the school could not teach alone, but he only needed to remind his old army comrade, Middendorf, of his promise, to induce him to interrupt his studies in Berlin, which were nearly completed, and join him. He also had his eye on Langethal, if his hope should be fulfilled. He knew what a treasure he would possess for his object in this rare man.

There was great joy in the little Griesheim circle, and the Thuringian (Froebel) did not regret for a moment that he had resigned his secure position; but the Westphalian (Middendorf) saw here the realization of the ideal which Froebel's kindling words had impressed upon his soul beside many a watch-fire.

The character of the two men is admirably described in the following passage from a letter of "the oldest pupil":

"Both had seen much of the serious side of life, and returned from the war with the higher inspiration which is hallowed by deep religious feeling. The idea of devoting their powers with self-denial and sacrifice to the service of their native land had become a fixed resolution; the devious paths which so many men entered were far from their thoughts. The youth, the young generation of their native land, were alone worthy of their efforts. They meant to train them to a harmonious development of mind and body; and upon these young people their pure spirit of patriotism exerted a vast influence. When we recall the mighty power which Froebel could exercise at pleasure over his fellowmen, and especially over children, we shall deem it natural that a child suddenly transported into this circle could forget its past."

When I entered it, though at that time it was much modified and established on firm foundations, I met with a similar experience. It was not only the open air, the forest, the life in Nature which so captivated new arrivals at Keilhau, but the moral earnestness and the ideal aspiration which consecrated and ennobled life. Then, too, there was that "nerve-strengthening" patriotism which pervaded everything, filling the place of the superficial philanthropy of the Basedow system of education.

But Froebel's influence was soon to draw, as if by magnetic power, the man who had formed an alliance with him amid blood and steel, and who was destined to lend the right solidity to the newly erected structure of the institute—I mean Heinrich Langethal, the most beloved and influential of my teachers, who stood beside Froebel's inspiring genius and Middendorf's lovable warmth of feeling as the character, and at the same time the fully developed and trained intellect, whose guidance was so necessary to the institute.

The life of this rare teacher can be followed step by step from the first years of his childhood in his autobiography and many other documents, but I can only attempt here to sketch in broad outlines the character of the man whose influence upon my whole inner life has been, up to the present hour, a decisive one.

The recollection of him makes me inclined to agree with the opinion to which a noble lady sought to convert me—namely, that our lives are far more frequently directed into a certain channel by the influence of an unusual personality than by events, experiences, or individual reflections.

Langethal was my teacher for several years. When I knew him he was totally blind, and his eyes, which are said to have flashed so brightly and boldly on the foe in war, and gazed so winningly into the faces of friends in time of peace, had lost their lustre. But his noble features seemed transfigured by the cheerful earnestness which is peculiar to the old man, who, even though only with the eye of the mind, looks back upon a well-spent, worthy life, and who does not fear death, because he knows that God who leads all to the goal allotted by Nature destined him also for no other. His tall figure could vie with Barop's, and his musical voice was unusually deep. It possessed a resistless power when, excited himself, he desired to fill our young souls with his own enthusiasm. The blind old man, who had nothing more to command and direct, moved through our merry, noisy life like a silent admonition to good and noble things. Outside of the lessons he never raised his voice for orders or censure, yet we obediently followed his signs. To be allowed to lead him was an honor and pleasure. He made us acquainted with Homer, and taught us ancient and modern history. To this day I rejoice that not one of us ever thought of using 'pons asinorum,' or copied passage, though he was perfectly sightless, and we were obliged to translate to him and learn by heart whole sections of the Iliad. To have done so would have seemed as shameful as the pillage of an unguarded sanctuary or the abuse of a wounded hero.

And he certainly was one!

We knew this from his comrades in the war and his stories of 1813, which were at once so vivid and so modest.

When he explained Homer or taught ancient history a special fervor animated him; for he was one of the chosen few whose eyes were opened by destiny to the full beauty and sublimity of ancient Greece.

I have listened at the university to many a famous interpreter of the Hellenic and Roman poets, and many a great historian, but not one of them ever gave me so distinct an impression of living with the ancients as Heinrich Langethal. There was something akin to them in his pure, lofty soul, ever thirsting for truth and beauty, and, besides, he had graduated from the school of a most renowned teacher.

The outward aspect of the tall old man was eminently aristocratic, yet his birthplace was the house of a plain though prosperous mechanic. He was born at Erfurt, in 1792. When very young his father, a man unusually sensible and well-informed for his station in life, entrusted him with the education of a younger brother, the one who, as I have mentioned, afterwards became a professor at Jena, and the boy's progress was so rapid that other parents had requested to have their sons share the hours of instruction.

After completing his studies at the grammar-school he wanted to go to Berlin, for, though the once famous university still existed in Erfurt, it had greatly deteriorated. His description of it is half lamentable, half amusing, for at that time it was attended by thirty students, for whom seventy professors were employed. Nevertheless, there were many obstacles to be surmounted ere he could obtain permission to attend the Berlin University; for the law required every native of Erfurt, who intended afterwards to aspire to any office, to study at least two years in his native city—at that time French. But, in defiance of all hindrances, he found his way to Berlin, and in 1811 was entered in the university just established there as the first student from Erfurt. He wished to devote himself to theology, and Neander, De Wette, Marheineke, Schleiermacher, etc., must have exerted a great power of attraction over a young man who desired to pursue that study.

At the latter's lectures he became acquainted with Middendorf. At first he obtained little from either. Schleiermacher seemed to him too temporizing and obscure. "He makes veils." He thought the young Westphalian, at their first meeting, merely "a nice fellow." But in time he learned to understand the great theologian, and the "favourite teacher" noticed him and took him into his house.

But first Fichte, and then Friedrich August Wolf, attracted him far more powerfully than Schleiermacher. Whenever he spoke of Wolf his calm features glowed and his blind eyes seemed to sparkle. He owed all that was best in him to the great investigator, who sharpened his pupil's appreciation of the exhaustless store of lofty ideas and the magic of beauty contained in classic antiquity, and had he been allowed to follow his own inclination, he would have turned his back on theology, to devote all his energies to the pursuit of philology and archaeology.

The Homeric question which Wolf had propounded in connection with Goethe, and which at that time stirred the whole learned world, had also moved Langethal so deeply that, even when an old man, he enjoyed nothing more than to speak of it to us and make us familiar with the pros and cons which rendered him an upholder of his revered teacher. He had been allowed to attend the lectures on the first four books of the Iliad, and—I have living witnesses of the fact—he knew them all verse by verse, and corrected us when we read or recited them as if he had the copy in his hand.

True, he refreshed his naturally excellent memory by having them all read aloud. I shall never forget his joyous mirth as he listened to my delivery of Wolf's translation of Aristophanes's Acharnians; but I was pleased that he selected me to supply the dear blind eyes. Whenever he called me for this purpose he already had the book in the side pocket of his long coat, and when, beckoning significantly, he cried, "Come, Bear," I knew what was before me, and would have gladly resigned the most enjoyable game, though he sometimes had books read which were by no means easy for me to understand. I was then fourteen or fifteen years old.

Need I say that it was my intercourse with this man which implanted in my heart the love of ancient days that has accompanied me throughout my life?

The elevation of the Prussian nation led Langethal also from the university to the war. Rumor first brought to Berlin the tidings of the destruction of the great army on the icy plains of Russia; then its remnants, starving, worn, ragged, appeared in the capital; and the street-boys, who not long before had been forced by the French soldiers to clean their boots, now with little generosity—they were only "street-boys"—shouted sneeringly, "Say, mounseer, want your boots blacked?"

Then came the news of the convention of York, and at last the irresolute king put an end to the doubts and delays which probably stirred the blood of every one who is familiar with Droysen's classic "Life of Field-Marshal York." From Breslau came the summons "To my People," which, like a warm spring wind, melted the ice and woke in the hearts of the German youth a matchless budding and blossoming.

The snow-drops which bloomed during those March days of 1813 ushered in the long-desired day of freedom, and the call "To arms!" found the loudest echo in the hearts of the students. It stirred the young, yet even in those days circumspect Langethal, too, and showed him his duty But difficulties confronted him; for Pastor Ritschel, a native of Erfurt, to whom he confided his intention, warned him not to write to his father. Erfurt, his own birthplace, was still under French rule, and were he to communicate his plan in writing and the letter should be opened in the "black room," with other suspicious mail matter, it might cost the life of the man whose son was preparing to commit high-treason by fighting against the ruler of his country—Napoleon, the Emperor of France.

"Where will you get the uniform, if your father won't help you, and you want to join the black Jagers?" asked the pastor, and received the answer:

"The cape of my cloak will supply the trousers. I can have a red collar put on my cloak, my coat can be dyed black and turned into a uniform, and I have a hanger."

"That's right!" cried the worthy minister, and gave his young friend ten thalers.

Middendorf, too, reported to the Lutzow Jagers at once, and so did the son of Professor Bellermann, and their mutual friend Bauer, spite of his delicate health which seemed to unfit him for any exertion.

They set off on the 11th of April, and while the spring was budding alike in the outside world and in young breasts, a new flower of friendship expanded in the hearts of these three champions of the same sacred cause; for Langethal and Middendorf found their Froebel. This was in Dresden, and the league formed there was never to be dissolved. They kept their eyes fixed steadfastly on the ideals of youth, until in old age the sight of all three failed. Part of the blessings which were promised to the nation when they set forth to battle they were permitted to see seven lustra later, in 1848, but they did not live to experience the realization of their fairest youthful dream, the union of Germany.

I must deny myself the pleasure of describing the battles and the marches of the Lutzow corps, which extended to Aachen and Oudenarde; but will mention here that Langethal rose to the rank of sergeant, and had to perform the duties of a first lieutenant; and that, towards the end of the campaign, Middendorf was sent with Lieutenant Reil to induce Blucher to receive the corps in his vanguard. The old commander gratified their wish; they had proved their fitness for the post when they won the victory at the Gohrde, where two thousand Frenchmen were killed and as many more taken prisoners. The sight of the battlefield had seemed unendurable to the gentle nature of Middendorf he had formed a poetical idea of the campaign as an expedition against the hereditary foe. Now that he had confronted the bloodstained face of war with all its horrors, he fell into a state of melancholy from which he could scarcely rouse himself.

After this battle the three friends were quartered in Castle Gohrde, and there enjoyed a delightful season of rest after months of severe hardships. Their corps had been used as the extreme vanguard against Davoust's force, which was thrice their superior in numbers, and in consequence they were subjected to great fatigues. They had almost forgotten how it seemed to sleep in a bed and eat at a table. One night march had followed another. They had often seized their food from the kettles and eaten it at the next stopping-place, but all was cheerfully done; the light-heartedness of youth did not vanish from their enthusiastic hearts. There was even no lack of intellectual aliment, for a little field-library had been established by the exchange of books. Langethal told us of his night's rest in a ditch, which was to entail disastrous consequences. Utterly exhausted, sleep overpowered him in the midst of a pouring rain, and when he awoke he discovered that he was up to his neck in water. His damp bed—the ditch—had gradually filled, but the sleep was so profound that even the rising moisture had not roused him. The very next morning he was attacked with a disease of the eyes, to which he attributed his subsequent blindness.

On the 26th of August there was a prospect of improvement in the condition of the corps. Davoust had sent forty wagons of provisions to Hamburg, and the men were ordered to capture them. The attack was successful, but at what a price! Theodor Korner, the noble young poet whose songs will commemorate the deeds of the Lutzow corps so long as German men and boys sing his "Thou Sword at my Side," or raise their voices in the refrain of the Lutzow Jagers' song:

"Do you ask the name of yon reckless band? 'Tis Lutzow's black troopers dashing swift through the land!"

Langethal first saw the body of the author of "Lyre and Sword" and "Zriny" under an oak at Wobbelin; but he was to see it once more under quite different circumstances. He has mentioned it in his autobiography, and I have heard him describe several times his visit to the corpse of Theodor Korner.

He had been quartered in Wobbelin, and shared his room with an Oberjager von Behrenhorst, son of the postmaster-general in Dessau, who had taken part in the battle of Jena as a young lieutenant and returned home with a darkened spirit.

At the summons "To my People," he had enlisted at once as a private soldier in the Lutzow corps, where he rose rapidly to the rank of Oberjager. During the war he had often met Langethal and Middendorf; but the quiet, reserved man, prematurely grave for his years, attached himself so closely to Korner that he needed no other friend.

After the death of the poet on the 26th of August, 1813, he moved silently about as though completely crushed. On the night which followed the 27th he invited his room-mate Langethal to go with him to the body of his friend. Both went first to the village church, where the dead Jagers lay in two long black rows. A solemn stillness pervaded the little house of God, which had become during this night the abode of death, and the nocturnal visitors gazed silently at the pallid, rigid features of one lifeless young form after another, but without finding him whom they sought.

During this mute review of corpses it seemed to Langethal as if Death were singing a deep, heartrending choral, and he longed to pray for these young, crushed human blossoms; but his companion led the way into the guard's little room. There lay the poet, "the radiance of an angel on his face," though his body bore many traces of the fury of the battle. Deeply moved, Langethal stood gazing down upon the form of the man who had died for his native land, while Behrenhorst knelt on the floor beside him, silently giving himself up to the anguish of his soul. He remained in this attitude a long time, then suddenly started up, threw his arms upward, and exclaimed, "Korner, I'll follow you!"

With these words Behrenhorst darted out of the little room into the darkness; and a few weeks after he, too, had fallen for the sacred cause of his native land.

They had seen another beloved comrade perish in the battle of Gohrde, a handsome young man of delicate figure and an unusually reserved manner.

Middendorf, with whom he—his name was Prohaska—had been on more intimate terms than the others, once asked him, when he timidly avoided the girls and women who cast kindly glances at him, if his heart never beat faster, and received the answer, "I have but one love to give, and that belongs to our native land."

While the battle was raging, Middendorf was fighting close beside his comrade. When the enemy fired a volley the others stooped, but Prohaska stood erect, exclaiming, when he was warned, "No bowing! I'll make no obeisance to the French!"

A few minutes after, the brave soldier, stricken by a bullet, fell on the greensward. His friends bore him off the field, and Prohaska—Eleonore Prohaska—proved to be a girl!

While in Castle Gohrde, Froebel talked with his friends about his favourite plan, which he had already had a view in Gottingen, of establishing a school for boys, and while developing his educational ideal to them and at the same time mentioning that he had passed his thirtieth birthday, and alluding to the postponement of his plan by the war, he exclaimed, to explain why he had taken up arms:

"How can I train boys whose devotion I claim, unless I have proved by my own deeds how a man should show devotion to the general welfare?"

These words made a deep impression upon the two friends, and increased Middendorf's enthusiastic reverence for the older comrade, whose experiences and ideas had opened a new world to him.

The Peace of Paris, and the enrolment of the Lutzow corps in the line, brought the trio back to Berlin to civil life.

There also each frequently sought the others, until, in the spring of 1817, Froebel resigned the permanent position in the Bureau of Mineralogy in order to establish his institute.

Middendorf had been bribed by the saying of his admired friend that he "had found the unity of life." It gave the young philosopher food for thought, and, because he felt that he had vainly sought this unity and was dissatisfied, he hoped to secure it through the society of the man who had become everything to him His wish was fulfilled, for as an educator he grew as it were into his own motto, "Lucid, genuine, and true to life."

Middendorf gave up little when he followed Froebel.

The case was different with Langethal. He had entered as a tutor the Bendemann household at Charlottenburg, where he found a second home. He taught with brilliant success children richly gifted in mind and heart, whose love he won. It was "a glorious family" which permitted him to share its rich social life, and in whose highly gifted circle he could be sure of finding warm sympathy in his intellectual interests. Protected from all external anxieties, he had under their roof ample leisure for industrious labour and also for intercourse with his own friends.

In July, 1817, he passed the last examination with the greatest distinction, receiving the "very good," rarely bestowed; and a brilliant career lay before him.

Directly after this success three pulpits were offered to him, but he accepted neither, because he longed for rest and quiet occupation.

The summons from Froebel to devote himself to his infant institute, where Langethal had placed his younger brother, also reached him. The little school moved on St. John's Day, 1817, from Griesheim to Keilhau, where the widow of Pastor Froebel had been offered a larger farm. The place which she and her children's teacher found was wonderfully adapted to Froebel's purpose, and seemed to promise great advantages both to the pupils and to the institute. There was much building and arranging to be accomplished, but means to do so were obtained, and the first pupil described very amusingly the entrance into the new home, the furnishing, the discovery of all the beauties and advantages which we found as an old possession in Keilhau, and the endeavour, so characteristic of Middendorf, to adapt even the less attractive points to his own poetic ideas.

Only the hours of instruction fared badly, and Froebel felt that he needed a man of fully developed strength in order to give the proper foundation to the instruction of the boys who were entrusted to his care. He knew a man of this stamp in the student F. A. Wolfs, whose talent for teaching had been admirably proved in the Bendemann family.

"Langethal," as the first pupil describes him, was at that time a very handsome man of five-and-twenty years. His brow was grave, but his features expressed kindness of heart, gentleness, and benevolence. The dignity of his whole bearing was enhanced by the sonorous tones of his voice—he retained them until old age—and his whole manner revealed manly firmness. Middendorf was more pleasing to women, Langethal to men. Middendorf attracted those who saw, Langethal those who heard him, and the confidence he inspired was even more lasting than that aroused by Middendorf.

What marvel that Froebel made every effort to win this rare power for the young institute? But Langethal declined, to the great vexation of Middendorf. Diesterweg called the latter "a St. John," but our dear, blind teacher added, "And Froebel was his Christus."

The enthusiastic young Westphalian, who had once believed he saw in this man every masculine virtue, and whose life appeared emblematical, patiently accepted everything, and considered every one a "renegade" who had ever followed Froebel and did not bow implicitly to his will. So he was angered by Langethal's refusal. The latter had been offered, with brilliant prospects for the present and still fairer ones for the future, a position as a tutor in Silesia, a place which secured him the rest he desired, combined with occupation suited to his tastes. He was to share the labour of teaching with another instructor, who was to take charge of the exact sciences, with which he was less familiar, and he was also permitted to teach his brother with the young Counts Stolberg.

He accepted, but before going to Silesia he wished to visit his Keilhau friends and take his brother away with him. He did so, and the "diplomacy" with which Froebel succeeded in changing the decision of the resolute young man and gaining him over to his own interests, is really remarkable.

It won for the infant institute in the person of Langethal—if the expression is allowable—the backbone.

Froebel had sent Middendorf to meet his friend, and the latter, on the way, told him of the happiness which he had found in his new home and occupation. Then they entered Keilhau, and the splendid landscape which surrounds it needs no praise.

Froebel received his former comrade with the utmost cordiality, and the sight of the robust, healthy, merry boys who were lying on the floor that evening, building forts and castles with the wooden blocks which Froebel had had made for them according to his own plan, excited the keenest interest. He had come to take his brother away; but when he saw him, among other happy companions of his own age, complete the finest structure of all—a Gothic cathedral—it seemed almost wrong to tear the child from this circle.

He gazed sadly at his brother when he came to bid him "good-night," and then remained alone with Froebel. The latter was less talkative than usual, waiting for his friend to tell him of the future which awaited him in Silesia. When he heard that a second tutor was to relieve Langethal of half his work, he exclaimed, with the greatest anxiety:

"You do not know him, and yet intend to finish a work of education with him? What great chances you are hazarding!"

The next morning Froebel asked his friend what goal in life he had set before him, and Langethal replied:

"Like the apostle, I would fain proclaim the gospel to all men according to the best of my powers, in order to bring them into close communion with the Redeemer."

Froebel answered, thoughtfully:

"If you desire that, you must, like the apostles, know men. You must be able to enter into the life of every one—here a peasant, there a mechanic. If you can not, do not hope for success; your influence will not extend far."

How wise and convincing the words sounded! And Froebel touched the sensitive spot in the young minister, who was thoroughly imbued with the sacred beauty of his life-task, yet certainly knew the Gospels, his classic authors, and apostolic fathers much better than he did the world.

He thoughtfully followed Froebel, who, with Middendorf and the boys, led him up the Steiger, the mountain whose summit afforded the magnificent view I have described. It was the hour when the setting sun pours its most exquisite light over the mountains and valleys. The heart of the young clergyman, tortured by anxious doubts, swelled at the sight of this magnificence, and Froebel, seeing what was passing in his mind, exclaimed:

"Come, comrade, let us have one of our old war-songs."

The musical "black Jager" of yore willingly assented; and how clearly and enthusiastically the chorus of boyish voices chimed in!

When it died away, the older man passed his arm around his friend's shoulders, and, pointing to the beautiful region lying before them in the sunset glow, exclaimed:

"Why seek so far away what is close at hand? A work is established here which must be built by the hand of God! Implicit devotion and self-sacrifice are needed."

While speaking, he gazed steadfastly into his friend's tearful eyes, as if he had found his true object in life, and when he held out his hand Langethal clasped it—he could not help it.

That very day a letter to the Counts Stolberg informed them that they must seek another tutor for their sons, and Froebel and Keilhau could congratulate themselves on having gained their Langethal.

The management of the school was henceforward in the hands of a man of character, while the extensive knowledge and the excellent method of a well-trained scholar had been obtained for the educational department. The new institute now prospered rapidly. The renown of the fresh, healthful life and the able tuition of the pupils spread far beyond the limits of Thuringia. The material difficulties with which the head-master had had to struggle after the erection of the large new buildings were also removed when Froebel's prosperous brother in Osterode decided to take part in the work and move to Keilhau. He understood farming, and, by purchasing more land and woodlands, transformed the peasant holding into a considerable estate.

When Froebel's restless spirit drew him to Switzerland to undertake new educational enterprises, and some one was needed who could direct the business management, Barop, the steadfast man of whom I have already spoken, was secured. Deeply esteemed and sincerely beloved, he managed the institute during the time that we three brothers were pupils there. He had found many things within to arrange on a more practical foundation, many without to correct: for the long locks of most of the pupils; the circumstance that three Lutzen Jagers, one of whom had delivered the oration at a students' political meeting, had established the school; that Barop had been persecuted as a demagogue on account of his connection with a students' political society; and, finally, Froebel's relations with

Switzerland and the liberal educational methods of the school, had roused the suspicions of the Berlin demagogue-hunters, and therefore demagogic tendencies, from which in reality it had always held aloof, were attributed to the institute.

Yes, we were free, in so far that everything which could restrict or retard our physical and mental development was kept away from us, and our teachers might call themselves so because, with virile energy, they had understood how to protect the institute from every injurious and narrowing outside influence. The smallest and the largest pupil was free, for he was permitted to be wholly and entirely his natural self, so long as he kept within the limits imposed by the existing laws. But license was nowhere more sternly prohibited than at Keilhau; and the deep religious feeling of its head-masters—Barop, Langethal, and Middendorf—ought to have taught the suspicious spies in Berlin that the command, "Render unto Caesar the things that are Caesar's," would never be violated here.

The time I spent in Keilhau was during the period of the worst reaction, and I now know that our teachers would have sat on the Left in the Prussian Landtag; yet we never heard a disrespectful word spoken of Frederick William IV, and we were instructed to show the utmost respect to the prince of the little country of Rudolstadt to which Keilhau belonged. Barop, spite of his liberal tendencies, was highly esteemed by this petty sovereign, decorated with an order, and raised to the rank of Councillor of Education. From a hundred isolated recollections and words which have lingered in my memory I have gathered that our teachers were liberals in a very moderate way, yet they were certainly guilty of "demagogic aspirations" in so far as that they desired for their native land only what we, thank Heaven, now possess its unity, and a popular representation, by a free election of all its states, in a German Parliament. What enthusiasm for the Emperor William, Bismarck, and Von Moltke, Langethal, Middendorf, and Barop would have inspired in our hearts had they been permitted to witness the great events of 1870 and 1871!

Besides, politics were kept from us, and this had become known in wider circles when we entered the institute, for most of the pupils belonged to loyal families. Many were sons of the higher officials, officers, and landed proprietors; and as long locks had long since become the exception, and the Keilhau pupils were as well mannered as possible, many noblemen, among them chamberlains and other court officials, decided to send their boys to the institute.

The great manufacturers and merchants who placed their sons in the institute were also not men favourable to revolution, and many of our comrades became officers in the German army. Others are able scholars, clergymen, and members of Parliament; others again government officials, who fill high positions; and others still are at the head of large industrial or mercantile enterprises. I have not heard of a single individual who has gone to ruin, and of very many who have accomplished things really worthy of note. But wherever I have met an old pupil of Keilhau, I have found in him the same love for the institute, have seen his eyes sparkle more brightly when we talked of Langethal, Middendorf, and Barop. Not one has turned out a sneak or a hypocrite.

The present institution is said to be an admirable one; but the "Realschule" of Keilhau, which has been forced to abandon its former humanistic foundation, can scarcely train to so great a variety of callings the boys now entrusted to its care.

CHAPTER XIV.
RUDOLSTADT

The little country of Rudolstadt in which Keilhau lies had had its revolution, though it was but a small and bloodless one. True, the insurrection had nothing to do with human beings, but involved the destruction of living creatures. Greater liberty in hunting was demanded.

This might seem a trivial matter, yet it was of the utmost importance to both disputants. The wide forests of the country had hitherto been the hunting-grounds of the prince, and not a gun could be fired there without his permission. To give up these "happy hunting-grounds" was a severe demand upon the eager sportsman who occupied the Rudolstadt throne, and the rustic population would gladly have spared him had it been possible.

But the game in Rudolstadt had become a veritable torment, which destroyed the husbandmen's hopes of harvests. The peasant, to save his fields from the stags and does which broke into them in herds at sunset, tried to keep them out by means of clappers and bad odours. I have seen and smelled the so-called "Frenchman's oil" with which the posts were smeared, that its really diabolical odour—I don't know from what horrors it was compounded—might preserve the crops. The ornament of the forests had become the object of the keenest hate, and as soon as—shortly before we entered Keilhau—hunting was freely permitted, the peasants gave full vent to their rage, set off for the woods with the old muskets they had kept hidden in the garrets, or other still more primitive weapons, and shot or struck down all the game they encountered. Roast venison was cheap for weeks on Rudolstadt tables, and the pupils had many an unexpected pleasure.

The hunting exploits of the older scholars were only learned by us younger ones as secrets, and did not reach the teachers' ears until long after.

But the woods furnished other pleasures besides those enjoyed by the sportsman. Every ramble through the forest enriched our knowledge of plants and animals, and I soon knew the different varieties of stones also; yet we did not suspect that this knowledge was imparted according to a certain system. We were taught as it were by stealth, and how many pleasant, delicious things attracted us to the class-rooms on the wooded heights!

Vegetation was very abundant in the richly watered mountain valley. Our favourite spring was the Schaalbach at the foot of the Steiger,—[We pupils bought it of the peasant who owned it and gave it to Barop.]—because there was a fowling-floor connected with it, where I spent many a pleasant evening. It could be used only after breeding-time, and consisted of a hut built of boughs where the birdcatcher lodged. Flowing water rippled over the little wooden rods on which the feathered denizens of the woods alighted to quench their thirst before going to sleep. When some of them—frequently six at a time—had settled on the perches in the trough, it was drawn into the hut by a rope, a net was spread over the water and there was nothing more to do except take the captives out.

The name of the director of this amusement was Merbod. He could imitate the voices of all the birds, and was a merry, versatile fellow, who knew how to do a thousand things, and of whom we boys were very fond.

The peasant Bredernitz often took us to his crow-hut, which was a hole in the ground covered with boughs and pieces of turf, where the hunters lay concealed. The owl, which lured the crows and other birds of prey, was fastened on a perch, and when they flew up, often in large flocks, to tease the old cross-patch which sat blinking angrily, they were shot down from loop-holes which had been left in the hut. The hawks which prey upon doves and hares, the crows and magpies, can thus easily be decimated.

We had learned to use our guns in the playground. The utmost caution was enforced, and although, as I have already remarked, we handled our own guns when we were only lads of twelve years old, I can not recall a single accident which occurred.

Once, during the summer, there was a Schutzenfest, in which a large wooden eagle was shot from the pole. Whoever brought down the last splinter became king. This honour once fell to my share, and I was permitted to choose a queen. I crowned Marie Breimann, a pretty, slender young girl from Brunswick, whose Greek profile and thick silken hair had captivated my fancy. She and Adelheid Barop, the head-master's daughter, were taught in our classes, but Marie attracted me more strongly than the diligent Keilhau lassies with their beautiful black eyes and the other two blooming and graceful Westphalian girls who were also schoolmates. But the girls occupied a very small place in our lives. They could neither wrestle, shoot, nor climb, so we gave them little thought, and anything like actual flirtation was unknown—we had so many better things in our heads. Wrestling and other sports threw everything else into the shade. Pretty Marie, however, probably suspected which of my school-mates I liked best, and up to the time of my leaving the institute I allowed no other goddess to rival her. But there were plenty of amusements at Keilhau besides bird-shooting.

I will mention the principal ones which came during the year, for to describe them in regular order would be impossible.

Of the longer walks which we took in the spring and summer the most beautiful was the one leading through Blankenburg to the entrance of the Schwarzathal, and thence through the lofty, majestically formed group of cliffs at whose foot the clear, swift Schwarza flows, dashing and foaming, to Schwarzburg.

How clearly our songs echoed from the granite walls of the river valley, and how lively it always was at "The Stag," whose landlord possessed a certain power of attraction to us boys in his own person; for, as the stoutest man in Thuringia, he was a feast for the eyes! His jollity equalled his corpulence, and how merrily he used to jest with us lads!

Of the shorter expeditions I will mention only the two we took most frequently, which led us in less than an hour to Blankenburg or Greifenstein, a large ruin, many parts of which were in tolerable preservation. It had been the home of Count Gunther von Schwarzburg, who paid with his life for the honour of wearing the German imperial crown a few short months.

We also enjoyed being sent to the little town of Blankenburg on errands, for it was the home of our drawing-master, the artist Unger, one of those original characters whom we rarely meet now. When we knew him, the handsome, broad-shouldered man, with his thick red beard, looked as one might imagine Odin. Summer and winter his dress was a grey woollen jacket, into which a short pipe was thrust, and around his hips a broad leather belt, from which hung a bag containing his drawing materials. He cared nothing for public opinion, and, as an independent bachelor, desired nothing except "to be let alone," for he professed the utmost contempt for the corrupt brood yclept "mankind." He never came to our entertainments, probably because he would be obliged to wear something in place of his woollen jacket, and because he avoided women, whom he called "the roots of all evil." I still remember how once, after emptying the vials of his wrath upon mankind, he said, in reply to the question whether he included Barop among the iniquitous brood, "Why, of course not; he doesn't belong to it!"

There was no lack of opportunity to visit him, for a great many persons employed to work for the school lived in Blankenburg, and we were known to be carefully watched there.

I remember two memorable expeditions to the little town. Once my brother burned his arm terribly during a puppet-show by the explosion of some powder provided for the toy cannon.

The poor fellow suffered so severely that I could not restrain my tears, and though it was dark, and snow lay on the mountains, off I went to Blankenburg to get the old surgeon, calling to some of my school-mates at the door to tell them of my destination. It was no easy matter to wade through the snow; but, fortunately, the stars gave me sufficient light to keep in the right path as I dashed down the mountain to Blankenburg. How often I plunged into ditches filled with snow and slid down short descents I don't know; but as I write these lines I can vividly remember the relief with which I at last trod the pavement of the little town. Old Wetzel was at home, and a carriage soon conveyed us over the only road to the institute. I was not punished. Barop only laid his hand on my head, and said, "I am glad you are back again, Bear."

Another trip to Blankenburg entailed results far more serious—nay, almost cost me my life.

I was then fifteen, and one Sunday afternoon I went with Barop's permission to visit the Hamburgers, but on condition that I should return by nine o'clock at latest.

Time, however, slipped by in pleasant conversation until a later hour, and as thunder-clouds were rising my host tried to keep me overnight. But I thought this would not be allowable, and, armed with an umbrella, I set off along the road, with which I was perfectly familiar.

But the storm soon burst, and it grew so dark that, except when the lightning flashed, I could not see my hand before my face. Yet on I went, though wondering that the path along which I groped my way led upward, until the lightning showed me that, by mistake, I had taken the road to Greifenstein. I turned back, and while feeling my way through the gloom the earth seemed to vanish under my feet, and I plunged headlong into a viewless gulf—not through empty space, however, but a wet, tangled mass which beat against my face, until at last there was a jerk which shook me from head to foot.

I no longer fell, but I heard above me the sound of something tearing, and the thought darted through my mind that I was hanging by my trousers. Groping around, I found vine-leaves, branches, and lattice-work, to which I clung, and tearing away with my foot the cloth which had caught on the end of a lath, I again brought my head where it should be, and discovered that I was hanging on a vine-clad wall. A flash of lightning showed me the ground not very far below and, by the help of the espalier and the vines I at last stood in a garden.

Almost by a miracle I escaped with a few scratches; but when I afterwards went to look at the scene of this disaster cold chills ran down my back, for half the distance whence I plunged into the garden would have been enough to break my neck.

Our games were similar to those which lads of the same age play now, but there were some additional ones that could only take place in a wooded mountain valley like Keilhau; such, for instance, were our Indian games, which engrossed us at the time when we were pleased with Cooper's "Leather-Stocking," but I need not describe them.

When I was one of the older pupils a party of us surprised some "Panzen"—as we called the younger ones—one hot afternoon engaged in a very singular game of their own invention. They had undressed to the skin in the midst of the thickest woods and were performing Paradise and the Fall of Man, as they had probably just been taught in their religious lesson. For the expulsion of Adam and our universal mother Eve, the angel—in this case there were two of them—used, instead of the flaming sword, stout hazel rods, with which they performed their part of warders so overzealously that a quarrel followed, which we older ones stopped.

Thus many bands of pupils invented games of their own, but, thank Heaven, rarely devised such absurdities. Our later Homeric battles any teacher would have witnessed with pleasure. Froebel would have greeted them as signs of creative imagination and "individual life" in the boys.

CHAPTER XV.
SUMMER PLEASURES AND RAMBLES

Wholly unlike these, genuinely and solely a product of Keilhau, was the great battle-game which we called Bergwacht, one of my brightest memories of those years.

Long preparations were needed, and these, too, were delightful.

On the wooded plain at the summit of the Kolm, a mountain which belonged mainly to the institute, war was waged during the summer every Saturday evening until far into the night, whenever the weather was fine, which does not happen too often in Thuringia.

The whole body of pupils was divided into three, afterwards into four sections, each of which had its own citadel. After two had declared war against two others, the battle raged until one party captured the strongholds of the other. This was done as soon as a combatant had set foot on the hearth of a hostile fortress.

The battle itself was fought with stakes blunted at the tops. Every one touched by the weapon of an enemy must declare himself a prisoner. To admit this, whenever it happened, was a point of honour.

In order to keep all the combatants in action, a fourth division was added soon after our arrival, and of course it was necessary to build a strong hold like the others. This consisted of a hut with a stone roof, in which fifteen or twenty boys could easily find room and rest, a strong wall which protected us up to our foreheads, and surrounded the front of the citadel in a semicircle, as well as a large altar-like hearth which rose in the midst of the semicircular space surrounded by the wall.

We built this fortress ourselves, except that our teacher of handicrafts, the sapper Sabum, sometimes gave us a hint. The first thing was to mark out the plan, then with the aid of levers pry the rocks out of the fields, and by means of a two-wheeled cart convey them to the site chosen, fit them neatly together, stuff the interstices with moss, and finally put on a roof made of pine logs which we felled ourselves, earth, moss, and branches.

How quickly we learned to use the plummet, take levels, hew the stone, wield the axes! And what a delight it was when the work was finished and we saw our own building! Perhaps we might not have accomplished it without the sapper, but every boy believed that if he were cast, like Robinson Crusoe, on a desert island, he could build a hut of his own.

As soon as this citadel was completed, preparations for the impending battle were made. The walls and encircling walls of all were prepared, and we were drilled in the use of the poles. This, too, afforded us the utmost pleasure. Touching the head of an enemy was strictly prohibited; yet many a slight wound was given while fighting in the gloom of the woods.

Each of the four Bergwachts had its leader. The captain of the first was director of the whole game, and instead of a lance wore a rapier. I considered it a great honour when this dignity was conferred on me. One of its consequences was that my portrait was sketched by "Old Unger" in the so-called "Bergwacht Book," which contained the likenesses of all my predecessors.

During the summer months all eyes, even as early as Thursday, were watching the weather. When Saturday evening proved pleasant and Barop had given his consent, there was great rejoicing in the institute, and the morning hours must have yielded the teachers little satisfaction.

Directly after dinner everybody seized his pole and the other "Bergwacht" equipments. The alliances were formed under the captain's guidance. We will say that the contest was to begin with the first and third Bergwacht pitted against the second and fourth, and be followed by another, with the first and second against the third and fourth.

We assembled in the court-yard just before sunset. Barop made a little speech, exhorting us to fight steadily, and especially to observe all the rules and yield ourselves captives as soon as an enemy's pole touched us. He never neglected on these occasions to admonish us that, should our native land ever need the armed aid of her sons, we should march to battle as joyously as we now did to the Bergwacht, which was to train us to skill in her defence.

Then the procession set off in good order, four or six pupils harnessing themselves voluntarily to the cart in which the kegs of beer were dragged up the Kolm. Off we went, singing merrily, and at the top the women were waiting for us with a lunch. Then the warriors scattered, the fire was lighted on every hearth, the plan of battle was discussed, some were sent out to reconnoitre, others kept to defend the citadel.

At last the conflict began. Could I ever forget the scenes in the forest! No Indian tribe on the war-path ever strained every sense more keenly to watch, surround, and surprise the foe. And the hand-to-hand fray! What delight it was to burst from the shelter of the thicket and touch with our poles two, three, or four of the surprised enemies ere they thought of defence! And what self-denial it required when—spite of the most skilful parry—we felt the touch of the pole, to confess it, and be led off as a prisoner!

Voices and shouts echoed through the woods, and the glare of five fires pierced the darkness—five—for flames were also blazing where the women were cooking the supper. But the light was brightest, the shouts of the combatants were loudest, in the vicinity of the forts. The effort of the besiegers was to spy out unguarded places, and occupy the attention of the garrison so that a comrade might leap over the wall and set his foot on the hearth. The object of the garrison was to prevent this.

What was that? An exulting cry rang through the night air. A warrior had succeeded in penetrating the hostile citadel untouched and setting his foot on the hearth!

Two or three times we enjoyed the delight of battle; and when towards midnight it closed, we threw ourselves-glowing from the strife and blackened by the smoke of the hearth-fires-down on the greensward around the women's fire, where boiled eggs and other good things were served, and meanwhile the mugs of foaming beer were passed around the circle. One patriotic song after another was sung, and at last each Bergwacht withdrew to its citadel and lay down on the moss to sleep under the sheltering roof. Two sentinels marched up and down, relieved every half hour until the early dawn of the summer Sunday brightened the eastern sky.

Then "Huup!"—the Keilhau shout which summoned us back to the institute-rang out, and a hymn, the march back, a bath in the pond, and finally the most delicious rest, if good luck permitted, on the heaps of hay which had not been gathered in. On the Sunday following the Bergwacht we were not required to attend church, where we should merely have gone to sleep. Barop, though usually very strict in the observance of religious duties, never demanded anything for the sake of mere appearances.

And the bed of my own planning! It consisted of wood and stones, and was covered with a thick layer of moss, raised at the head in a slanting direction. It looked like other beds, but the place where it stood requires some description, for it was a Keilhau specialty, a favour bestowed by our teachers on the pupils.

Midway up the slope of the Kolm where our citadels stood, on the side facing the institute, each boy had a piece of ground where he might build, dig, or plant, as he chose. They descended from one to another: Ludo's and mine had come down from Martin and another pupil who left the school at the same time. But I was not satisfied with what my predecessors had created. I spared the beautiful vine which twined around a fir-tree, but in the place of a flower-bed and a bench which I found there Ludo and I built a hearth, and for myself the bed already mentioned, which my brother of course was permitted to occupy with me.

How many hours I have spent on its soft cushions, reading or dreaming or imagining things! If I could only remember them as they hovered before me, what epics and tales I could write!

No doubt we ought to be grateful to God for this as well as for so many other blessings; but why are we permitted to be young only once in our lives, only once to be borne aloft on the wings of a tireless power of imagination, so easily satisfied with ourselves, so full of love, faith, and hope, so open to every joy and so blind to every care and doubt, and everything which threatens to cloud and extinguish the sunlight in the soul?

Dear bed in my plot of ground at Keilhau, you ought, in accordance with a remark of Barop, to cause me serious self-examination, for he said, probably with no thought of my mossy couch, "From the way in which the pupils use their plots of ground and the things they place in them, I can form a very correct opinion of their dispositions and tastes." But you, beloved couch, should have the best place in my garden if you could restore me but for one half hour the dreams which visited me on your grey-green pillows, when I was a lad of fourteen or fifteen.

I have passed over the Rudolstadt Schutzenfest, its music, its merry-go-round, and the capital sausages cooked in the open air, and have intentionally omitted many other delightful things. I cannot help wondering now where we found time for all these summer pleasures.

True, with the exception of a few days at Whitsuntide, we had no vacation from Easter until the first of September. But even in August one thought, one joyous anticipation, filled every heart. The annual autumn excursion was coming!

After we were divided into travelling parties and had ascertained which teacher was to accompany us—a matter that seemed very important—we diligently practised the most beautiful songs; and on many an evening Barop or Middendorf told us of the places through which we were to pass, their history, and the legends which were associated with them. They were aided in this by one of the sub-teachers, Bagge, a poetically gifted young clergyman, who possessed great personal beauty and a heart capable of entering into the intellectual life of the boys who were entrusted to his care.

He instructed us in the German language and literature. Possibly because he thought that he discovered in me a talent for poetic expression, he showed me unusual favor, even read his own verses aloud to me, and set me special tasks in verse-writing, which he criticised with me when I had finished. The first long poem I wrote of my own impulse was a description of the wonderful forms assumed by the stalactite formations in the Sophie Cave in Switzerland, which we had visited. Unfortunately, the book containing it is lost, but I remember the following lines, referring to the industrious sprites which I imagined as the sculptors of the wondrous shapes:

"Priestly robes and a high altar the sprites created here,

And in the rock-hewn cauldron poured the holy water clear,

Within whose depths reflected, by the torches' flickering rays,

Beneath the surface glimmering my own face met my gaze;

And when I thus beheld it, so small it seemed to me,

That yonder stone-carved giant looked on with mocking glee.

Ay, laugh, if that's your pleasure, Goliath huge and old,

I soon shall fare forth singing, you still your place must hold."

Another sub-teacher was also a favourite travelling-companion. His name was Schaffner, and he, too, with his thick, black beard, was a handsome man. To those pupils who, like my brother Ludo, were pursuing the study of the sciences, he, the mathematician of the institute, must have been an unusually clear and competent teacher. I was under his charge only a short time, and his branch of knowledge was unfortunately my weak point. Shortly before my departure he married a younger sister of Barop's wife, and established an educational institution very similar to Keilhau at Gumperda, at Schwarza in Thuringia.

Herr Vodoz, our French teacher, a cheery, vigorous Swiss, with a perfect forest of curls on his head, was also one of the most popular guides; and so was Dr. Budstedt, who gave instruction in the classics. He was not a handsome man, but he deserved the name of "anima candida." He used to storm at the slightest occasion, but he was quickly appeased again. As a teacher I think he did his full duty, but I no longer remember anything about his methods.

The travelling party which Barop accompanied were very proud of the honour. Middendorf's age permitted him to go only with the youngest pupils, who made the shortest trips.

These excursions led the little boys into the Thuringian Forest, the Hartz Mountains, Saxony and Bohemia, Nuremberg and Wurzburg, and the older ones by way of Baireuth and Regensburg to Ulm. The large boys in the first travelling party, which was usually headed by Barop himself, extended their journey as far as Switzerland.

I visited in after-years nearly all the places to which we went at that time, and some, with which important events in my life were associated, I shall mention later. It would not be easy to reproduce from memory the first impressions received without mingling with them more recent ones.

Thus, I well remember how Nuremberg affected me and how much it pleased me. I express this in my description of the journey; but in the author of Gred, who often sought this delightful city, and made himself familiar with life there in the days of its mediaval prosperity, these childish impressions became something wholly new. And yet they are inseparable from the conception and contents of the Nuremberg novel.

My mother kept the old books containing the accounts of these excursions, which occupied from two to three weeks, and they possessed a certain interest for me, principally because they proved how skilfully our teachers understood how to carry out Froebel's principles on these occasions. Our records of travel also explain in detail what this educator meant by the words "unity with life"; for our attention was directed not only to beautiful views or magnificent works of art and architecture, but to noteworthy public institutions or great manufactories. Our teachers took the utmost care that we should understand what we saw.

The cultivation of the fields, the building of the peasants' huts, the national costumes, were all brought under our notice, thus making us familiar with life outside of the school, and opening our eyes to things concerning which the pupil of an ordinary model grammar-school rarely inquires, yet which are of great importance to the world to which we belong.

Our material life was sensibly arranged. During the rest at noon a cold lunch was served, and an abundant hot meal was not enjoyed until evening.

In the large cities we dined at good hotels at the table d'hote, and—as in Dresden, Prague, and Coburg—were taken to the theatre.

But we often spent the night in the villages, and then chairs were turned upside down, loose straw was spread on the backs and over the floor, and, wrapped in the shawl which almost every boy carried buckled to his knapsack, we slept, only half undressed, as comfortably as in the softest bed.

While walking we usually sung songs, among them very nonsensical ones, if only we could keep step well to their time. Often one of the teachers told us a story. Schaffner and Bagge could do this best, but we often met other pedestrians with whom we entered into conversation. How delightful is the memory of these tramps! Progress on foot is slow, but not only do we see ten times better than from a carriage or the window of a car, but we hear and learn something while talking with the mechanics, citizens, and peasants who are going the same way, or the landlords, bar-maids, and table companions we meet in the taverns, whose guests live according to the custom of the country instead of the international pattern of our great hotels.

As a young married man, I always anticipated as the greatest future happiness taking pedestrian tours with my sons like the Keilhau ones; but Fate ordained otherwise.

On our return to the institute we were received with great rejoicing; and how much the different parties, now united, had to tell one another!

Study recommenced on the first of October, and during the leisure days before that time the village church festival was celebrated under the village linden, with plenty of cakes, and a dance of the peasants, in which we older ones took part. But we were obliged to devote several hours of every day to describing our journey for our relatives at home. Each one filled a large book, which was to be neatly written. The exercise afforded better practice in describing personal experiences than a dozen essays which had been previously read with the teacher.

CHAPTER XVI.
AUTUMN, WINTER, EASTER AND DEPARTURE

Autumn had come, and this season of the year, which afterwards was to be the most fraught with suffering, at that time seemed perhaps the pleasantest; for none afforded a better opportunity for wrestling and playing. It brought delicious fruit, and never was the fire lighted more frequently on the hearth in the plots of ground assigned to the pupils—baking and boiling were pleasant during the cool afternoons.

No month seemed to us so cheery as October. During its course the apples and pears were gathered, and an old privilege allowed the pupils "to glean"—that is, to claim the fruit left on the trees. This tested the keenness of our young eyes, but it sometimes happened that we confounded trees still untouched with those which had been harvested. "Nitimur in vetitum semper cupimusque negata,"—[The forbidden charms, and the unexpected lures us.]—is an excellent saying of Ovid, whose truth, when he tested it in person, was the cause of his exile. It sometimes brought us into conflict with the owners of the trees, and it was only natural that "Froebel's youngsters" often excited the peasants' ire.

Gellert, it is true, has sung:

"Enjoy what the Lord has granted,

Grieve not for aught withheld."

but the popular saying is, "Forbidden fruit tastes sweetest," and the proverb was right in regard to us Keilhau boys.

Whatever fruit is meant in the story related in Genesis of the fall of man, none could make it clearer to German children than the apple. The Keilhau ones were kept in a cellar, and through the opening we thrust a pole to which the blade of a rapier was fastened. This sometimes brought us up four or five apples at once, which hung on the blade like the flock of ducks that Baron Munchausen's musket pierced with the ramrod.

We were all honest boys, yet not one, not even the sons of the heads of the institute, ever thought of blaming or checking the zest for this appropriation of other people's property.

The apple and morality must stand in a very peculiar relation to each other.

Scarcely was the last fruit gathered, when other pleasures greeted us.

The 18th of October, the anniversary of the battle of Leipsic, was celebrated in Thuringia by kindling bonfires on the highest mountains, but ours was always the largest and brightest far and wide. While the flames soared heavenward, we enthusiastically sang patriotic songs. The old Lutzow Jagers, who had fought for the freedom of Germany, led the chorus and gazed with tearful eyes at the boys whom they were rearing for the future supporters and champions of their native land.

Then winter came.

Snow and ice usually appeared in our mountain valley in the latter half of November. We welcomed them, for winter brought coasting parties down the mountains, skating, snow-balling, the clumsy snow-man, and that most active of mortals, the dancing-master, who not only instructed us in the art of Terpsichore, but also gave us rules of decorum which were an abomination to Uncle Froebel.

An opportunity to put them into practice was close at hand, for the 29th of November was Barop's birthday, which was celebrated by a little dance after the play.

Those who took part in the performance were excused from study for several days before, for with the sapper's help we built the stage, and even painted the scenes. The piece was rehearsed till it was absolutely faultless.

I took an active part in all these matters during my entire residence at the institute, and we three Ebers brothers had the reputation of being among the best actors, though Martin far surpassed us. We had invented another variety of theatrical performances which we often enjoyed on winter evenings after supper, unless one of the teachers read aloud to us, or we boys performed the classic dramas. While I was one of the younger pupils, we used the large and complete puppet-show which belonged to the institute; but afterwards we preferred to act ourselves, and arranged the performance according to a plan of our own.

One of us who had seen a play during the vacation at home told the others the plot. The whole was divided into scenes, and each character was assigned to some representative who was left to personate it according to his own conception, choosing the words and gestures which he deemed most appropriate.

I enjoyed nothing more than these performances; and my mother, who witnessed several of them during one of her visits, afterwards said that it was surprising how well we had managed the affair and acted our parts.

For a long time I was the moving spirit in this play, and we had no lack of talented mimes, personators of sentimental heroes, and droll comedians.

The women's parts, of course, were also taken by boys. Ludo made a wonderfully pretty girl. I was sometimes one thing, sometimes another, but almost always stage manager.

These merry improvisations were certainly well fitted to strengthen the creative power and activity of our intellects. There was no lack of admirable stage properties, for the large wardrobe of the institute was at our disposal whenever we wanted to act, which was at least once a week during the whole winter, except in the Advent season, when everything was obliged to yield to the demand of the approaching Christmas festival. Then we were all busy in making presents for our relatives. The younger ones manufactured various cardboard trifles; the older pupils, as embryo cabinet-makers, all sorts of pretty and useful things, especially boxes.

Unluckily, I did not excel as a cabinet-maker, though I managed to finish tolerable boxes; but my mother had two made by the more skilful hands of Ludo, which were provided with locks and hinges, so neatly finished, veneered, and polished that many a trained cabinet-maker's apprentice could have done no better. It was one of Froebel's principles—as I have already mentioned—to follow the "German taste for manual labor," and have us work with spades and pickaxes (in our plots of ground), and with squares, chisels, and saws (in the pasteboard and carving lessons).

A clever elderly man, the sapper, or Sabuim, already mentioned—I think I never heard his real name—instructed us in the trades of the book binder and cabinet-maker. He was said to have served under Napoleon as a sapper, and afterwards settled in our neighbourhood, and found occupation in Keilhau. He was skilful in all kinds of manual labour, and an excellent teacher. The nearer Christmas came the busier were the workshops; and while usually there was no noise, they now resounded with Christmas songs, among which:

"Up, up, my lads! why do ye sleep so long?

The night has passed, and day begins to dawn";

or our Berlin one:

"Something will happen to-morrow, my children,"

were most frequently heard.

Christmas thoughts filled our hearts and minds. Christmas at home had been so delightful that the first year I felt troubled by the idea that the festival must be celebrated away from my mother and without her. But after we had shared the Keilhau holiday, and what preceded and followed it, we could not decide which was the most enjoyable.

Once our mother was present, though the cause of her coming was not exactly a joyous one. About a week before the Christmas of my third year at Keilhau I went to the hayloft at dusk, and while scuffling with a companion the hay slipped with us and we both fell to the barn-floor. My school-mate sustained an internal injury, while I escaped with the fracture of two bones, fortunately only of the left arm. The severe suffering which has darkened so large a portion of my life has been attributed to this fracture, but the idea is probably incorrect; otherwise the consequences would have appeared earlier.

At first the arm was very painful; yet the thought of having lost the Christmas pleasures was almost worse. But the experience that the days from which we expect least often afford us most happiness was again verified. Barop had thought it his duty to inform my mother of this serious accident, and two or three days later she arrived. Though I could not play out of doors with the others, there was enough to enjoy in the house with her and some of my comrades.

Every incident of that Christmas has remained in my memory, and, though Fate should grant me many more years of life, I would never forget them. First came the suspense and excitement when the wagon from Rudolstadt filled with boxes drove into the court-yard, and then the watching for those which might be meant for us.

On Christmas eve, when at home the bell summoned us to the Christmas-tree the delight of anticipation reached its climax, and expressed itself in song, in gayer talk, and now and then some harmless scuffle.

Then we went to bed, with the firm resolve of waking early; but the sleep of youth is sounder than any resolution, and suddenly unwonted sounds roused us, perhaps from the dreams of the manger at Bethlehem and the radiant Christmas-tree.

Was it the voice of the angels which appeared to the shepherds? The melody was a Christmas choral played by the Rudolstadt band, which had been summoned to waken us thus pleasantly.

Never did we leave our beds more quickly than in the darkness of that early morning, illuminated as usual only by a tallow dip. Rarely was the process of washing more speedily accomplished—in winter we were often obliged to break a crust of ice which had formed over the water; but this time haste was useless, for no one was admitted into the great hall before the signal was given. At last it sounded, and when we had pressed through the wide-open doors, what splendours greeted our enraptured eyes and ears!

The whole room was most elaborately decorated with garlands of pine. Wherever the light entered the windows we saw transparencies representing biblical Christmas scenes. Christmas-trees—splendid firs of stately height and size, which two days before were the ornaments of the forest-glittered in the light of the candles, which was reflected from the ruddy cheeks of the apples and the gilded and silvered nuts. Meanwhile the air, "O night so calm, so holy!" floated from the instruments of the musicians.

Scarcely had we taken our places when a chorus of many voices singing the angel's greeting, "Glory to God in the highest, peace on earth," recalled to our happy hearts the sacredness of the morning. Violins and horns blended with the voices; then, before even the most excited could feel the least emotion of impatience, the music ceased. Barop stepped forward, and in the deep, earnest tones peculiar to him exclaimed, "Now see what pleasures the love of your friends has prepared for you!"

The devout, ennobling feelings which had inspired every heart were scattered to the four winds; we dispersed like a flock of doves threatened by a hawk, and the search for the places marked by a label began.

One had already seen his name; a near-sighted fellow went searching from table to table; and here and there one boy called to another to point out what his sharp eyes had detected. On every table stood a Stolle, the Saxon Christmas bread called in Keilhau Schuttchen, and a large plate of nuts and cakes, the gift of the institute. Beside these, either on the tables or the floor, were the boxes from home. They were already opened, but the unpacking was left to us—a wise thing; for what pleasure it afforded us to take out the various gifts, unwrap them, admire, examine, and show them to others!

Those were happy days, for we saw only joyous faces, and our own hearts had room for no other feelings than the heaven-born sisters Love, Joy, and Gratitude.

We entered with fresh zeal upon the season of work which followed. It was the hardest of the twelve months, for it carried us to Easter, the close of the school year, and was interrupted only by the carnival with its merry masquerade.

All sorts of examinations closed the term of instruction. On Palm Sunday the confirmation services took place, which were attended by the parents of many of the pupils, and in which the whole institute shared.

Then came the vacation. It lasted three weeks, and was the only time we were allowed to return home. And what varied pleasures awaited us there! Martha, whom we left a young lady of seventeen, remained unaltered in her charming, gentle grace, but Paula changed every year. One Easter we found the plump school-girl transformed into a slender young lady. The next vacation she had been confirmed, wore long dresses, had lost every trace of boyishness, even rarely showed any touch of her former drollery.

She did not care to go to the theatre, of which Martha was very fond, unless serious dramas were performed. We, on the contrary, liked farces. I still remember a political quip which was frequently repeated at the Konigstadt Theatre, and whose point was a jeer at the aspirations of the revolution: "Property is theft, or a Dream of a Red Republican."

We were in the midst of the reaction and those who had fought at the barricades on the 18th of March applauded when the couplet was sung, of which I remember these lines:

"Ah! what bliss is the aspiration

To dangle from a lamp-post

As a martyr for the nation!"

During these vacations politics was naturally a matter of utter indifference to us, and toward their close we usually paid a visit to my grandmother and aunt in Dresden.

So the years passed till Easter (1852) came, and with it our confirmation and my separation from Ludo, who was to follow a different career. We had double instruction in confirmation, first with the village boys from the pastor of Eichfeld, and afterwards from Middendorf at the institute.

Unfortunately, I have entirely forgotten what the Eichfeld clergyman taught us, but Middendorf's lessons made all the deeper impression.

He led us through life to God and the Saviour, and thence back again to life.

How often, after one of these lessons, silence reigned, and teachers and pupils rose from their seats with tearful eyes!

Afterwards I learned from a book which had been kept that what he gave us had been drawn chiefly from the rich experiences of his own life and the Gospels, supplemented by the writings of his favourite teacher, Schleiermacher. By contemplation, the consideration of the universe with the soul rather than with the mind, we should enter into close relations with God and become conscious of our dependence upon him, and this consciousness Middendorf with his teacher Schleiermacher called "religion."

But the old Lutzow Jager, who in the year 1813 had taken up arms at the Berlin University, had also sat at the feet of Fichte, and therefore crowned his system by declaring, like the latter, that religion was not feeling but perception. Whoever attained this, arrived at a clear understanding of his own ego (Middendorf's mental understanding of life), perfect harmony with himself and the true sanctification of his soul. This man who, according to our Middendorf, is the really religious human being, will be in harmony with God and Nature, and find an answer to the highest of all questions.

Froebel's declaration that he had found "the unity of life," which had brought Middendorf to Keilhau, probably referred to Fichte. The phrase had doubtless frequently been used by them in conversations about this philosopher, and neither needed an explanation, since Fichte's opinions were familiar to both.

We candidates for confirmation at that time knew the Berlin philosopher only by name, and sentences like "unity with one's self," "to grasp and fulfil," "inward purity of life," etc., which every one who was taught by Middendorf must remember, at first seemed perplexing; but our teacher, who considered it of the utmost importance to be understood, and whose purpose was not to give us mere words, but to enrich our souls with possessions that would last all our lives, did not cease his explanations until even the least gifted understood their real meaning.

This natural, childlike old man never lectured; he was only a pedagogue in the sense of the ancients—that is, a guide of boys. Though precepts tinctured by philosophy mingled with his teachings, they only served as points of departure for statements which came to him from the soul and found their way to it.

He possessed a comprehensive knowledge of the religions of all nations, and described each with equal love and an endeavour to show us all their merits. I remember how warmly he praised Confucius's command not to love our fellow-men but to respect them, and how sensible and beautiful it seemed to me, too, in those days. He lingered longest on Buddhism; and it surprises me now to discover how well, with the aids then at his command, he understood the touching charity of Buddha and the deep wisdom and grandeur of his doctrine.

But he showed us the other religions mainly to place Christianity and its renewing and redeeming power in a brighter light. The former served, as it were, for a foil to the picture of our Saviour's religion and character, which he desired to imprint upon the soul. Whether he succeeded in bringing us into complete "unity" with the personality of Christ, to which he stood in such close relations, is doubtful, but he certainly taught us to understand and love him; and this love, though I have also listened to the views of those who attribute the creation and life of the world to mechanical causes, and believe the Deity to be a product of the human intellect, has never grown cold up to the present day.

The code of ethics which Middendorf taught was very simple. His motto, as I have said, was, "True, pure, and upright in life." He might have added, "and with a heart full of love"; for this was what distinguished him from so many, what made him a Christian in the most beautiful sense of the word, and he neglected nothing to render our young hearts an abiding-place for this love.

Of course, our mother came to attend our confirmation, which first took place with the peasant boys—who all wore sprigs of lavender in their button-holes—in the village church at Eichfeld, and then, with Middendorf officiating, in the hall of the institute at Keilhau.

Few boys ever approached the communion-table for the first time in a more devout mood, or with hearts more open to all good things, than did we two brothers that day on our mother's right and left hand.

No matter how much I may have erred, Middendorf's teachings and counsels have not been wholly lost in any stage of my career.

After the confirmation I went away with my mother and Ludo for the vacation, and three weeks later I returned to the institute without my brother.

I missed him everywhere. His greater discretion had kept me from many a folly, and my need of loving some one found satisfaction in him. Besides, his mere presence was a perpetual reminder of my mother.

Keilhau was no longer what it had been. New scenes always seem desirable to young people, and for the first time I longed to go away, though I knew nothing of my destination except that it would be a gymnasium.

Yet I loved the institute and its teachers, though I did not realize until later how great was my debt of gratitude. Here, and by them, the foundation of my whole future life was laid, and if I sometimes felt it reel under my feet, the Froebel method was not in fault.

The institute could not dismiss us as finished men; the desired "unity with life" can be attained only upon its stage—the world—in the motley throng of fellow-men, but minds and bodies were carefully trained according to their individual peculiarities, and I might consider myself capable of receiving higher lessons. True, my character was not yet steeled sufficiently to resist every temptation, but I no longer need fear the danger of crossing the barrier which Froebel set for men "worthy" in his sense.

My acquirements were deficient in many respects what the French term "justesse d'esprit" had to a certain degree become mine, as in the case of every Keilhau boy, through our system of education.

Though I could not boast of "being one with Nature," we had formed a friendly alliance, and I learned by my own experience the truth of Goethe's words, that it was the only book which offers valuable contents on every page.

I was not yet familiar with life, but I had learned to look about with open eyes.

I had not become a master in any handicraft, but I had learned with paste-pot and knife, saw, plane, and chisel—nay, even axe and handspike—what manual labour meant and how to use my hands.

I had by no means attained to union with God, but I had acquired the ability and desire to recognize his government in Nature as well as in life; for Middendorf had understood how to lead us into a genuine filial relation with him and awaken in our young hearts love for him who kindles in the hearts of men the pure flame of love for their neighbours.

The Greek words which Langethal wrote in my album, and which mean "Be truthful in love," were beginning to be as natural to me as abhorrence of cowardice and falsehood had long been.

Love for our native land was imprinted indelibly on my soul, and lives there joyously, ready to sacrifice for the freedom and greatness of Germany even what I hold dearest.

CHAPTER XVII.
THE GYMNASIUM AND THE FIRST PERIOD OF UNIVERSITY LIFE.

It was hard for me to leave Keilhau, but our trip to Rudolstadt, to which my dearest companions accompanied me, was merry enough. With Barop's permission we had a banquet in the peasant tavern there, whose cost was defrayed by the kreutzers which had been paid as fines for offences against table rules. At one of these tables where we larger boys sat, only French was spoken; at another only the purest German; and we had ourselves made the rule that whoever used a word of his native tongue at one, or a foreign one at the other, should be fined a kreutzer.

How merry were these banquets, at which usually several teachers were welcome guests!

One of the greatest advantages of Keilhau was that our whole lives, and even our pleasures, were pure enough not to shun a teacher's eyes. And yet we were true, genuine boys, whose overplus of strength found vent not only in play, but all sorts of foolish tricks.

A smile still hovers around my lips when I think of the frozen snow-man on whose head we put a black cap and then placed in one of the younger teacher's rooms to personate a ghost, and the difficulty we had in transporting the monster, or when I remember our pranks in the dormitory.

I believe I am mentioning these cheerful things here to give myself a brief respite, for the portion of my life which followed is the one I least desire to describe.

Rousseau says that man's education is completed by art, Nature, and circumstances. The first two factors had had their effect upon me, and I was now to learn for the first time to reckon independently with the last; hitherto they had been watched and influenced in my favour by others. This had been done not only by masters of the art of pedagogy, but by their no less powerful co-educators, my companions, among whom there was not a single corrupt, ill-disposed boy. I was now to learn what circumstances I should find in my new relations, and in what way they would prove teachers to me.

I was to be placed at school in Kottbus, at that time still a little manufacturing town in the Mark. My mother did not venture to keep me in Berlin during the critical years now approaching. Kottbus was not far away, and knowing that I was backward in the science that Dr. Boltze, the mathematician, taught, she gave him the preference over the heads of the other boarding-schools in the Mark.

I was not reluctant to undertake the hard work, yet I felt like a colt which is led from the pastures to the stable.

A visit to my grandmother in Dresden, and many pleasures which I was permitted to share with my brothers and sisters, seemed to me like the respite before execution.

My mother accompanied me to my new school, and I can not describe the gloomy impression made by the little manufacturing town on the flat plains of the Mark, which at that time certainly possessed nothing that could charm a boy born in Berlin and educated in a beautiful mountain valley.

In front of Dr. Boltze's house we found the man to whose care I was to be entrusted. At that time he was probably scarcely forty years old, short in stature and very erect, with a shrewd face whose features indicated an iron sternness of character, an impression heightened by the thick, bushy brows which met above his nose.

He himself said that people in Pomerania believed that men with such eyebrows stood in close relations to Satan. Once, while on his way in a boat from Greifswald to the island of Rugen, the superstitious sailors were on the point of throwing him overboard because they attributed their peril to him as the child of the devil, yet, he added—and he was a thoroughly truthful man—the power which these strange eyebrows gave him over others, and especially over men of humble station, induced them to release him.

But after we had learned what a jovial, indulgent comrade was hidden behind the iron tyrant who gazed so threateningly at us from the black eyes beneath the bushy brows, our timidity vanished, and at last we found it easy enough to induce him to change a resolute "No" into a yielding "Yes."

His wife, on the contrary, was precisely his opposite, for she wielded the sceptre in the household with absolute sway, though so fragile a creature that it seemed as if a breath would blow her away. No one could have been a more energetic housekeeper. She was as active an assistant to her husband with her pen as with her tongue. Most of my reports are in her writing. Besides this, one pretty, healthy child after another was born, and she allowed herself but a brief time for convalescence. I was the godfather of one of these babies, an honour shared by my school-mate, Von Lobenstein. The baptismal ceremony was performed in the Boltze house. The father and we were each to write a name on a slip of paper and lay it beside the font. We had selected the oddest ones we could think of, and when the pastor picked up the slips he read Gerhard and Habakkuk. Thanks to the care and wisdom of his excellent mother, the boy throve admirably in spite of his cognomen, and I heard to my great pleasure that he has become an able man.

This boyish prank is characteristic of our relations. If we did not go too far, Frau Boltze always took our part, and understood how to smooth her husband's frowning brow quickly enough. Besides, it was a real pleasure to be on good terms with her, for, as the daughter of a prominent official, she had had an excellent education, and her quick wit did honour to her native city, Berlin.

Had Dr. Boltze performed his office of tutor with more energy, it would have been better for us; but in other respects I can say of him nothing but good.

The inventions he made in mechanics, I have been told by experts, were very important for the times and deserved greater success. Among them was a coach moved by electricity.

My mother and I were cordially welcomed by this couple, on conversing with whom my first feeling of constraint vanished.

The examination next morning almost placed me higher than I expected, for the head-master who heard me translate at first thought me prepared for the first class; but Pro-Rector Braune, who examined me in Latin grammar, said that I was fitted only for the second.

When I left the examination hall I was introduced by Dr. Boltze to one of my future school-fellows in the person of an elegant young gentleman who had just alighted from a carriage and was patting the necks of the horses which he had driven himself.

I had supposed him to be a lieutenant in civilian's dress, for his dark mustache, small whiskers, and the military cut of his hair, which already began to be somewhat thin, made me add a lustrum to his twenty-one years.

After my new tutor had left us this strange school-fellow entered into conversation with me very graciously, and after telling me many things about the school and its management which seemed incredible, he passed on to the pupils, among whom were some "nice fellows," and mentioned a number of names, principally of noble families whose bearers had come here to obtain the graduation certificate, the key without which so many doors are closed in Prussia.

Then he proceeded to describe marvels which I was afterwards to witness, but which at that time I did not know whether I ought to consider delightful or quite the contrary.

Of course, I kept my doubts to myself and joined in when he laughed; but my heart was heavy. Could I avoid these companions? Yet I had come to be industrious, prepare quickly for the university, and give my mother pleasure.

Poor woman! She had made such careful inquiries before sending me here; and what a dangerous soil for a precocious boy just entering the years of youth was this manufacturing town and an institution so badly managed as the Kottbus School! I had come hither full of beautiful ideals and animated by the best intentions; but the very first day made me suspect how many obstacles I should encounter; though I did not yet imagine the perils which lay in my companion's words. All the young gentlemen who had been drawn hither by the examination were sons of good families, but the part which these pupils, and I with them, played in society, at balls, and in all the amusements of the cultivated circle in the town was so prominent, the views of life and habits which they brought with them so completely contradicted the idea which every sensible person has of a grammar-school boy, that their presence could not fail to injure the school.

Of course, all this could not remain permanently concealed from the higher authorities. The old head-master was suddenly retired, and one of the best educators summoned in his place man who quickly succeeded in making the decaying Kottbus School one of the most excellent in all Prussia. I had the misfortune of being for more than two years a pupil under the government of the first head-master, and the good luck of spending nearly the same length of time under the charge of his successor.

My mother was satisfied with the result of the examination, and the next afternoon she drove with me to our relatives at Komptendorf. Frau von Berndt, the youngest daughter of our beloved kinsman, Moritz von Oppenfeld, united to the elegance of a woman reared in a large city the cordiality of the mistress of a country home. Her husband won the entire confidence of every one who met the gaze of his honest blue eyes. He had given up the legal profession to take charge of his somewhat impoverished paternal estate, and soon transformed it into one of the most productive in the whole neighbourhood.

He was pleased that I, a city boy, knew so much about field and forest, so at my very first visit he invited me to repeat it often.

The next morning I took leave of my mother, and my school life began. In many points I was in advance of the other pupils in the second class, in others behind them; but this troubled me very little—school seemed a necessary evil. My real life commenced after its close, and here also my natural cheerfulness ruled my whole nature. The town offered me few attractions, but the country was full of pleasures. Unfortunately, I could not go to Komptendorf as often as I wished, for it was a two hours' walk, and horses and carriages were not always at my disposal. Yet many a Saturday found me there, enjoying the delight of chatting with my kind hostess about home news and other pleasant things, or reading aloud to her.

Even in the second year of my stay at Kottbus I went to every dance given on the estates in the neighbourhood and visited many a delightful home in the town. Then there were long walks—sometimes with Dr. Boltze and my school-mates, sometimes with friends, and often alone.

We frequently took a Sunday walk, which often began on Saturday afternoon, usually with merry companions and in the society of our stern master, who, gayer than the youngest of us, needed our care rather than we his. In this way I visited the beautiful Muskau, and still more frequently the lovely woodlands of the Spree, a richly watered region intersected by numerous arms of the river and countless canals, resting as quietly under dense masses of foliage as a child asleep at noontide beneath the shadow of a tree.

The alders and willows, lindens and oaks, which grow along the banks, are superb; flocks of birds fly twittering and calling from one bush and branch to another; but all human intercourse is carried on, as in Venice, by boats which glide noiselessly to and fro.

Whoever desires a faithful and minute picture of this singular region, which reminded me of many scenes in Holland and many of Hobbema's paintings, should read The Goddess of Noon. It contains a number of descriptions whose truth and vividness are matchless.

Every trip into the woodlands of the Spree offered an abundance of beautiful and pleasurable experiences, but I remember with still greater enjoyment my leafy nooks on the river-bank.

CHAPTER XVIII.
THE TIME OF EFFERVESCENCE, AND MY SCHOOL MATES.

Although the events of my school-days at Kottbus long since blended together in my memory, my life there is divided into two sharply defined portions. The latter commences with Professor Tzschirner's appointment and the reform in the school.

From the first day of the latter's government I can recall what was taught us in the class and how it influenced me, while I have entirely forgotten what occurred during the interim. This seems strange; for, while Langethal's, Middendorf's, and Barop's instruction, which I received when so much younger, remains vividly impressed on my memory, and it is the same with Tzschirner's lessons, the knowledge I acquired between my fifteenth and seventeenth year is effaced as completely as though I had passed a sponge over the slate of my memory. A chasm yawns between these periods of instruction, and I cannot ascribe this circumstance entirely to the amusements which withdrew my thoughts from study; for they continued under Tzschirner's rule, though with some restrictions. I wish I could believe that everything which befel me then had remained entirely without influence on my inner life.

A demon—I can find no other name—urged me to all sorts of follies, many of which I still remember with pleasure, and, thank Heaven, not a single one which a strict teacher—supposing that he had not forgotten how to put himself into the place of a youth—would seriously censure. The effervescing spirits which did not find vent in such pranks obtained expression in a different form.

I had begun to write, and every strong emotion was uttered in verses, which I showed to the companions from whom I could expect sympathy. My school-mates were very unlike. Among the young gentlemen who paid a high price to attend the school not a single one had been really industrious and accomplished anything. But neither did any one of the few lads whose fathers were peasants, or who belonged to the lower ranks, stand at the head of his class. They were very diligent, but success rarely corresponded with the amount of labour employed. The well-educated but by no means wealthy middle class supplied the school with its best material.

The evolution of the human soul is a strange thing. The period during which, in my overflowing mirth, I played all sorts of wild pranks, and at school worked earnestly for one teacher only, often found me toiling late at night for hours with burning head over a profound creation—I called it The Poem of the World—in which I tried to represent the origin of cosmic and human life.

Many other verses, from a sonnet to the beautiful ears of a pretty cousin to the commencement of the tragedy of Panthea and Abradatus, were written at that time; but I owe The Poem of the World special gratitude, for it kept me from many a folly, and often held me for weeks at my desk during the evening hours which many of my comrades spent in the tavern. Besides, it attracted the new head-master's attention to my poetical tastes, for a number of verses had been left by mistake in an exercise-book. He read them, and asked to see the rest. But I could not fulfil the wish, for they contained many things which could not fail to offend him; so I gave him only a few of the tamest passages, and can still see him smile in his peculiar way as he read them in my presence. He said something about "decided talent," and when preparations for the celebration of the birthday of King Frederick William IV were made he gave me the task of composing an original poem. I gladly accepted it. Writing was a great pleasure, and though my productions at school were far too irregular for me to call them good, I was certainly the best declaimer.

THE NEW HEAD OF THE SCHOOL.

Before passing on to other subjects, I must devote a few words to the remodelling of the school and its new head.

At the end of my first term in the first class we learned that we were to have a new teacher, and one who would rule with a rod of iron. Terrible stories of his Draconian severity were in circulation, and his first address gave us reason to fear the worst, for the tall man of forty in the professor's chair was very imposing in his appearance. His smoothly shaven upper lip and brown whiskers, his erect bearing and energetic manner, reminded one of an English parliamentary leader, but his words sounded almost menacing. He said that an entirely new house must be erected. We and the teachers must help him. To the obedient he would be a good friend; but to the refractory, no matter what might be their position, he would——What followed made many of us nudge one another, and the young men who attended the school merely for the sake of the examination left it in a body. Many a teacher even changed colour.

This reorganizer, Professor Tzschirner, had formerly been principal of the Magdalen Gymnasium at Breslau. In energy and authoritative manner he resembled Barop, but he was also an eminent scholar and a thorough man of the world. The authorities in Berlin made an excellent choice, and we members of the first class soon perceived that he not only meant kindly by us, but that we had obtained in him a teacher far superior to any we had possessed before. He required a great deal, but he was a good friend to every one who did his duty. His kindly intention and inspiring influence made themselves felt in our lives; for he invited to his house the members of the first class whom he desired to influence, and his charming, highly educated wife helped him entertain us, so that we preferred an evening there to almost any other amusements. Study began to charm us, and I can only repeat that he seemed to recall Langethal's method and awaken many things which the latter had given me, and which, as it were, had fallen asleep during the interval. He again aroused in my soul the love for the ancients, and his interpretations of Horace or Sophocles were of great service to me in after-years.

Nor did he by any means forget grammar, but in explaining the classics he always laid most stress upon the contents, and every lesson of his was a clever archaeological, aesthetic, and historical lecture. I listened to none more instructive at the university. Philological and linguistic details which were not suited for the senior pupils who were being fitted for other callings than those of the philologist were omitted. But he insisted upon grammatical correctness, and never lost sight of his maxim, "The school should teach its pupils to do thoroughly whatever they do at all."

He urged us especially to think for ourselves, and to express our ideas clearly and attractively, not only in writing but verbally.

It seemed as though a spring breeze had melted the snow from the land, such bourgeoning and blossoming appeared throughout the school.

Creative work was done by fits and starts. If the demon seized upon me, I raved about for a time as before, but I did my duty for the principal. I not only honoured but loved him, and censure from his lips would have been unbearable.

The poem which I was to read on the king's birthday has been preserved, and as I glanced over it recently I could not help smiling.

It was to describe the life of Henry the Fowler, and refer to the reigning king, Frederick William IV. The praise of my hero had come from my heart, so the poem found favour, and in circles so wide that the most prominent man in the neighbourhood, Prince Puckler-Muskau, sent for my verses.

I was perfectly aware that they did not represent my best work, but what father does not find something to admire in his child? So I copied them neatly, and gave them to Billy, the dwarf, the prince's factotum. A short time after, while I was walking with some friends in Branitz Park, the prince summoned me, and greeted me with the exclamation, "You are a poet!"

These four words haunted me a long while; nay, at times they even echo in my memory now. I had heard a hundred anecdotes of this prince, which could not fail to charm a youth of my disposition. When a young officer of the Garde-du-Corps in Dresden, after having been intentionally omitted from the invitations to a court-ball, he hired all the public conveyances in the city, thus compelling most of the gentlemen and ladies who were invited either to wade through the snow or forego the dance.

When the war of 1813 began he entered the service of "the liberators," as the Russians were then called, and at the head of his regiment challenged the colonel of a French one to a duel, and seriously wounded him.

It was apparently natural to Prince Puckler to live according to his own pleasure, undisturbed by the opinions of his fellow-men, and this pleasure urged him to pursue a different course in almost every phase of life. I said "apparently," because, although he scorned the censure of the people, he never lost sight of it. From a child his intense vanity was almost a passion, and unfortunately this constant looking about him, the necessity of being seen, prevented him from properly developing an intellect capable of far higher things; yet there was nothing petty in his character.

His highest merit, however, was the energy with which he understood how to maintain his independence in the most difficult circumstances in which life placed him. To one department of activity, especially, that of gardening, he devoted his whole powers. His parks can vie with the finest pleasure-grounds of all countries.

At the time I first met him he was sixty-nine years old, but looked much younger, except when he sometimes appeared with his hair powdered until it was snow-white. His figure was tall and finely proportioned, and though a sarcastic smile sometimes hovered around his lips, the expression of his face was very kindly. His eyes, which I remember as blue, were somewhat peculiar. When he wished to please, they sparkled with a warm—I might almost say tender-light, which must have made many a young heart throb faster. Yet I think he loved himself too much to give his whole affection to any one.

A great man has always seemed to me the greatest of created things, and though Prince Puckler can scarcely be numbered among the great men of mankind, he was undoubtedly the greatest among those who surrounded him at Branitz. In me, the youth of nineteen, he awakened admiration, interest, and curiosity, and his "You are a poet" sometimes strengthened my courage, sometimes disheartened me. My boyish ambitions in those days had but one purpose, and that was the vocation of a poet.

I was still ignorant that the Muse kisses only those who have won her love by the greatest sufferings. Life as yet seemed a festal hall, and as the bird flies from bough to bough wherever a red berry tempts him, my heart was attracted by every pair of bright eyes which glanced kindly at me. When I entered upon my last term, my Leporello list was long enough, and contained pictures from many different classes. But my hour, too, seemed on the point of striking, for when I went home in my last Christmas vacation I thought myself really in love with the charming daughter of the pleasant widow of a landed proprietor. Nay, though only nineteen, I even considered whether I should not unite her destiny with mine, and formally ask her hand. My father had offered himself to my mother at the same age.

In Kottbus I was treated with the respect due to a man, but at home I was still "the boy," and the youngest of us three "little ones." Ludo, as a lieutenant, had a position in society, while I was yet a schoolboy. Amid these surroundings I realized how hasty and premature my intention had been.

Only four of us came to keep Christmas at home, for Martha now lived in Dresden as the wife of Lieutenant Baron Curt von Brandenstein, the nephew of our Aunt Sophie's husband. Her wedding ceremony in the cathedral was, of course, performed by the court-chaplain Strauss.

My grandmother had died, but my Aunt Sophie still lived in Dresden, and spent her summers in Blasewitz. Her hospitable house always afforded an atmosphere very stimulating to intellectual life, so I spent more time there than in my mother's more quiet residence at Pillnitz.

I had usually passed part of the long—or, as it was called, the "dog-day"—vacation in or near Dresden, but I also took pleasant pedestrian tours in Bohemia, and after my promotion to the senior class, through the Black Forest.

It was a delightful excursion! Yet I can never recall it without a tinge of sadness, for my two companions, a talented young artist named Rothermund, and a law student called Forster, both died young. We had met in a railway carriage between Frankfort and Heidelberg and determined to take the tour together, and never did the Black Forest, with its mountains and valleys, dark forests and green meadows, clear streams and pleasant villages, seem to me more beautiful. But still fairer days were in store after parting from my friends.

I went to Rippoldsau, where a beloved niece of my mother with her charming daughter Betsy expected me. Here in the excellent Gohring hotel I found a delightful party, which only lacked young gentlemen. My arrival added a pair of feet which never tired of dancing, and every evening our elders were obliged to entreat and command in order to put an end to our sport. The mornings were occupied in walks through the superb forests around Rippoldsau, and the afternoons in bowling, playing graces, and running races. I speedily lost my susceptible heart to a charming young lady named Leontine, who permitted me to be her Knight, and I fancied myself very unjustly treated when, soon after our separation, I received her betrothal cards.

The Easter and Christmas vacations I usually spent in Berlin with my mother, where I was allowed to attend entertainments given by our friends, at which I met many distinguished persons, among others Alexander von Humboldt.

Of political life in the capital at that time there is nothing agreeable to be said. I was always reminded of the state of affairs immediately after my arrival; for during the first years of my school life at Kottbus no one was permitted to enter the city without a paper proving identity, which was demanded by constables at the exits of railway stations or in the yards of post-houses. Once, when I had nothing to show except my report, I was admitted, it is true, but a policeman was sent with me to my mother's house to ascertain that the boy of seventeen was really the person he assumed to be, and not a criminal dangerous to the state.

The beautiful aspirations of the Reichstag in Paulskirche were baffled, the constitution of the empire had become a noble historical monument which only a chosen few still remembered. The king, who had had the opportunity to place himself at the head of united Germany, had preferred to suppress the freedom of his native land rather than to promote its unity. Yet we need not lament his refusal. Blood shed together in mutual enthusiasm is a better cement than the decree of any Parliament.

The ruling powers at that time saw in the constitution only a cage whose bars prevented them from dealing a decisive blow, but whatever they could reach through the openings they tore and injured as far as lay in their power. The words "reactionary" and "liberal" had become catch terms which severed families and divided friends.

At Komptendorf, and almost everywhere in the country, there was scarcely any one except Conservatives. Herr von Berndt had driven into the city to the election. Pastor Albin, the clergyman of his village, voted for the Liberal candidate. When the pastor asked the former, who was just getting into his carriage, to take him home, the usually courteous, obliging gentleman, who was driving, exclaimed, "If you don't vote with me you don't ride with me," and, touching the spirited bays, dashed off, leaving the pastor behind.

Dr. Boltze was a "Liberal," and had to endure many a rebuff because his views were known to the ministry. Our religious instruction might serve as a mirror of the opinions which were pleasing to the minister. It had made the man who imparted it superintendent when comparatively young. The term "mob marriage" for "civil marriage" originated with him, and it ought certainly to be inscribed in the Golden Book above.

He was a fiery zealot, who sought to induce us to share his wrath and scorn when he condemned Bauer, David Strauss, and Lessing.

When discussing the facts of ecclesiastical history, he understood how to rouse us to the utmost, for he was a talented man and a clever speaker, but no word of appeal to the heart, no exhortation to love and peace, ever crossed his lips.

The vacations were the only time which I spent with my mother. I ceased to think of her in everything I did, as was the case in Keilhau. But after I had been with her for a while, the charm of her personality again mastered my soul, her love rekindled mine, and I longed to open my whole heart to her and tell her everything which interested me. She was the only person to whom I read my Poem of the World, as far as it was completed. She listened with joyful astonishment, and praised several passages which she thought beautiful. Then she warned me not to devote too much time to such things at present, but kissed and petted me in a way too charming to describe. During the next few days her eyes rested on me with an expression I had always longed to see. I felt that she regarded me as a man, and she afterwards confessed how great her hopes were at that time, especially as Professor Tzschirner had encouraged her to cherish them.

CHAPTER XIX.
A ROMANCE WHICH REALLY HAPPENED.

After returning to Kottbus from the Christmas vacation I plunged headlong into work, and as I exerted all my powers I made rapid progress.

Thus January passed away, and I was so industrious that I often studied until long after midnight. I had not even gone to the theatre, though I had heard that the Von Hoxar Company was unusually good. The leading lady, especially, was described as a miracle of beauty and remarkably talented. This excited my curiosity, and when a school-mate who had made the stage manager's acquaintance told us that he would be glad to have us appear at the next performance of The Robbers, I of course promised to be present.

We went through our parts admirably, and no one in the crowded house suspected the identity of the chorus of robbers who sang with so much freshness and vivacity.

I was deeply interested in what was passing on the stage, and, concealed at the wings, I witnessed the greater part of the play.

Rarely has so charming an Amalie adorned the boards as the eighteen-year-old actress, who, an actor's child, had already been several years on the stage.

The consequence of this visit to the theatre was that, instead of studying historical dates, as I had intended, I took out Panthea and Abradatus, and on that night and every succeeding one, as soon as I had finished my work for the manager, I added new five-foot iambics to the tragedy, whose material I drew from Xenophon.

Whenever the company played I went to the theatre, where I saw the charming Clara in comedy parts, and found that all the praises I had heard of her fell short of the truth. Yet I did not seek her acquaintance. The examination was close at hand, and it scarcely entered my mind to approach the actress. But the Fates had undertaken to act as mediators and make me the hero of a romance which ended so speedily, and in a manner which, though disagreeable, was so far from tragical, that if I desired to weave the story of my own life into a novel I should be ashamed to use the extensive apparatus employed by Destiny.

Rather more than a week had passed since the last performance of The Robbers, when one day, late in the afternoon, the streets were filled with uproar. A fire had broken out, and as soon as Professor Braune's lesson was over I joined the human flood. The boiler in the Kubisch cloth factory had burst, a part of the huge building near it was in flames, and a large portion of the walls had fallen.

When, with several school-mates, I reached the scene of the disaster, the fire had already been mastered, but many hands were striving to remove the rubbish and save the workmen buried underneath. I eagerly lent my aid.

Meanwhile it had grown dark, and we were obliged to work by the light of lanterns. Several men, fortunately all living, had been brought out, and we thought that the task of rescue was completed, when the rumour spread that some girls employed in one of the lower rooms were still missing.

It was necessary to enter, but the smoke and dust which filled the air seemed to preclude this, and, besides, a high wall above the cleared space in the building threatened to fall. An architect who had directed with great skill the removal of the debris was standing close beside me and gave orders to tear down the wall, whose fall would cost more lives.

Just at that moment I distinctly heard an inexpressibly mournful cry of pain. A narrow shouldered, sickly-looking man, who spite of his very plain clothing, seemed to belong to the better classes, heard it too, and the word "Horrible!" in tones of the warmest sympathy escaped his lips. Then he bent over the black smoking space, and I did the same.

The cry was repeated still louder than before, my neighbour and I looked at each other, and I heard him whisper, "Shall we?"

In an instant I had flung off my coat, put my handkerchief over my mouth, and let myself down into the smoking pit, where I pressed forward through a stifling mixture of lime and particles of sand.

The groans and cries of the wounded guided me and my companion, who had instantly followed, and at last two female figures appeared amid the smoke and dust on which the lanterns, held above, cast flickering rays of light.

One was lying prostrate, the other, kneeling, leaned against the wall. We seized the first one, and staggered towards the spot where the lanterns glimmered, and loud shouts greeted us.

Our example had induced others to leap down too.

As soon as we were released from our burden we returned for the second victim. My companion now carried a lantern. The woman was no longer kneeling, but lay face downward several paces nearer to the narrow passage choked with stones and lime dust which separated her from us. She had fainted while trying to follow. I seized her feet, and we staggered on, but ere we could leave the passage which led into the larger room I heard a loud rattling and thundering above, and the next instant something struck my head and everything reeled around me. Yet I did not drop the blue yarn stockings, but tottered on with them into the large open space, where I fell on my knees.

Still I must have retained my consciousness, for loud shouts and cries reached my ears. Then came a moment with which few in life can compare—the one when I again inhaled draughts of the pure air of heaven.

I now felt that my hair was stained with blood, which had flowed from a wound in my head, but I had no time to think of it, for people crowded around me saying all sorts of pleasant things. The architect, Winzer, was most cordial of all. His words, "I approve of such foolhardiness, Herr Ebers," echoed in my ears long afterwards.

A beam had fallen on my head, but my thick hair had broken the force of the blow, and the wound in a few days began to heal.

My companion in peril was at my side, and as my blood-stained face looked as if my injuries were serious he invited me to his house, which was close by the scene of the accident. On the way we introduced ourselves to each other. His name was Hering, and he was the prompter at the theatre. When the doctor who had been sent to me had finished his task of sewing up the wound and left us, an elderly woman entered, whose rank in life was somewhat difficult to determine. She wore gay flowers in her bonnet, and a cloak made of silk and velvet, but her yellow face was scarcely that of a "lady." She came to get a part for her daughter; it was one of the prompter's duties to copy the parts for the various actors.

But who was this daughter?

Fraulein Clara, the fair Amalie of The Robbers, the lovely leading lady of the theatre.

My daughter has an autograph of Andersen containing the words, "Life is the fairest fairy tale."

Ay, our lives are often like fairy tales.

The Scheherezade "Fate" had found the bridge to lead the student to the actress, and the means employed were of no less magnitude than a conflagration, the rescue of a life, and a wound, as well as the somewhat improbable combined action of a student and a prompter. True, more simple methods would scarcely have brought the youth with the examination in his head and a pretty girl in his heart to seek the acquaintanceship of the fair actress.

Fate urged me swiftly on; for Clara's mother was an enthusiastic woman, who in her youth had herself been an ornament of the stage, and I can still hear her exclamation, "My dear young sir, every German girl ought to kiss that wound!"

I can see her indignantly forbid the prompter to tie his gay handkerchief over the injury and draw a clean one from her own velvet bag to bind my forehead. Boltze and my school-mates greeted me very warmly. Director Tzschirner said something very similar to Herr Winzer's remark.

And so matters would have remained, and in a few weeks, after passing the examination, I should have returned to my happy mother, had not a perverse Fate willed otherwise.

This time a bit of linen was the instrument used to lead me into the path allotted, for when the wound healed and the handkerchief which Clara's mother had tied round it came back from the wash, I was uncertain whether to return it in person or send it by a messenger with a few words of thanks. I determined on the latter course; but when, that same evening, I saw Clara looking so pretty as the youthful Richelieu, I cast aside my first resolve, and the next day at dusk went to call on the mother of the charming actress. I should scarcely have ventured to do so in broad daylight, for Herr Ebeling, our zealous religious instructor, lived directly opposite.

The danger, however, merely gave the venture an added zest and, ere I was aware of it I was standing in the large and pretty sitting-room occupied by the mother and daughter.

It was a disappointment not to meet the latter, yet I felt a certain sense of relief. Fate intended to let me escape the storm uninjured, for my heart had been by no means calm since I mounted the narrow stairs leading to the apartments of the fair actress. But just as I was taking leave the pavement echoed with the noise of hoofs and the rattle of wheels. Prince Puckler's coupe stopped in front of the house and the young girl descended the steps.

She entered the room laughing merrily, but when she saw me she became graver, and looked at her mother in surprise.

A brief explanation, the cry, "Oh, you are the man who was hurt!" and then the proof that the room did not owe its neat appearance to her, for her cloak flew one way, her hat another, and her gloves a third. After this disrobing she stood before me in the costume of the youthful Richelieu, so bewitchingly charming, so gay and bright, that I could not restrain my delight.

She had come from old Prince Puckler, who, as he never visited the theatre in the city, wished to see her in the costume whose beauty had been so much praised. The vigorous, gay old gentleman had charmed her, and she declared that she liked him far better than any of the young men. But as she knew little of his former life and works, I told her of his foolish pranks and chivalrous deeds.

It seemed as if her presence increased my powers of description, and when I at last took leave she exclaimed: "You'll come again, won't you? After one has finished one's part, it's the best time to talk."

Did I wait to be asked a second time? Oh, no! Even had I not been the "foolhardy Ebers," I should have accepted her invitation. The very next evening I was in the pleasant sitting-room, and whenever I could slip away after supper I went to the girl, whom I loved more and more ardently. Sometimes I repeated poems of my own, sometimes she recited and acted passages from her best parts, amid continual jesting and laughter. My visits seemed like so many delightful festivals, and Clara's mother took care that they were not so long as to weary her treasure. She often fell asleep while we were reading and talking, but usually she sent me away before midnight with "There's another day coming to-morrow." Long before my first visit to the young actress I had arranged a way of getting into the house at any time, and Dr. Boltze had no suspicion of my expeditions, since on my return I strove the more zealously to fulfil all my school duties.

This sounds scarcely credible, yet it is strictly true, for from a child up to the present time I have always succeeded, spite of interruptions of every kind, in devoting myself to the occupation in which I was engaged. Loud noises in an adjoining room, or even tolerably severe physical pain, will not prevent my working on as soon as the subject so masters me as to throw the external world and my own body into the background. Only when the suffering becomes very intense, the whole being must of necessity yield to it.

During the hours of the night which followed these evening visits I often succeeded in working earnestly for two or three hours in preparation for the examination. During my recitations, however, weariness asserted itself, and even more strongly the new feeling which had obtained complete mastery over me. Here I could not shake off the delightful memories of these evenings because I did not strive to battle with them.

I am not without talent for drawing, and even at that time it was an easy matter to reproduce anything which had caught my eye, not only distinctly, but sometimes attractively and with a certain degree of fidelity to nature. So my note-book was filled with figures which amazed me when I saw them afterwards, for my excited imagination had filled page after page with a perfect Witch's Sabbath of compositions, in which the oddest scrolls and throngs of genii blended with flowers, buds, and all sorts of emblems of love twined around initial letters or the picture of the person who had captured my heart at a time so inopportune.

I owe the suggestion of some verses which were written at that time to the memory of a dream. I was on the back of a swan, which bore me through the air, and on another swan flying at my side sat Clara. Our hands were clasped. It was delightful until I bent to kiss her; then the swan I rode melted into mist, and I plunged headlong down, falling, falling, until I woke.

I had this dream on the Friday before the beginning of the week in which the first examination was to take place; and it is worthy of mention, for it was fulfilled.

True, I needed no prophetic vision to inform me that this time of happiness was drawing to a close. I had long known that the company was to remove from Kottbus to Guben, but I hoped that the separation would be followed by a speedy meeting.

It was certainly fortunate that she was going, yet the parting was hard to bear; for the evening hours I had spent with her in innocent mirth and the interchange of all that was best in our hearts and minds were filled with exquisite enjoyment. The fact that our intercourse was in a certain sense forbidden fruit merely doubled its charm.

How cautiously I had glided along in the shadows of the houses, how anxiously I had watched the light in the minister's study opposite, when I went home!

True, he would have seen nothing wrong or even unseemly, save perhaps the kiss which Clara gave me the last time she lighted me down stairs, yet that would have been enough to shut me out of the examination. Ah! yes, it was fortunate that she was going.

March had come, the sun shone brightly, the air was as warm as in May, and I had carried the mother and daughter some violets which I had gathered myself. Suddenly I thought how delightful it would be to drive with Clara in an open carriage through the spring beauty of the country. The next day was Sunday. If I went with them and spent the night in Guben I could reach home in time the next day. I need only tell Dr. Boltze I was going to Komptendorf, and order the carriage, to transform the dear girl's departure into a holiday.

Again Fate interfered with the course of this story; for on my way to school that sunny Saturday morning I met Clara's mother, and at sight of her the wish merged into a resolve. I followed her into the shop she entered and explained my plan. She thought it would be delightful, and promised to wait for me at a certain place outside of the city.

The plan was carried out. I found them at the appointed spot, my darling as fresh as a rose. If love and joy had any substantial weight, the horses would have found it a hard matter to drag the vehicle swiftly on.

But at the first toll-house, while the toll-keeper was changing some money, I experienced the envy of the gods which hitherto I had known only in Schiller's ballad. A pedestrian passed—the teacher whom I had offended by playing all sorts of pranks during his French lesson. Not one of the others disliked me.

He spoke to me, but I pretended not to understand, hastily took the change from the toll-keeper, and, raising my hat, shouted, "Drive on!"

This highly virtuous gentleman scorned the young actress, and as, on account of my companions, he had not returned my greeting, Clara flashed into comical wrath, which stifled in its germ my thought of leaving the carriage and going on foot to Komptendorf, where Dr. Boltze believed me to be.

Clara rewarded my courageous persistence by special gaiety, and when we had reached Guben, taken supper with some other members of the company, and spent the evening in merriment, danger and all the ills which the future might bring were forgotten.

The next morning I breakfasted with Clara and her mother, and in bidding them good-bye added "Till we meet again," for the way to Berlin was through Guben, where the railroad began.

The carriage which had brought us there took me back to Kottbus. Several members of the company entered it and went part of the way, returning on foot. When they left me twilight was gathering, but the happiness I had just enjoyed shone radiantly around me, and I lived over for the second time all the delights I had experienced.

But the nearer I approached Kottbus the more frequently arose the fear that the French teacher might make our meeting the cause of an accusation. He had already complained of me for very trivial delinquencies and would hardly let this pass. And yet he might.

Was it a crime to drive with a young girl of stainless reputation under her mother's oversight? No. I had done nothing wrong, except to say that I was going to Komptendorf—and that offence concerned only Dr. Boltze, to whom I had made the false statement.

At last I fell asleep, until the wheels rattled on the pavement of the city streets. Was my dream concerning the swan to be fulfilled?

I entered the house early. Dr. Boltze was waiting for me, and his wife's troubled face betrayed what had happened even more plainly than her husband's frown.

The French teacher had instantly informed my tutor where and with whom he had met me, and urged him to ascertain whether I had really gone to Komptendorf. Then he went to Clara's former residence, questioned the landlady and her servant, and finally interrogated the livery-stable keeper.

The mass of evidence thus gathered proved that I had paid the actress numerous visits, and always at dusk. My dream seemed fulfilled, but after I had told Dr. Boltze and his wife the whole truth a quiet talk followed. The former did not give up the cause as lost, though he did not spare reproaches, while his wife's wrath was directed against the informer rather than the offence committed by her favourite.

After a restless night I went to Professor Tzschirner and told him everything, without palliation or concealment. He censured my frivolity and lack of consideration for my position in life, but every word, every feature of his expressive face showed that he grieved for what had happened, and would have gladly punished it leniently. In after years he told me so. Promising to make every effort to save me from exclusion from the examination in the conference which he was to call at the close of the afternoon session, he dismissed me—and he kept his word.

I know this, for I succeeded in hearing the discussion. The porter of the gymnasium was the father of the boy whom my friend Lebenstein and I kept to clean our boots, etc. He was a conscientious, incorruptible man, but the peculiar circumstances of the case led him to yield to my entreaties and admit me to a room next to the one where the conference was held. I am grateful to him still, for it is due to this kindness that I can think without resentment of those whose severity robbed me of six months of my life.

This conference taught me how warm a friend I possessed in Professor Tzschirner, and showed that Professor Braune was kindly disposed. I remember how my heart overflowed with gratitude when Professor Tzschirner sketched my character, extolled my rescue of life at the Kubisch factory, and eloquently urged them to remember their own youth and judge what had happened impartially. I should have belied my nature had I not availed myself of the chain of circumstances which brought me into association with the actress to make the acquaintance of so charming a creature.

To my joyful surprise Herr Ebeling agreed with him, and spoke so pleasantly of me and of Clara, concerning whom he had inquired, that I began to hope he was on my side.

Unfortunately, the end of his speech destroyed all the prospects held out in the beginning.

Space forbids further description of the discussion. The majority, spite of the passionate hostility of the informer, voted not to expel me, but to exclude me from the examination this time, and advise me to leave the school. If, however, I preferred to remain, I should be permitted to do so.

At the close of the session I was standing in the square in front of the school when Professor Tzschirner approached, and I asked his permission to leave school that very day. A smile of satisfaction flitted over his manly, intellectual face, and he granted my request at once.

So my Kottbus school-days ended, and, unfortunately, in a way unlike what I had hoped. When I said farewell to Professor Tzschirner and his wife I could not restrain my tears. His eyes, too, were dim, and he repeated to me what I had already heard him say in the conference, and wrote the same thing to my mother in a letter explaining my departure from the school. The report which he sent with it contains not a single word to indicate a compulsory withdrawal or the advice to leave it.

When I had stopped at Guben and said goodbye to Clara my dream was literally fulfilled. Our delightful intercourse had come to a sudden end. Fortunately, I was the only sufferer, for to my great joy I heard a few months after that she had made a successful debut at the Dresden court theatre.

I was, of course, less joyfully received in Berlin than usual, but the letters from Professor Tzschirner and Frau Boltze put what had occurred in the right light to my mother—nay, when she saw how I grieved over my separation from the young girl whose charms still filled my heart and mind, her displeasure was transformed into compassion. She also saw how difficult it was for me to meet the friends and guardian who had expected me to return as a graduate, and drew her darling, whom for the first time she called her "poor boy," still closer to her heart.

Then we consulted about the future, and it was decided that I should graduate from the gymnasium of beautiful Quedlinburg. Professor Schmidt's house was warmly recommended, and was chosen for my home.

I set out for my new abode full of the best resolutions. But at Magdeburg I saw in a show window a particularly tasteful bonnet trimmed with lilies of the valley and moss-rose buds. The sight brought Clara's face framed in it vividly be fore my eyes, and drew me into the shop. It was a Paris pattern-hat and very expensive, but I spent the larger part of my pocket-money in purchasing it and ordered it to be sent to the girl whose image still filled my whole soul. Hitherto I had given her nothing except a small locket and a great many flowers.

CHAPTER XX.
AT THE QUEDLINBURG GYMNASIUM

The atmosphere of Quedlinburg was far different from that of the Mark factory town of Kottbus. How fresh, how healthful, how stimulating to industry and out-door exercise it was!

Everything in the senior class was just as it should be.

In Kottbus the pupils addressed each other formally. There were at the utmost, I think, not more than half a dozen with whom I was on terms of intimacy. In Quedlinburg a beautiful relation of comradeship united all the members of the school. During study hours we were serious, but in the intervals we were merry enough.

Its head, Professor Richter, the learned editor of the fragments of Sappho, did not equal Tzschirner in keenness of intellect and bewitching powers of description, yet we gladly followed the worthy man's interpretations.

Many a leisure day and hour we spent in the beautiful Hartz Mountains. But, best of all, was my home in Quedlinburg, the house of my tutor, Professor Adalbert Schmidt, an admirable man of forty, who seemed extremely gentle and yielding, but when necessary could be very peremptory, and allowed those under his charge to make no trespass on his authority.

His wife was a model of amiable, almost timid womanliness. Her sister-in-law, the widow of a magistrate, Frau Pauline Schmidt, shared the care of the pupils and the beautiful, large garden; while her pretty, bright young sons and daughters increased the charm of the intercourse.

How pleasant were the evenings we spent in the family circle! We read, talked, played, and Frau Pauline Schmidt was a ready listener when ever I felt disposed to communicate to any one what I had written.

Among my school friends were some who listened to my writings and showed me their own essays. My favorite was Carl Hey, grandson of Wilhelm Hey, who understood child nature so well, and wrote the pretty verses accompanying the illustrations in the Speckter Fables, named for the artist, a book still popular with little German boys and girls. I was also warmly attached to the enthusiastic Hubotter, who, under the name of "Otter," afterwards became the ornament of many of the larger German theatres. Lindenbein, Brosin, the talented Gosrau, and the no less gifted Schwalbe, were also dear friends.

At first I had felt much older than my companions, and I really had seen more of life; but I soon perceived that they were splendid, lovable fellows. My wounded heart speedily healed, and the better my physical and mental condition became the more my demon stirred within me. It was no merit of mine if I was not dubbed "the foolhardy Ebers" here also. The summer in Quedlinburg was a delightful season of mingled work and pleasure. An Easter journey through the Hartz with some gay companions, which included an ascent of the Brocken—already once climbed from Keilhau—is among my most delightful memories.

Like the Thuringian Mountains, the Hartz are also wreathed with a garland of legends and historical memories. Some of its fairest blossoms are in the immediate vicinity of Quedlinburg. These and the delight in nature with which I here renewed my old bond tempted more than one of us to write, and very different poems, deeper and with more true feeling, than those produced in Kottbus. A poetic atmosphere from the Hercynian woods and the monuments of ancient days surrounded our lives. It was delightful to dream under the rustling beeches of the neighbouring forest; and in the church with its ancient graves and the crypt of St. Wiperti Cloister, the oldest specimen of Christian art in that region, we were filled with reverence for the days of old.

The life of the great Henry, which I had celebrated in verse at Kottbus, became a reality to me here; and what a powerful influence a visit to the ancient cloister exerted on our young souls! The nearest relatives of mighty sovereigns had dwelt as abbesses within its walls. But two generations ago Anna Amalie, the hapless sister of Frederick the Great, died while holding this office.

A strange and lasting impression was wrought upon me by a corpse and a picture in this convent. Both were in a subterranean chamber which possessed the property of preserving animal bodies from corruption. In this room was the body of Countess Aurora von Konigsmark, famed as the most beautiful woman of her time. After a youth spent in splendour she had retired to the cloister as superior, and there she now lay unveiled, rigid, and yellow, although every feature had retained the form it had in death. Beside the body hung her portrait, taken at the time when a smile on her lips, a glance from her eyes, was enough to fire the heart of the coldest man.

A terrible antithesis!

Here the portrait of the blooming, beautiful husk of a soul exulting in haughty arrogance; yonder that husk itself, transformed by the hand of death into a rigid, colourless caricature, a mummy without embalming.

Art, too, had a place in Quedlinburg. I still remember with pleasure Steuerwald's beautiful winter landscapes, into which he so cleverly introduced the mediaeval ruins of the Hartz region.

Thus, Quedlinburg was well suited to arouse poetic feelings in young hearts, steep the soul with love for the beautiful, time-honoured region, and yet fill it with the desire to make distant lands its own. Every one knows that this was Klopstock's birthplace; but the greatest geographer of all ages, Karl Ritter, whose mighty mind grasped the whole universe as if it were the precincts of his home, also first saw the light of the world here.

Gutsmuths, the founder of the gymnastic system, Bosse, the present Minister of Public Worship and Instruction, and Julius Wolff, are children of Quedlinburg and pupils of its gymnasium.

The long vacation came between the written and verbal examinations, and as I had learned privately that my work had been sufficiently satisfactory, my mother gave me permission to go to the Black Forest, to which pleasant memories attracted me. But my friend Hey had seen nothing of the world, so I chose a goal more easily attained, and took him with me to the Rhine. I went home by the way of Gottingen, and what I saw there of the Saxonia corps filled me with such enthusiasm that I resolved to wear the blue, white, and blue ribbon.

The oral was also successfully examination passed, and I returned to my mother, who received me at Hosterwitz with open arms. The resolve to devote myself to the study of law and to commence in Gottingen was formed, and received her approval.

For what reason I preferred the legal profession it would be hard to say. Neither mental bias nor interest gained by any searching examination of the science to which I wished to devote myself, turned the scale. I actually gave less thought to my profession and my whole mental and external life than I should have bestowed upon the choice of a residence.

In the ideal school, as I imagine it, the pupils of the senior class should be briefly made acquainted with what each one of the principal professions offers and requires from its members. The principal of the institution should also aid by his counsel the choice of the young men with whose talents and tastes long intercourse had rendered him familiar.

[It should never contain more than seventy pupils. Barop, when I met him after I attained my maturity, named sixty as the largest number which permitted the teacher to know and treat individually the boys confided to his care. He would never receive more at

Keilhau.]

Of course I imagine this man not only a teacher but an educator, familiar not alone with the school exercises, but with the mental and physical characteristics of those who are to graduate from the university.

Had not the heads of the Keilhau Institute lost their pupils so young, they would undoubtedly have succeeded in guiding the majority to the right profession.

CHAPTER XXI.
AT THE UNIVERSITY.

The weeks following my graduation were as ill suited as possible to the decision of any serious question.

After a gay journey through Bohemia which ended in venerable Prague, I divided my time between Hosterwitz, Blasewitz, and Dresden. In the latter city I met among other persons, principally old friends, the son of my uncle Brandenstein, an Austrian lieutenant on leave of absence. I spent many a pleasant evening with him and his comrades, who were also on leave. These young gentlemen considered the Italians, against whom they fought, as rebels, while a cousin of my uncle, then Colonel von Brandenstein, but afterwards promoted in the Franco-Austrian war in 1859 and 1866 to the rank of master of ordnance, held a totally different opinion. This clever, warmhearted soldier understood the Italians and their struggle for unity and freedom, and judged them so justly and therefore favorably, that he often aroused the courteous opposition of his younger comrades. I did not neglect old friends, however, and when I did not go to the theatre in the evening I ended the day with my aunt at Blasewitz. But, on my mother's account, I was never long absent from Hosterwitz. I enjoyed being with her so much. We drove and walked together, and discussed everything the past had brought and the future promised.

Yet I longed for academic freedom, and especially to sit at the feet of an Ernst Curtius, and be initiated by Waitz into the methodical study of history.

The evening before my departure my mother drove with me to Blasewitz, where there was an elegant entertainment at which the lyric poet Julius Hammer, the author of "Look Around You and Look Within You," who was to become a dear friend of mine, extolled in enthusiastic verse the delights of student liberty and the noble sisters Learning and Poesy.

The glowing words echoed in my heart and mind after I had torn myself from the arms of my mother and of the woman who, next to her, was dearest to me on earth, my aunt, and was travelling toward my goal. If ever the feeling that I was born to good fortune took possession of me, it was during that journey.

I did not know what weariness meant, and when, on reaching Gottingen, I learned that the students' coffee-house was still closed and that no one would arrive for three or four days, I went to Cassel to visit the royal garden in Wilhelmshohe.

At the station I saw a gentleman who looked intently at me. His face, too, seemed familiar. I mentioned my name, and the next instant he had embraced and kissed me. Two Keilhau friends had met, and, with sunshine alike in our hearts and in the blue sky, we set off together to see everything of note in beautiful Cassel.

When it was time to part, Von Born told me so eagerly how many of our old school-mates were now living in Westphalia, and how delightful it would be to see them, that I yielded and went with him to the birthplace of Barop and Middendorf. The hours flew like one long revel, and my exuberant spirits made my old school-mates, who, engaged in business enterprises, were beginning to look life solemnly in the face, feel as if the carefree Keilhau days had returned. On going back to Gottingen, I still had to wait a few days for the real commencement of the term, but I was received at the station by the "Saxons," donned the blue cap, and engaged pleasant lodgings—though the least adapted to serious study in the "Schonhutte," a house in Weenderstrasse whose second story was occupied by our corps room.

My expectations of the life with young men of congenial tastes were completely fulfilled. Most of them belonged to the nobility, but the beloved "blue, white, and blue" removed all distinctions of birth.

By far the most talented of its members was Count (now Prince) Otto von Stolberg-Wernegerode, who was afterwards to hold so high a position in the service of the Prussian Government.

Among the other scions of royal families were the hereditary Prince Louis of Hesse-Darmstadt and his brother Henry. Both were vivacious, agreeable young men, who entered eagerly into all the enjoyments of student and corps life. The older brother, who died as Grand Duke, continued his friendship for me while sovereign of his country. I was afterwards indebted to him for the pleasure of making the acquaintance of his wife Alice, one of the most remarkable women whom I have ever met.—[Princess Alice of England, the daughter of Queen Victoria.-TR.]

Oh, what delightful hours we spent in the corps room, singing and revelling, in excursions through the beautiful scenes in the neighbourhood, and on the fencing ground, testing our strength and skill, man to man! Every morning we woke to fresh pleasures, and every evening closed a spring festal day, radiant with the sunlight of liberty and the magic of friendship.

Our dinner was eaten together at the "Krone" with the most jovial of hosts, old Betmann, whose card bore the pictures of a bed and a man. Then came coffee, drunk at the museum or at some restaurant outside of the city, riding, or a duel, or there was some excursion, or the entertainment of a fellow-student from some other university, and finally the tavern.

Many an evening also found me with some friends at the Schuttenhof, where the young Philistines danced with the little burgher girls and pretty dressmakers. They were all, however, of unsullied reputation, and how merrily I swung them around till the music ceased! These innocent amusements could scarcely have injured my robust frame, yet when some unusual misfortune happens it is a trait of human nature to seek its first germ in the past. I, too, scanned the period immediately preceding my illness, but reached the conclusion that it was due to acute colds, the first of which ran into a very violent fever.

Had the result been otherwise I certainly should not have permitted my sons to enjoy to the utmost the happy period which in my case was too soon interrupted.

True, the hours of the night which I devoted to study could scarcely have been beneficial to my nervous system; for when, with burning head and full of excitement, I returned from the tavern which was closed, by rule, at eleven—from the "Schuttenhof," or some ball or entertainment, I never went to rest; that was the time I gave the intellect its due. Legal studies were pursued during the hours of the night only at the commencement of my stay in Gottingen, for I rarely attended the lectures for which I had entered my name, though the brevity of the Roman definitions of law, with which Ribbentropp's lectures had made me familiar, afforded me much pleasure. Unfortunately, I could not attend the lectures of Ernst Curtius, who had just been summoned to Gottingen, on account of the hours at which they were given. My wish to join Waitz's classes was also unfulfilled, but I went to those of the philosopher Lotze, and they opened a new world to me. I was also one of the most eager of Professor Unger's hearers.

Probably his "History of Art" would have attracted me for its own sake, but I must confess that at first his charming little daughter was the sole magnet which drew me to his lectures; for on account of displaying the pictures he delivered them at his own house.

Unfortunately, I rarely met the fair Julie, but, to make amends, I found through her father the way to that province of investigation to which my after-life was to be devoted.

In several lessons he discussed subtly and vividly the art of the Egyptians, mentioning Champollion's deciphering of the hieroglyphics.

This great intellectual achievement awakened my deepest interest. I went at once to the library, and Unger selected the books which seemed best adapted to give me further instruction.

I returned with Champollion's Grammaire Hieroglyphique, Lepsius's Lettre a Rosellini, and unfortunately with some misleading writings by Seyffarth.

How often afterward, returning in the evening from some entertainment, I have buried myself in the grammar and tried to write hieroglyphics.

True, I strove still more frequently and persistently to follow the philosopher Lotze.

Obedient to a powerful instinct, my untrained intellect had sought to read the souls of men. Now I learned through Lotze to recognize the body as the instrument to which the emotions of the soul, the harmonies and discords of the mental and emotional life, owe their origin.

I intended later to devote myself earnestly to the study of physiology, for without it Lotze could be but half understood; and from physiologists emanated the conflict which at that time so deeply stirred the learned world.

In Gottingen especially the air seemed, as it were, filled with physiological and other questions of the natural sciences.

In that time of the most sorrowful reaction the political condition of Germany was so wretched that any discussion concerning it was gladly avoided. I do not remember having attended a single debate on that topic in the circles of the students with which I was nearly connected.

But the great question "Materialism or Antimaterialism" still agitated the Georgia Augusta, in whose province the conflict had assumed still sharper forms, owing to Rudolf Wagner's speech during the convention of the Guttingen naturalists three years prior to my entrance.

Carl Vogt's "Science and Bigotry" exerted a powerful influence, owing to the sarcastic tone in which the author attacked his calmer adversary. In the honest conviction of profound knowledge, the clever, vigorous champion of materialism endeavoured to brand the opponents of his dogmas with the stigma of absurdity, and those who flattered themselves with the belief that they belonged to the ranks of the "strong-minded" followed his standard.

Hegel's influence was broken, Schelling's idealism had been thrust aside. The solid, easily accessible fare of the materialists was especially relished by those educated in the natural sciences, and Vogt's maxim, that thought stands in a similar relation to the brain as the gall to the liver and the excretions of the other organs, met with the greater approval the more confidently and wittily it was promulgated. The philosopher could not help asserting that the nature of the soul could be disclosed neither by the scalpel nor the microscope; yet the discoveries of the naturalist, which had led to the perception of the relation existing between the psychical and material life seemed to give the most honest, among whom Carl Vogt held the first rank; a right to uphold their dogmas.

Materialism versus Antimaterialism was the subject under discussion in the learned circles of Germany. Nay, I remember scarcely any other powerful wave of the intellect visible during this period of stagnation.

Philosophy could not fail to be filled with pity and disapproval to see the independent existence of the soul, as it were, authoritatively reaffirmed by a purely empirical science, and also brought into the field all the defensive forces at her command. But throngs flocked to the camp of Materialism, for the trumpets of her leaders had a clearer, more confident sound than the lower and less readily understood opposing cries of the philosophers.

Vogt's wrath was directed with special keenness against my teacher, Lotze. These topics were rarely discussed at the tavern or among the members of the corps. I first heard them made the subject of an animated exchange of thought in the Dirichlet household, where Professor Baum emerged from his aristocratic composure to denounce vehemently materialism and its apostles. Of course I endeavoured to gain information about things which so strongly moved intellectual men, and read in addition to Lotze's books the polemical writings which were at that time in everybody's hands.

Vogt's caustic style charmed me, but it was not due solely to the religious convictions which I had brought from my home and from Keilhau that I perceived that here a sharp sword was swung by a strong arm to cut water. The wounds it dealt would not bleed, for they were inflicted upon a body against which it had as little power as Satan against the cross.

When, before I became acquainted with Feuerbach, I flung my books aside, wearied or angered, I often seized in the middle of the night my monster Poem of the World, my tragedy of Panthea and Abradatus, or some other poetical work, and did not retire till the wick of the lamp burned out at three in the morning.

When I think how much time and earnest labour were lavished on that poem, I regret having yielded to the hasty impulse to destroy it.

I have never since ventured to undertake anything on so grand a scale. I could repeat only a few lines of the verses it contained; but the plan of the whole work, as I rounded it in Gottingen and Hosterwitz, I remember perfectly, and I think, if only for the sake of its peculiarity and as the mirror of a portion of my intellectual life at that time, its main outlines deserve reproduction here.

I made Power and Matter, which I imagined as a formless element; the basis of all existence. These two had been cast forth by the divine Ruler of a world incomprehensible to human intelligence, in which the present is a moment, space a bubble, as out of harmony with the mighty conditions and purposes of his realm. But this supreme Ruler offered to create for them a world suited to their lower plane of existence. Power I imagined a man, Matter a woman. They were hostile to each other, for he despised his quiet, inert companion, she feared her restless, unyielding partner; yet the power of the ruler of the higher world forced them to wed.

From their loveless union sprang the earth, the stars-in short, all inorganic life.

When the latter showed its relation to the father, Power, by the impetuous rush of the stars through space, by terrible eruptions, etc., the mother, Matter, was alarmed, and as, to soothe them, she drew into her embrace the flaming spheres, which dashed each other to pieces in their mad career, and restrained the fiercest, her chill heart was warmed by her children's fire.

Thus, as it were, raised to a higher condition, she longed for less unruly children, and her husband, Power, who, though he would have gladly cast her off, was bound to her by a thousand ties, took pity upon her, because her listlessness and coldness were transformed to warmth and motion, and another child sprang from their union, love.

But she seemed to have been born to misery, and wandered mournfully about, weeping and lamenting because she lacked an object for which to labour. True, she drew from the flaming, smoking bodies which she kissed a soft, beneficent light, she induced some to give up their former impetuosity and respect the course of others, and plants and trees sprang from the earth where her lips touched it, yet her longing to receive something which would be in harmony with her own nature remained unsatisfied.

But she was a lovely child and the darling of her father, whom, by her entreaties, she persuaded to animate with his own nature the shapes which she created in sport, those of the animals.

From this time there were living creatures moved by Power and Love. But again they brought trouble to the mother; for they were stirred by fierce passions, under whose influence they attacked and rent each other. But Love did not cease to form new shapes until she attained the most beautiful, the human form.

Yet human beings were stirred by the same feelings as the animals, and Love's longing for something in which she could find comfort remained unsatisfied, till, repelled by her savage father and her listless mother, she flung herself in despair from a rock. But being immortal, she did not perish.

Her blood sprinkled the earth, and from her wounds exhaled an exquisite fragrance, which rose higher and higher till it reached the realm whence came her parents; and its supreme ruler took pity on the exile's child, and from the blood of Love grew at his sign a lily, from which arose, radiant in white garments, Intellect, which the Most High had breathed into the flower.

He came from that higher world to ours, but only a vague memory of his former home was permitted, lest he should compare his present abode with the old one and scorn it.

As soon as he met Love he was attracted towards her, and she ardently accepted his suit; yet the first embrace chilled her, and her fervour startled and repelled him. So, each fearing the other's tenderness, they shunned each other, though an invincible charm constantly drew them together.

Love continued to yearn for him even after she had sundered the bond; but he often yielded to the longing for his higher home, of whose splendours he retained a memory, and soared upward. Yet whenever he drew near he was driven back to the other.

There he directed sometimes with Love, sometimes alone, the life of everything in the universe, or in unison with her animated men with his breath.

He did this sometimes willingly, sometimes reluctantly, with greater or less strength, according to the nearness he had attained to his heavenly home; but when he had succeeded in reaching its circle of light, he returned wonderfully invigorated. Then whoever Love and he joined in animating with their breath became an artist.

There was also a thoroughly comic figure and one with many humorous touches. Intellect's page, Instinct, who had risen from the lily with him, was a comical fellow. When he tried to follow his master's flight he fell after the first few strokes of his wings, and usually among nettles. Only when some base advantage was to be gained on earth did this servant succeed better than his master. The mother, Matter, whom for the sake of the verse I called by her Greek name Hyle, was also invested with a shade of comedy as a dissatisfied wife and the mother-in-law of Intellect.

In regard to the whole Poem of the World I will observe that, up to the time I finished the last line, I had never studied the kindred systems of the Neo-Platonics or the Gnostics.

The verses which described the moment when Matter drew her fiery children to her heart and thus warmed it, another passage in which men who were destitute of intellect sought to destroy themselves and Love resolved to sacrifice her own life, and, lastly, the song where Intellect rises from the lily, besides many others, were worthy, in my opinion, of being preserved.

What first diverted my attention from the work was, as has been mentioned, the study of Feuerbach, to which I had been induced by a letter from the geographer Karl Andree. I eagerly seized his books, first choosing his "Axioms of the Philosophy of the Future," and afterwards devoured everything he had written which the library contained. And at that time I was grateful to my friend the geographer for his advice. True, Feuerbach seemed to me to shatter many things which from a child I had held sacred; yet I thought I discovered behind the falling masonry the image of eternal truth.

The veil which I afterwards saw spread over so many things in Feuerbach's writings at that time produced the same influence upon me as the mist whence rise here the towers, yonder the battlements of a castle. It might be large or small; the grey mist which forbids the eye from definitely measuring its height and width by no means prevents the traveller, who knows that a powerful lord possesses the citadel, from believing it to be as large and well guarded as the power of its ruler would imply.

True, I was not sufficiently mature for the study of this great thinker, whom I afterwards saw endanger other unripe minds. As a disciple of this master there were many things to be destroyed which from childhood had become interlaced by a thousand roots and fibres with my whole intellectual organism, and such operations are not effected without pain.

What I learned while seeking after truth during those night hours ought to have taught me the connection between mind and body; yet I was never farther from perceiving it. A sharp division had taken place in my nature. By night, in arduous conflict, I led a strange mental life, known to myself alone; by day all this was forgotten, unless—and how rarely this happened—some conversation recalled it.

From my first step out of doors I belonged to life, to the corps, to pleasure. What was individual existence, mortality, or the eternal life of the soul! Minerva's bird is an owl. Like it, these learned questions belonged to the night. They should cast no shadow on the brightness of my day. When I met the first friend in the blue cap no one need have sung our corps song, "Away with cares and crotchets!"

At no time had the exuberant joy in mere existence stirred more strongly within me. My whole nature was filled with the longing to utilize and enjoy this brief earthly life which Feuerbach had proved was to end with death.

> Better an hour's mad revel,
>
> E'en a kiss from a Moenad's lip,
>
> Than a year of timid doubting,
>
> Daring only to taste and sip,

were the closing lines of a song which I composed at this time.

So my old wantonness unfolded its wings, but it was not to remain always unpunished.

My mother had gone to Holland with Paula just before Advent, and as I could not spend my next vacation at home, she promised to furnish me with means to take a trip through the great German Hanse cities.

In Bremen I was most cordially received in the family of Mohr, a member of my corps, in whose circle I spent some delightful hours, and also an evening never to be forgotten in the famous old Rathskeller.

But I wished to see the harbour of the great commercial city, and the ships which ploughed the ocean to those distant lands for which I had often longed.

Since I had shot my first hare in Komptendorf and brought down my first partridge from the air, the love of sport had never slumbered; I gratified it whenever I could, and intended to take a boat from Bremerhaven and go as near as possible to the sea, where I could shoot the cormorants and the bald-headed eagles which hunters on the seashore class among the most precious booty.

In Bremerhaven an architect whose acquaintance I had made on the way became my cicerone, and showed me all the sights of the small but very quaint port. I had expected to find the bustle on shore greater, but what a throng of ships and boats, masts and smoke-stacks I saw!

My guide showed me the last lighthouse which had been built, and took me on board of a mail steamer which was about to sail to America.

I was deeply interested in all this, but my companion promised to show me things still more remarkable if I would give up my shooting excursion.

Unfortunately, I insisted upon my plan, and the next morning sailed in a pouring rain through a dense mist to the mouth of the Weser and out to sea. But, instead of pleasure and booty, I gained on this expedition nothing but discomfort and drenching, which resulted in a violent cold.

What I witnessed and experienced in my journey back to Cuttingen is scarcely worth mentioning. The only enjoyable hours were spent at the theatre in Hanover, where I saw Niemann in Templar and Jewess, and for the first time witnessed the thoroughly studied yet perfectly natural impersonations of Marie Seebach. I also remember with much pleasure the royal riding-school in charge of General Meyer. Never have I seen the strength of noble chargers controlled and guided with so much firmness, ease, and grace as by the hand of this officer, the best horseman in Germany.

CHAPTER XXII.
THE SHIPWRECK

The state of health in which, still with a slight fever recurring every afternoon, I returned to Gottingen was by no means cheering.

Besides, I was obliged at once to undergo the five days' imprisonment to which I had been justly sentenced for reckless shooting across the street.

During the day I read, besides some very trashy novels, several by Jean Paul, with most of which I had become familiar while a school-boy in the first class.

They had given me so much pleasure that I was vexed with the indifference with which some of my friends laid the works of the great humorist aside.

There were rarely any conversations on the more serious scientific subjects among the members of the corps, though it did not lack talented young men, and some of the older ones were industrious.

Nothing, perhaps, lends the life of the corps a greater charm than the affectionate intercourse which unites individuals.

I was always sure of finding sympathizers for everything that touched my feelings.

With regard to the results of my nocturnal labour the case was very different. If any one else had "bored" me at the tavern about his views of Feuerbach and Lotze, I should undoubtedly have stopped him with Goethe's "Ergo bibamus."

There was one person in Gottingen, however, Herbert Pernice, from whom I might expect full sympathy. Though only five years my senior, he was already enrolled among the teachers of the legal faculty. The vigour and keenness of his intellect and the extent of his knowledge were as amazing as his corpulence.

One evening I had met him at the Krone and left the table at which he presided in a very enthusiastic state of mind; for while emptying I know not how many bottles of Rhine wine he directed the conversation apparently unconsciously.

Each of his statements seemed to strike the nail on the head.

The next day, to my great delight, I met him again at Professor Baum's. He had retreated from the ladies, whom he always avoided, and as we were alone in the room I soon succeeded in turning the conversation upon Feuerbach, for I fairly longed to have another person's opinion of him. Besides, I was certain of hearing the philosopher criticised by the conservative antimaterialistic Pernice in an original manner—that is, if he knew him at all. True, I might have spared myself the doubt; for into what domain of humanistic knowledge had not this highly talented man entered!

Feuerbach was thoroughly familiar to him, but he condemned his philosophy with pitiless severity, and opposed with keen wit and sharp dialectics his reasons for denying the immortality of the soul, inveighing especially against the phrase and idea "philosophy of religion" as an absurdity which genuine philosophy ought not to permit because it dealt only with thought, while religion concerned faith, whose seat is not in the head, the sacred fount of all philosophy, but the heart, the warm abode of religion and faith. Then he advised me to read Bacon, study Kant, Plato, and the other ancient philosophers—Lotze, too, if I desired—and when I had them all by heart, take up the lesser lights, and even then be in no hurry to read Feuerbach and his wild theology.

I met and conversed with him again whenever I could, and he availed himself of the confidence he inspired to arouse my enthusiasm for the study of jurisprudence. So I am indebted to Pernice for many benefits. In one respect only my reverence for him entailed a certain peril.

He knew what I was doing, but instead of warning me of the danger which threatened me from toiling at night after such exciting days, he approved my course and described episodes of his own periods of study.

One of the three essays for which he received prizes had been written to compel his father to retract the "stupid fellow" with which he had insulted him. At that time he had sat over his books day and night for weeks, and, thank Heaven, did not suffer from it.

His colossal frame really did seem immovable, and I deemed mine, though much slighter, capable of nearly equal endurance. It required severe exertions to weary me, and my mind possessed the capacity to devote itself to strenuous labour directly after the gayest amusements, and there was no lack of such "pastimes" either in Gottingen or just beyond its limits.

Among the latter was an excursion to Cassel which was associated with an adventure whose singular course impressed it firmly on my memory.

When we arrived, chilled by the railway journey, an acquaintance of the friend who accompanied me ordered rum and water for us, and we laughed and jested with the landlord's pretty daughters, who brought it to us.

As it had been snowing heavily and the sleighing was excellent, we determined to return directly after dinner, and drive as far as Munden. Of course the merry girls would be welcome companions, and we did not find it very difficult to persuade them to go part of the way with us.

So we hired two sleighs to convey us to a village distant about an hour's ride, from which we were to send them back in one, while my friend and I pursued our journey in the other.

After a lively dinner with our friends they joined us.

The snow-storm, which had ceased for several hours, began again, growing more and more violent as we drove on. I never saw such masses of the largest flakes, and just outside the village where the girls were to turn back the horses could barely force their way through the white mass which transformed the whole landscape into a single snowy coverlet.

The clouds seemed inexhaustible, and when the time for departure came the driver declared that it would be impossible to go back to Cassel.

The girls, who, exhilarated by the swift movement through the cold, bracing air, had entered into our merriment, grew more and more anxious. Our well-meant efforts to comfort them were rejected; they were angry with us for placing them in such an unpleasant position.

The lamps were lighted when I thought of taking the landlady into our confidence and asking her to care for the poor frightened children. She was a kind, sensible woman, and though she at first exclaimed over their heedlessness, she addressed them with maternal tenderness and showed them to the room they were to occupy.

They came down again at supper reassured, and we ate the rustic meal together very merrily. One of them wrote a letter to her father, saying that they had been detained by the snow at the house of an acquaintance, and a messenger set off with it at sunrise, but we were told that the road would not be passable before noon.

Yet, gay as our companions were at breakfast, the thought of entertaining them longer seemed irksome, and as the church bells were ringing some one proposed that we should go.

A path had been shovelled, and we were soon seated in the country church. The pastor, a fine-looking man of middle age, entered, and though I no longer remember his text, I recollect perfectly that he spoke of the temptations which threaten to lure us from the right paths and the means of resisting them.

One of the most effectual, he said, was the remembrance of those to whom we owe love and respect. I thought of my mother and blind old Langethal, of Tzschirner, and of Herbert Pernice, and, dissatisfied with myself, resolved to do in the future not only what was seemly, but what the duty of entering more deeply into the science which I had chosen required.

The childish faith which Feuerbach's teachings had threatened to destroy seemed to gaze loyally at me with my mother's eyes. I felt that Pernice was right—it was the warm heart, not the cool head, which should deal with these matters, and I left the church, which I had entered merely to shorten an hour, feeling as if released from a burden.

Our return home was pleasant, and I began to attend the law lectures at Gottingen with tolerable regularity.

I was as full of life, and, when occasion offered, as reckless, as ever, though a strange symptom began to make itself unpleasantly felt. It appeared only after severe exertion in walking, fencing, or dancing, and consisted of a peculiar, tender feeling in the soles of my feet, which I attributed to some fault of the shoemaker, and troubled myself the less about it because it vanished soon after I came in.

But the family of Professor Baum, the famous surgeon, where I was very intimate, had thought ever since my return from the Christmas vacation that I did not look well.

With Marianne, the second daughter of this hospitable household, a beautiful girl of remarkably brilliant mind, I had formed so intimate, almost fraternal, a friendship, that both she and her warm-hearted mother called me "Cousin Schorge."

Frau Dirichlet, the wife of the great mathematician, the sister of Felix Mendelssohn Bartholdy, in whose social and musical home I spent hours of pleasure which will never be forgotten, also expressed her anxiety about my loss of flesh. When a girl she had often met my mother, and at my first visit she won my affection by her eager praise of that beloved woman's charms.

As the whole family were extremely musical they could afford themselves and their friends a great deal of enjoyment. I have never heard Joachim play so entrancingly as to her accompaniment. At a performance in her own house, where the choruses from Cherubini's Water-Carrier were given, she herself had rehearsed the music with those who were to take part, and to hear her play on the piano was a treat.

This lady, a remarkable woman in every respect, who gave me many tokens of maternal affection, insisted on the right to warn me. She did this by reminding me, with delicate feminine tact, of my mother when she heard of a wager which I now remember with grave disapproval. This was to empty an immense number of bottles of the heavy Wurzburg Stein wine and yet remain perfectly sober. My opponent, who belonged to the Brunswick Corps, lost, but as soon after I was attacked by illness, though not in consequence of this folly, which had occurred about a fortnight before, he could not give the breakfast which I had won. But he fulfilled his obligation; for when, several lustra later, I visited his native city of Hamburg as a Leipsic professor, to deliver an address before the Society of Art and Science, he arranged a splendid banquet, at which I met several old Gottingen friends.

The term was nearly over when an entertainment was given to the corps by one of its aristocratic members. It was a very gay affair. A band of music played, and we students danced with one another. I was one of the last to depart, long after midnight, and on looking for my overcoat I could not find it. One of the guests had mistaken it for his, and the young gentleman's servant had carried his own home. This was unfortunate, for mine contained my door-key.

Heated by dancing, in a dress-coat, with a thin white necktie, I went out into the night air. It was cold, and, violently as I pounded on the door of the Schonhutte, no one opened it. At last I thought of pounding on the gutter-spout, which I did till I roused the landlord. But I had been at least fifteen minutes in the street, and was fairly numbed. The landlord was obliged to open the room and light my lamp, because I could not use my fingers.

If I had been intoxicated, which I do not believe, the cold would have sobered me, for what happened is as distinct as if it had occurred yesterday.

I undressed, went to bed, and when I was roused by a strange burning sensation in my throat I felt so weak that I could scarcely lift my arm. There was a peculiar taste of blood in my mouth, and as I moved I touched something moist. But my exhaustion was so great that I fell asleep again, and the dream which followed was so delightful that I did not forget it. Perhaps the distinctness of my recollection is due to my making it the subject of a poem, which I still possess. It seemed as if I were lying in an endless field of poppies, with the notes of music echoing around me. Never did I have a more blissful vision.

The awakening was all the more terrible. Only a few hours could have passed since I went to rest. Dawn was just appearing, and I rang for the old maid-servant who waited on me. An hour later Geheimrath Baum stood beside my bed.

The heavy tax made upon my physical powers by exposure to the night air had caused a severe haemorrhage. The excellent physician who took charge of my case said positively that my lungs were sound, and the attack was due to the bursting of a blood-vessel. I was to avoid sitting upright in bed, to receive no visitors, and have ice applied. I believed myself destined to an early death, but the departure from life caused me no fear; nay, I felt so weary that I desired nothing but eternal sleep. Only I wanted to see my mother again.

Then let my end come!

I was in the mood to write, and either the day after the haemorrhage or the next one I composed the following verses:

> A field of poppies swaying to and fro,
>
> Their blossoms scarlet as fresh blood,
>
> I see, While o'er me, radiant in the noontide glow,
>
> The sky, blue as corn-flowers, arches free.
>
> Low music echoes through the breezes warm;
>
> The violet lends the poppy her sweet breath;
>
> The song of nightingales is heard, a swarm
>
> Of butterflies flit hov'ring o'er the heath.
>
> While thus I lie, wrapped in a morning dream,
>
> Half waking, half asleep, 'mid poppies red,
>
> A fresh breeze cools my burning cheeks; a gleam
>
> Of light shines in the East. Hath the night sped?
>
> Then upward from an opening bud hath flown
>
> A poppy leaf toward the azure sky,
>
> But close beside it, from a flower full-blown,
>
> The scattered petals on the brown earth lie.
>
> The leaflet flutters, a fair sight to view,
>
> By the fresh matin breezes heavenward borne,
>
> The faded poppy falls, the fields anew
>
> To fertilize, which grateful thanks return.

> Starting from slumber round my room I gaze
>
> My hand of my own life-blood bears the stain;
>
> I am the poppy-leaf, with the first rays
>
> Of morning snatched away from earth's domain.
>
> Not mine the fate the world's dark ways to wend,
>
> And perish, wearied, at the goal of life;
>
> Still glad and blooming, I leave every friend;
>
> The game is lost—but with what joys 'twas rife!

I cannot express how these verses relieved my heart; and when on the third day I again felt comparatively well I tried to believe that I should soon recover, enjoy the pleasures of corps life, though with some caution, and devote myself seriously to the study of jurisprudence under Pernice's direction.

The physician gave his permission for a speedy return, but his assurance that there was no immediate danger if I was careful did not afford me unmixed pleasure. For my mother's sake and my own I desired to live, but the rules he prescribed before my departure were so contradictory to my nature that they seemed unbearably cruel. They restricted every movement. He feared the haemorrhage far less than the tender feeling in the soles of my feet and other small symptoms of the commencement of a chronic disease.

Middendorf had taught us to recognize God's guidance in Nature and our own lives, and how often I succeeded in doing so! But when I examined myself and my condition closely it seemed as if what had befallen me was the result of a malicious or blind chance.

Never before or since have I felt so crushed and destitute of support as during those days, and in this mood I left the city where the spring days of life had bloomed so richly for me, and returned home to my mother. She had learned what had occurred, but the physician had assured her that with my vigorous constitution I should regain my health if I followed his directions.

CHAPTER XXIII.
THE HARDEST TIME IN THE SCHOOL OF LIFE.

The period which now followed was the most terrible of my whole life. Even the faithful love that surrounded me could do little to relieve it.

Medicines did not avail, and I had not yet found the arcanum which afterwards so greatly benefitted my suffering soul.

The props which my mother and Middendorf had bestowed upon me when a boy had fallen; and the feeling of convalescence, which gives the invalid's life a sense of bliss the healthy person rarely knows, could not aid me, for the disease increased with wonderful speed.

When autumn came I was so much worse that Geheimrath von Ammon, a learned and experienced physician, recalled his advice that my mother and I should spend the winter in the south. The journey would have been fatal. The correctness of his judgment was proved by the short trip to Berlin which I took with my mother, aided by my brother Martin, who was then a physician studying with the famous clinical doctor Schonlein. It was attended with cruel suffering and the most injurious results, but it was necessary for me to return to my comfortable winter quarters. Our old friend and family physician, who had come to Hosterwitz in September to visit me, wished to have me near him, and in those days there was probably no one who deserved more confidence; for Heinrich Moritz Romberg was considered the most distinguished pathologist in nervous diseases in Germany, and his works on his own specialty are still valued.

In what a condition I entered the home which I had left so strong and full of youthful vigour! And Berlin did not receive me kindly; for the first months I spent there brought days of suffering with fever in the afternoon, and nights whose condition was no less torturing than pain.

But our physician had been present at my birth, he was my godfather, and as kind as if I were his son. He did everything in his power to relieve me, but the remedies he used were not much easier to bear than many a torturing disease. And hardest of all, I was ordered to keep perfectly still in bed. What a prospect! But when I had once resolved to follow the doctor's advice, I controlled with the utmost care every movement of my body. I, who had so often wished to fly, lay like my own corpse. I did not move, for I did not want to die, and intended to use every means in my power to defer the end. Death, which after the haemorrhage had appeared as the beautiful winged boy who is so easily mistaken for the god of love—Death, who had incited me to write saucy, defiant verses about him, now confronted me as a hollow-eyed, hideous skeleton.

In the guise of the most appalling figure among the apocalyptic riders of Cornelius, who had used me when a child for the model of a laughing angel, he seemed to be stretching his hand toward me from his emaciated steed. The poppy leaf was not to flutter toward the sky, but to wither in the dust.

Once, several weeks after our return home, I saw the eyes of my mother, who rarely wept, reddened with tears after a conversation with Dr. Romberg. When I asked my friend and physician if he would advise me to make my will, he said that it could do no harm.

Soon after Hans Geppert, who meanwhile had become a notary, arrived with two witnesses, odd-looking fellows who belonged to the working class, and I made my will in due form. The certainty that when I was no more what I possessed would be divided as I wished was a ray of light in this gloomy time.

No one knows the solemnity of Death save the person whom his cold hand has touched, and I felt it for weeks upon my heart.

What days and nights these were!

Yet in the presence of the open grave from which I shrank something took place which deeply moved my whole nature, gave it a new direction, led me to self-examination, and thence to a knowledge of my own character which revealed many surprising and unpleasing things. But I also felt that it was not yet too late to bring the good and evil traits, partly hereditary, partly acquired, into harmony with one another and render them of use to the same higher objects.

Yes, if I were permitted time to do so!

I had learned how quickly and unexpectedly the hour strikes which puts an end to all struggle towards a goal.

Besides, I now knew what would protect me from a relapse into the old careless waste of strength, what could aid me to do my utmost, for the mother's heart had again found the son's, fully and completely.

I had been forced to become as helpless as a child in order again to lay my head upon her breast and belong to her as completely as during the first years of life. During the long nights when fever robbed me of sleep she sat beside my bed, holding my hands in hers.

At last one came which contained hours of the most intense suffering, and in its course she asked, "Can you still pray?" The answer, which came from my inmost heart, was, "When you are with me, and with you, certainly."

We remained silent a long time, and whenever impatience, suffering, and faintness threatened to overpower me, I found, like Antaeus when he touched the earth that had given him birth, new strength in my mother's heart.

My old life seemed henceforward to lie far behind me.

I did not take up Feuerbach's writings again; his way could never again have been mine. In my suffering it had become evident from what an Eden he turns away and into what a wilderness he leads. But I still value this thinker as an honest, virile, and brilliantly gifted seeker after truth.

I also laid aside the other philosophers whose works I had been studying.

I never resumed Lotze, though later, with two other students, I attended Trendelenburg's difficult course, and tried to comprehend Kant's "critiques."

I first became familiar with Schopenhauer in Jena.

On the other hand, I again devoted many leisure hours to Egyptological works.

I felt that these studies suited my powers and would satisfy me. Everything which had formerly withheld me from the pursuits of learning now seemed worthless. It was as if I stood in a new relation to all things. Even the one to my mother had undergone a transformation. I realized for the first time what I possessed in her, how wrong I had been, and what I owed to her. One day during this period I remembered my Poem of the World, and instantly had the box brought in which I kept it among German favours, little pink notes, and similar trophies.

For the first time I perceived, in examining the fruits of the labour of so many days and nights, the vast disproportion between the magnitude of the subject and my untrained powers. One passage seemed faulty, another so overstrained and inadequate, that I flung it angrily back among the rest. At the same time I thought that the verses I had addressed to various beauties and the answers which I had received ought not to be seen by other eyes. I was alone with the servant, a bright fire was blazing in the stove, and, obedient to a hasty impulse, I told him to throw the whole contents of the box into the fire.

When the last fragment was consumed to ashes I uttered a sigh of relief.

Unfortunately, the flames also destroyed the greater part of my youthful poems. Even the completed acts of my tragedy had been overtaken by destruction, like the heroes of Panthea and Abradatus.

If I had formerly obeyed the physician's order to lie motionless, I followed it after the first signs of convalescence so rigidly that even the experienced Dr. Romberg admitted that he had not given me credit for so much self-control. Toward the end of the winter my former cheerfulness returned, and with it I also learned to use the arcanum I have formerly mentioned, which makes even the most bitter things enjoyable and lends them a taste of sweetness. I might term it "the practice of gratitude." Without intending it, I acquired the art of thankfulness by training my eyes to perceive the smallest trifle which gave cause for it. And this recognition of even the least favour of Fortune filled the rude wintry days with so much sunshine, that when children of my own were given me my first effort was to train them to gratitude, and especially to an appreciation of trifles.

The motto 'Carpe diem,' which I had found in my father's Horace and had engraved upon my seal ring, unexpectedly gained a new significance by no longer translating it "enjoy," but "use the day," till the time came when the two meanings seemed identical.

CHAPTER XXIV.
THE APPRENTICESHIP.

Firmly as I had resolved to follow the counsel of Horace, and dear as earnest labour was becoming, I still lacked method, a fixed goal towards which to move with firm tread in the seclusion to which my sufferings still condemned me.

I had relinquished the study of the law. It seemed more than doubtful whether my health would ever permit me to devote myself to a practical profession or an academic career, and my interest in jurisprudence was too slight to have it allure me to make it the subject of theoretical studies.

Egyptology, on the contrary, not only attracted me but permitted me to devote my whole strength to it so far as my health would allow. True, Champollion, the founder of this science, termed it "a beautiful dowerless maiden," but I could venture to woo her, and felt grateful that, in choosing my profession, I could follow my inclination without being forced to consider pecuniary advantages.

The province of labour was found, but with each step forward the conviction of my utter lack of preparation for the new science grew clearer.

Just then the kind heart of Wilhelm Grimm's wife brought her to me with some delicious fruit syrup made by her own hands. When I told her what I was doing and expressed a wish to have a guide in my science, she promised to tell "the men" at home, and within a few days after his sister-in-law's visit Jacob was sitting with me.

He inquired with friendly interest how my attention had been called to Egyptology, what progress I had made, and what other sciences I was studying.

After my reply he shook his venerable head with its long grey locks, and said, smiling:

"You have been putting the cart before the horse. But that's the way with young specialists. They want to become masters in the workshops of their sciences as a shoemaker learns to fashion boots. Other things are of small importance to them; and yet the special discipline first gains value in connection with the rest or the wider province of the allied sciences. Your deciphering of hieroglyphics can only make you a dragoman, and you must become a scholar in the higher sense, a real and thorough one. The first step is to lay the linguistic foundation."

This was said with the engaging yet impressively earnest frankness characteristic of him. He himself had never investigated Egyptian matters closely, and therefore did not seek to direct my course minutely, but advised me, in general, never to forget that the special science was nothing save a single chord, which could only produce its full melody with those that belonged to the same lute.

Lepsius had a broader view than most of those engaged in so narrow a field of study. He would speak of me to him.

The next Thursday Lepsius called on me. I know this because that day was reserved for his subsequent visits.

After learning what progress I had made by my own industry, he told me what to do next, and lastly promised to come again.

He had inquired about my previous education, and urged me to study philology, archaeology, and at least one Semitic language. Later he voluntarily informed me how much he, who had pursued philological, archaeological, Sanscrit, and Germanistic studies, had been impeded in his youth by having neglected the Semitic languages, which are more nearly allied to the Egyptian. It would be necessary also for me to understand English and Italian, since many things which the Egyptologist ought to know were published in these languages, as well as in French. Lastly he advised me to obtain some insight into Sanscrit, which was the point of departure for all linguistic studies.

His requirements raised mountain after mountain in my path, but the thought of being compelled to scale these heights not only did not repel me, but seemed extremely attractive. I felt as if my strength increased with the magnitude and multiplicity of the tasks imposed, and, full of joyous excitement, I told Lepsius that I was ready to fulfil his requirements in every detail.

We now discussed in what sequence and manner I should go to work, and to this day I admire the composure, penetration, and lucidity with which he sketched a plan of study that covered years.

I have reason to be grateful to this great scholar for the introduction to my special science, but still more for the wisdom with which he pointed out the direction of my studies. Like Jacob Grimm, he compelled me, as an Egyptologist, to remain in connection with the kindred departments.

Later my own experience was to teach me the correctness of his assertion that it would be a mistake to commence by studying so restricted a science as Egyptology.

My pupils can bear witness that during my long period of teaching I always strove to urge students who intended to devote themselves to Egyptology first to strengthen the foundations, without which the special structure lacks support.

Lepsius's plan of instruction provided that I should follow these principles from the beginning. The task I had to perform was a great and difficult one. How infinitely easier it was for those whom I had the privilege of introducing to this science! The lecture-rooms of famous teachers stood open to them, while my physical condition kept me for weeks from the university; and how scanty were the aids to which the student could turn! Yet the zeal—nay, the enthusiasm—with which I devoted myself to the study was so great that it conquered every difficulty.

[I had no dictionary and no grammar for the hieroglyphic language save Champollion's. No Stern had treated Coptic in a really scientific manner. I was obliged to learn it according to Tuki, Peyron, Tattam, and Steinthal-Schwarze. For the hieratic there was no aid save my own industry and the lists I had myself compiled from the scanty texts then at the disposal of the student. Lepsius had never devoted much time to them. Brugsch's demotic grammar had appeared, but its use was rendered very difficult by the lack of conformity between the type and the actual signs.]

When I recall the amount of knowledge I mastered in a few terms it seems incredible; yet my labour was interrupted every summer by a sojourn at the springs—once three months, and never for a less period than six weeks. True, I was never wholly idle while using the waters, but, on the other hand, I was obliged to consider the danger that in winter constantly threatened my health. All night-work was strictly forbidden and, if I sat too long over my books by day, my mother reminded me of my promise to the doctor, and I was obliged to stop.

During the first years I worked almost exclusively at home, for I was permitted to go out only in very pleasant weather.

Dr. Romberg had wisely considered my reluctance to interrupt my studies by a residence in the south, because he deemed life in a well-ordered household more beneficial to sufferers from spinal diseases than a warmer climate, when leaving home, as in my case, threatened to disturb the patient's peace of mind.

For three winters I had been denied visiting the university, the museum, and the libraries. On the fourth I was permitted to begin, and now, with mature judgment and thorough previous preparation, I attended the academic lectures, and profited by the treasures of knowledge and rich collections of the capital.

After my return from Wildbad Lepsius continued his Thursday visits, and during the succeeding winters still remained my guide, even when I had also placed myself, in the department of the ancient Egyptian languages, under the instruction of Heinrich Brugsch.

At school, of course, I had not thought of studying Hebrew. Now I took private lessons in that language, to which I devoted several hours daily. I had learned to read Sanscrit and to translate easy passages in the chrestomathy, and devoted myself with special zeal to the study of the Latin grammar and prosody. Professor Julius Geppert, the brother of our most intimate family friend, was my teacher for four terms.

The syntax of the classic languages, which had been my weak point as a school-boy, now aroused the deepest interest, and I was grateful to Lepsius for having so earnestly insisted upon my pursuing philology. I soon felt the warmest appreciation of the Roman comedies, which served as the foundation of these studies. What sound wit, what keenness of observation, what a happy gift of invention, the old comic writers had at their disposal! I took them up again a few years ago, after reading with genuine pleasure in Otto Ribbeck's masterpiece, The History of Roman Poetry, the portions devoted to Plautus and Terence.

The types of character found in these comedies strengthened my conviction that the motives of human actions and the mental and emotional peculiarities of civilized men in every age always have been and always will be the same.

With what pleasure, when again permitted to go out in the evening, I witnessed the performances of Plautus's pieces given by Professor Geppert's pupils!

The refreshed and enlarged knowledge of school Latin was of great service in writing, and afterwards discussing, a Latin dissertation. I devoted perhaps a still larger share of my time to Greek, and, as the fruit of these studies, still possess many translations from Anacreon, Sappho, and numerous fragments from the Bergk collection of Greek lyrics, but, with the exception of those introduced into my novels, none have been printed.

During my leisure hours translating afforded me special pleasure. An exact rendering of difficult English authors soon made Shakespeare's language in both prose and poetry as intelligible as German or French.

After mastering the rules of grammar, I needed no teacher except my mother. When I had conquered the first difficulties I took up Tennyson's Idyls of the King, and at last succeeded in translating two of these beautiful poems in the metre of the original.

My success with Enid I think was very tolerable. The manuscript still lies in my desk unpublished.

As I was now engaged in studying the languages I easily learned to read Italian, Spanish, and Dutch books.

In view of this experience, which is not wholly personal, I have wondered whether the instruction of boys might not be shortened to give them more outdoor exercise. In how brief a time the pupils, as men studying for their own benefit, not the teacher's, would acquire many things! Besides the languages, I studied, at first exclusively under Lepsius's thoroughly admirable instruction, ancient history and archeology.

Later I owed most to Gerhard, Droysen, Friederichs, and August Bockh.

A kind fate afterwards brought me into personal relations with the latter, whose lectures on the Athenian financial system were the finest and the most instructive I have ever heard. What clearness, what depth of learning, what a subtle sense of humour this splendid old man possessed! I attended his lectures in 1863, and how exquisite were the allusions to the by no means satisfactory political conditions of the times with which he spiced them. I also became sincerely attached to Friederichs, and it made me happy to be able to requite him in some small degree in Egypt for the kindness and unselfishness he had shown me in Berlin.

Bopp's lectures, where I tried to increase my meagre knowledge of Sanscrit, I attended, unfortunately, only a few hours.

The lectures of the African traveller Heinrich Earth supplied rich sources of material, but whoever expected to hear bewitching narratives from him would have been disappointed. Even in more intimate intercourse he rarely warmed up sufficiently to let others share the rich treasure of his knowledge and experience. It seemed as if, during his lonely life in Africa, he had lost the necessity of exchanging thoughts with his fellow-men. During this late period Heinrich Brugsch developed in the linguistic department of Egyptology what I had gained from Lepsius and by my own industry, and I gladly term myself his pupil.

I have cause to be grateful for the fresh and helpful way in which this great and tireless investigator gave me a private lecture; but Lepsius had opened the door of our science, and though he could carry me only to a certain stage in the grammar of the ancient Egyptians, in other departments I owe him more than any other of my intellectual guides. I am most indebted to him for the direction to use historical and archaeological authorities critically, and his correction of the tasks he set me; but our conversations on archaeological subjects have also been of the greatest interest.

After his death I tried to return in some small degree what his unselfish kindness had bestowed by accepting the invitation to become his biographer. In "Richard Lepsius," I describe reverently but without deviating one step from the truth, this wonderful scholar, who was a faithful and always affectionate friend.

I can scarcely believe it possible that the dignified man, with the grave, stern, clear-cut, scholarly face and snow-white hair, was but forty-five years old when he began to direct my studies; for, spite of his erect bearing and alert, movements, he seemed to me at that time a venerable old man. There was something in the aristocratic reserve of his nature and the cool, penetrating sharpness of his criticism, which is usually found only in men of more mature years. I should have supposed him incapable of any heedless word, any warm emotion, until I afterwards met him under his own roof and enjoyed the warm-hearted cheerfulness of the father of the family and the graciousness of the host.

It certainly was not the cool, calculating reason, but the heart, which had urged him to devote so many hours of his precious time to the young follower of his science.

Heinrich Brugsch, my second teacher, was far superior to Lepsius as a decipherer and investigator of the various stages of the ancient Egyptian languages. Two natures more totally unlike can scarcely be imagined.

Brugsch was a man of impulse, who maintained his cheerfulness even when life showed him its serious side. Then, as now, he devoted himself with tireless energy to hard work. In this respect he resembled Lepsius, with whom he had other traits in common-first, a keen sense of order in the collection and arrangement of the abundant store of scientific material at his disposal; and, secondly, the circumstance that Alexander von Humboldt had smoothed the beginning of the career of investigation for both. The attention of this great scholar and influential man had been attracted by Brugsch's first Egyptological works, which he had commenced before he left school, and his keen eye recognized their value as well as the genius of their author. As soon as he began to win renown Humboldt extended his powerful protection to him, and induced his friend, the king, to afford him means for continuing his education in Paris and for a journey to Europe.

Though it was Bunsen who first induced Lepsius to devote himself to Egyptology, that he might systematize the science and prune with the knife of philological and historical criticism the shoots which grew so wildly after Champollion's death, Humboldt had opened the paths to learning which in Paris were closed to the foreigner.

Finally, it was the great naturalist who had lent the aid of his powerful influence with Frederick William IV to the enterprise supported by Bunsen of an expedition to Egypt under the direction of Lepsius. But for the help of the most influential man of his day it would have been difficult—nay, perhaps impossible—to obtain for themselves and German investigation the position which, thanks to their labour, it now occupies.

I had the privilege of meeting Alexander von Humboldt at a small dinner party, and his image is vividly imprinted on my memory. He was at that time far beyond the span of life usually allotted to man, and what I heard him say was hardly worth retaining, for it related to the pleasures of the table, ladies' toilettes, court gossip, etc. When he afterwards gave me his hand I noticed the numerous blue veins which covered it like a network. It was not until later that I learned how many important enterprises that delicate hand had aided.

Heinrich Brugsch is still pursuing with fresh creative power the profession of Egyptological research. The noble, simple-hearted woman who was so proud of her son's increasing renown, his mother, died long ago. She modestly admired his greatness, yet his shrewdness, capacity for work, and happy nature were a heritage from her.

Heinrich Brugsch's instruction extended beyond the actual period of teaching.

With the commencement of convalescence and the purposeful industry which then began, a time of happiness dawned for me. The mental calmness felt by every one who, secluded from the tumult of the world, as I was at that time, devotes himself to the faithful fulfilment of duty, rendered it comparatively easy for me to accommodate myself patiently to a condition which a short time before would have seemed insupportable.

True, I was forced to dispense with the companionship of gay associates of my own age. At first many members of my old corps, who were studying in Berlin, sought me, but gradually their places were filled by other friends.

The dearest of these was Dr. Adolf Baeyer, son of the General. He is now one of the leaders in his chosen science, chemistry, and is Justus Liebig's successor in the Munich University.

My second friend was a young Pole who devoted himself eagerly to Egyptology, and whom Lepsius had introduced as a professional comrade. He called me Georg and I him Mieczy (his name was Mieczyslaw).

So, during those hard winters, I did not lack friendship. But they also wove into my life something else which lends their memory a melancholy charm.

The second daughter of my mother's Belgian niece, who had married in Berlin the architect Fritz Hitzig, afterwards President of the Academy of Arts, was named Eugenie and nicknamed "Nenny."

If ever any woman fulfilled the demands of the fairy tale, "White as snow and black as ebony," it was she. Only the "red as blood" was lacking, for usually but a faint roseate hue tinged her cheeks. Her large blue eyes had an innocent, dreamy, half-melancholy expression, which I was not the only person who found unspeakably charming. Afterwards it seemed to me, in recalling her look, that she beheld the fair boy Death, whose lowered torch she was so soon to follow.

About the time that I returned to Berlin seriously ill she had just left boarding-school, and it is difficult to describe the impression she made when I saw her for the first time; yet I found in the opening rose all that had lent the bud so great a charm.

I am not writing a romance, and shall not permit the heart to beautify or transfigure the image memory retains, yet I can assert that Nenny lacked nothing which art and poesy attribute to the women who allegorically personate the magic of Nature or the fairest emotions and ideals of the human soul. In this guise poet, sculptor, or artist might have represented Imagination, the Fairy Tale, Lyric Poetry, the Dream, or Compassion.

The wealth of raven hair, the delicate lines of the profile, the scarlet lips, the pearly teeth, the large, long-lashed blue eyes, whose colour formed a startling contrast to the dark hair, the slender little hands and dainty feet, united to form a beauty whose equal Nature rarely produces. And this fair body contained a tender, loving, pure, childlike heart, which longed for higher gifts than human life can bestow.

Thus she appeared before me like an apparition from a world opened only to the poet. She came often, for she loved my mother, and rarely approached my couch without a flower, a picture which pleased her, or a book containing a poem which she valued.

When she entered I felt as if happiness came with her. Doubtless my eyes betrayed this distinctly enough, though I forced my lips to silence; for what love had she, before whom life was opening like a path through a blooming garden, to bestow on the invalid cousin who was probably destined to an early death, and certainly to many a year of illness? At our first meeting I felt that I loved her, but for that very reason I desired to conceal it.

I had grown modest. It was enough for me to gaze at her, hear her dear voice, and sometimes—she was my cousin—clasp her little hand.

Science was now the object of my devotion. My intellect, passion, and fire were all hers. A kind fortune seemed to send me Nenny in order to bestow a gift also upon the heart, the soul, the sense of beauty.

This state of affairs could not last; for no duty commanded her to share the conflict raging within me, and a day came when I learned from her own lips that she loved me, that her heart had been mine when she was a little school-girl, that during my illness she had never wearied of praying for me, and had wept all night long when the physician told her mother of the danger in which I stood.

This confession sounded like angel voices. It made me infinitely happy, yet I had strength to entreat Nenny to treasure this blissful hour with me as the fairest jewel of our lives, and then help me to fulfil the duty of parting from her.

But she took a different view of the future. It was enough for her to know that my heart was hers. If I died young, she would follow me.

And now the devout child, who firmly believed in a meeting after death face to face, permitted me a glimpse of the wondrous world in which she hoped to have her portion after the end here.

I listened in astonishment, with sincere emotion. This was the faith which moved mountains, which brings heaven itself to earth.

Afterwards I again beheld the eyes with which, gazing into vacancy, she tried to conjure up before my soul these visions of hope from the realm of her fairest dreams—they were those of Raphael's Saint Cecilia in Bologna and Munich. I also saw them long after Nenny's death in one of Murillo's Madonnas in Seville, and even now they rise distinctly before my memory.

To disturb this childish faith or check the imagination winged by this devout enthusiasm would have seemed to me actually criminal. And I was young. Even the suffering I had endured had neither silenced the yearning voice of my heart nor cooled the warmth of my blood. I, who had believed that the garden of love was forever closed against me, was beloved by the most beautiful girl, who was even dearer to me than life, and with new hope, which Nenny's faith in God's goodness bedewed with warm spring rain, I enjoyed this happiness.

Yet conscience could not be silenced. The warning voice of my mother, to whom I had opened my heart, sharpened the admonitions of mine; and when Wildbad brought me only relief, by no means complete recovery, I left the decision to the physician. It was strongly adverse. Under the most favourable circumstances years must pass ere I should be justified in binding any woman's fate to mine.

So this beginning of a beautiful and serious love story became a swiftly passing dream. Its course had been happy, but the end dealt my heart a blow which healed very slowly. It opened afresh when in her parents' house, where during my convalescence I was a frequent guest, I myself advised her to marry a young land-owner, who eagerly wooed her. She became his wife, but only a year later entered that other world which she had regarded as her true home even while here. Her beloved image occupies the most sacred place in the shrine of my memory.

I denied myself the pleasure of introducing her character in one of my novels, for I felt that if I should succeed in limning it faithfully the modern reader would be justified in considering her an impossible figure for our days. She would perhaps have suited a fairy tale; and when I created Bianca in The Elixir I gave her Nenny's form. The gratitude which I owe her will accompany me to my life's end, for it was she who brought to my sick-room the blue sky, sunlight, and the thousand gifts of a blooming Garden of Eden.

CHAPTER XXV.
THE SUMMERS OF MY CONVALESCENCE.

While I spent the winters in my mother's house in industrious work and pleasant social life, the summers took me out of the city into the open air. I always went first with my faithful nurse and companion to Wildbad; the remainder of the warm season I spent on the Elbe, sometimes with my mother, sometimes with my aunt.

I used the Wildbad springs in all seventeen times. For two summers, aided by a servant, I descended from a wheel-chair into the warm water; in the third I could dispense with assistance; and from the fourth for several lustra I moved unchecked with a steady step. After a long interval, owing to a severe relapse of the apparently conquered disease, I returned to them.

The Wurtemberg Wildbad is one of the oldest cures in Germany. The legend of the Count Mirtemberg, who discovered its healing powers by seeing a wild boar go down to the warm spring to wash its wound, has been rendered familiar by Uhland to every German. Ulrich von Hutten also used it. It rises in a Black Forest valley inclosed by stately mountains, a little stream, the Enz, crystal clear, and abounding in trout.

The small town on both banks of the river expands, ere the Enz loses itself in the leafage, into the Kurplatz, where one stately building of lightred sandstone adjoins another. The little white church stands at the left. But the foil, the background for everything, is the beautiful foliage, which is as beneficial to the eyes as are the springs to the suffering body. This fountain of health has special qualities. The Swabian says, "just right, like Wildbad." It gushes just the right degree of heat for the bath from the gravelly sand. After bathing early in the morning I rested an hour, and when I rose obeyed any other directions of the physician in charge of the watering-place.

The remainder of the day, if the weather was pleasant, I spent out of doors, usually in the grounds under the leafy trees and groups of shrubs on the shore of the Enz. On the bank of the clear little stream stood a wooden arbour, where the murmur of the waves rippling over the mossy granite blocks invited dreams and meditation. During my whole sojourn in Wildbad I always passed several hours a day here. During my period of instruction I was busied with grammatical studies in ancient Egyptian text or archaeological works. In after years, instead of Minerva, I summoned the muse and committed to paper the thoughts and images which had been created in my mind at home. I wrote here the greater portion of An

Egyptian Princess, and afterwards many a chapter of Uarda, Homo Sum, and other novels.

I was rarely interrupted, for the report had spread that I wished to be alone while at work; yet even the first year I did not lack acquaintances.

Even during our first stay at Wildbad, which, with the Hirsau interruption, lasted more than three months, my mother had formed an intimate friendship with Frau von Burckhardt, in which I too was included. The lady possessed rare tact in harmonizing the very diverse elements which her husband, the physician in charge, brought to her. Every one felt at ease in her house and found congenial society there. So it happened that for a long time the Villa Burckhardt was the rendezvous of the most eminent persons who sought the healing influence of the Wildbad spring. Next to this, it was the Burckhardts who constantly drew us back to the Enz.

Were I to number the persons whom I met here and whose acquaintanceship I consider a benefit, the list would be a long one. Some I shall mention later. The first years we saw most frequently the song-writer Silcher, from Tubingen, Justus von Liebig, the Munich zoologist von Siebold, the Belgian artist Louis Gallait, the author Moritz Hartmann, Gervinus, and, lastly, the wife of the Stuttgart publisher Eduard Hallberger, and the never-to-be-forgotten Frau Puricelli and her daughter Jenny.

Silcher, an unusually attractive old man, joined us frequently. No other composer's songs found their way so surely to the hearts of the people. Many, as "I know not what it means," "I must go hence to-morrow," are supposed to be folk-songs. It was a real pleasure to hear him sing them in our little circle in his weak old voice. He was then seventy, but his freshness and vivacity made him appear younger. The chivalrous courtesy he showed to all ladies was wonderfully winning.

Justus Liebig's manners were no less attractive, but in him genuine amiability was united to the elegance of the man of the world who had long been one of the most distinguished scholars of his day. He must have been remarkably handsome in his youth, and though at that time past fifty, the delicate outlines of his profile were wholly unmarred.

Conversation with him was always profitable and the ease with which he made subjects farthest from his own sphere of investigation—chemistry perfectly clear was unique in its way. Unfortunately, I have been denied any deeper insight into the science which he so greatly advanced, but I still remember how thoroughly I understood him when he explained some results of agricultural chemistry. He eagerly endeavoured to dissuade the gentlemen of his acquaintance from smoking after dinner, which he had found by experiment to be injurious.

For several weeks we played whist with him every evening, for Liebig, like so many other scholars, regarded card-playing as the best recreation after severe tension of the mind. During the pauses and the supper which interrupted the game, he told us many things of former times. Once he even spoke of his youth and the days which determined his destiny. The following event seems to me especially worth recording.

When a young and wholly unknown student he had gone to Paris to bring his discovery of fulminic acid to the notice of the Academy. On one of the famous Tuesdays he had waited vainly for the introduction of his work, and at the close of the session he rose sadly to leave the hall, when an elderly academician in whose hand he thought he had seen his treatise addressed a few words to him concerning his discovery in very fluent French and invited him to dine the following Thursday. Then the stranger suddenly disappeared, and Liebig, with the painful feeling of being considered a very uncivil fellow, was obliged to let the Thursday pass without accepting the invitation so important to him. But on Saturday some one knocked at the door of his modest little room and introduced himself as Alexander von Humboldt's valet. He had been told to spare no trouble in the search, for the absence of his inexperienced countryman from the dinner which would have enabled him to make the acquaintance of the leaders of his science in Paris had not only been noticed by Humboldt, but had filled him with anxiety. When Liebig went that very day to his kind patron he was received at first with gay jests, afterwards with the kindest sympathy.

The great naturalist had read his paper and perceived the writer's future promise. He at once made him acquainted with Gay Lussac, the famous Parisian chemist, and Liebig was thus placed on the road to the lofty position which he was afterwards to occupy in all the departments of science.

The Munich zoologist von Siebold we first knew intimately years after. I shall have more to say of him later, and also of the historian Gervinus, who, behind apparently repellant arrogance, concealed the noblest human benevolence.

After the first treatment, which occupied six weeks, the physician ordered an intermission of the baths. I was to leave Wildbad to strengthen in the pure air of the Black Forest the health I had gained. On the Enz we had been in the midst of society. The new residence was to afford me an opportunity to lead a lonely, quiet life with my mother and my books, which latter, however, were only to be used in moderation.

Shortly before our departure we had taken a longer drive with our new friends Fran Puricelli and her daughter Jenny to the Hirsau cloister.

The daughter specially attracted me. She was pretty, well educated, and possessed so much independence and keenness of mind that this alone would have sufficed to render her remarkable.

Afterwards I often thought simultaneously of her and Nenny, yet they were totally unlike in character, having nothing in common save their steadfast faith and the power of looking with happy confidence beyond this life into death.

The devout Protestant had created a religion of her own, in which everything that she loved and which she found beautiful and sacred had a place.

Jenny's imagination was no less vivid, but she used it merely to behold in the form most congenial to her nature and sense of beauty what faith commanded her to accept. For Jenny the Church had already devised and arranged what Nenny's poetic soul created. The Protestant had succeeded in blending Father and Son into one in order to pray to love itself. The Catholic, besides the Holy Trinity, had made the Virgin Mother the embodiment of the feeling dearest to her girlish heart and bestowed on her the form of the person whom she loved best on earth, and regarded as the personification of everything good and beautiful. This was her older sister Fanny, who had married a few years before a cousin of the same name.

When she at last appeared I was surprised, for I had never met a woman who combined with such rare beauty and queenly dignity so much winning amiability. Nothing could be more touching than the manner in which this admired, brilliant woman of the world devoted herself to the sick girl.

This lady was present during our conversations, which often turned upon religious questions.

At first I had avoided the subject, but the young girl constantly returned to it, and I soon perceived that I must summon all my energies to hold my ground against her subtle dialectics. Once when I expressed my scruples to her sister, she answered, smiling: "Don't be uneasy on that score; Jenny's armour is strong, but she has sharp arrows in her quiver."

And so indeed it proved.

She felt so sure of her own convictions that she might investigate without peril the views of those who held a different belief, and beheld in me, as it were, the embodiment of this opportunity, so she gave me no peace until I had explained the meaning of the words pantheism, atheism, materialism, etc.

At first I was very cautious, but when I perceived that the opinions of the doubters and deniers merely inspired her with pity, I spoke more freely.

Her soul was like a polished plate of metal on which a picture is etched. This, her belief, remained uninjured. Whatever else might be reflected from the mirror-like surface soon vanished, leaving no trace.

The young girl died shortly after our separation the following year. She had grown very dear to my heart. Her beloved image appears to me most frequently as she looked in the days when she was suffering, with thick, fair hair falling in silken masses on her white dress, but amid keen physical pain the love of pleasure natural to youth still lingered. She went with me—both in wheel-chairs—to a ball at the Kursaal, and looked so pretty in an airy, white dress which her mother and sister had arranged for their darling, that I should have longed to dance with her had not this pleasure been denied me.

Hirsau had first been suggested as a resting-place, but it was doubtful whether we should find what we needed there. If not, the carriage was to convey us to beautiful, quiet Herrenalb, between Wildbad and Baden-Baden.

But we found what we sought, the most suitable house possible, whose landlady proved to have been trained as a cook in a Frankfort hotel.

The lodgings we engaged were among the most "romantic" I have ever occupied, for our landlord's house was built in the ruins of the monastery just beside the old refectory. The windows of one room looked out upon the cloisters and the Virgin's chapel, the only part of the once stately building spared by the French in 1692.

A venerable abode of intellectual life was destroyed with this monastery, founded by a Count von Calw early in the ninth century. The tower which has been preserved is one of the oldest and most interesting works of Romanesque architecture in Germany.

A quieter spot cannot be imagined, for I was the first who sought recreation here. Surrounded by memories of olden days, and absolutely undisturbed, I could create admirably. But one cannot remain permanently secluded from mankind.

First came the Herr Kameralverwalter, whose stately residence stood near the monastery, and in his wife's name invited us to use their pretty garden.

This gentleman's title threw his name so far into the shade that I had known the pleasant couple five weeks before I found it was Belfinger.

We also made the acquaintance of our host, Herr Meyer. Strange and varied were the paths along which Fate had led this man. As a rich bachelor he had welcomed guests to his ever-open house with salvos of artillery, and hence was still called Cannon Meyer, though, after having squandered his patrimony, he remained absent from his home for many years. His career in America was one of perpetual vicissitudes and full of adventures. More than once he barely escaped death. At last, conquered by homesickness, he returned to the Black Forest, and with a good, industrious wife.

His house in the monastery suited his longing for rest; he obtained a position in the morocco factory in the valley below, which afforded him a support, and his daughters provided for his physical comfort.

The big, broad-shouldered man with the huge mustache and deep, bass voice looked like some grey-haired knight whose giant arm could have dealt that Swabian stroke which cleft the foe from skull to saddle, and yet at that time he was occupied from morning until night in the delicate work splitting the calf skin from whose thin surfaces, when divided into two portions, fine morocco is made.

We also met the family of Herr Zahn, in whose factory this leather was manufactured; and when in the East I saw red, yellow, and green slippers on the feet of so many Moslems, I could not help thinking of the shady Black Forest.

Sometimes we drove to the little neighbouring town of Calw, where we were most kindly received. The mornings were uninterrupted, and my work was very successful. Afternoon sometimes brought visitors from Wildbad, among whom was the artist Gallait, who with his wife and two young daughters had come to use the water of the springs. His paintings, "Egmont in Prison," "The Beheaded Counts Egmont and Horn," and many others, had aroused the utmost admiration. Praise and honours of all kinds had consequently been lavished upon him. This had brought him to the Spree, and he had often been a welcome guest in our home.

Like Menzel, Cornelius, Alma Tadema, and Meissonier, he was small in stature, but the features of his well-formed face were anything but insignificant. His whole person was distinguished by something I might term "neatness." Without any touch of dudishness he gave the impression of having "just stepped out of a bandbox." From the white cravat which he always wore, to the little red ribbon of the order in his buttonhole, everything about him was faultless.

Madame Gallait, a Parisian by birth, was the very embodiment of the French woman in the most charming sense of the word, and the bond which united her to her husband seemed enduring and as if woven by the cheeriest gods of love. Unfortunately, it did not last.

After leaving Hirsau, we again met the Gallaits in Wildbad and spent some delightful days with them. The Von Burckhardts, Fran Henrietta Hallberger, the wife of the Stuttgart publisher, the Puricellis, ourselves, and later the author Moritz Hartmann, were the only persons with whom they associated. We always met every afternoon at a certain place in the grounds, where we talked or some one read aloud. On these occasions, at Gallait's suggestion, everybody who was so disposed sketched. My portrait, which he drew for my mother at that time in black and red pencils, is now in my wife's possession. I also took my sketch-book, for he had seen the school volume I had filled with arabesques just before leaving Keilhau, and I still remember the 'merveilleux and incroyable, inoui, and insense' which he lavished on the certainly extravagant creatures of my love-sick imagination.

During these exercises in drawing he related many incidents of his own life, and never was he more interesting than while describing his first success.

He was the son of a poor widow in the little Belgian town of Tournay. While a school-boy he greatly enjoyed drawing, and an able teacher perceived his talent.

Once he saw in the newspaper an Antwerp competition for a prize. A certain subject—if I am not mistaken, Moses drawing water from the rock in the wilderness—was to be executed with pencil or charcoal. He went to work also, though with his defective training he had not the least hope of success. When he sent off the finished drawing he avoided taking his mother into his confidence in order to protect her from disappointment.

On the day the prize was to be awarded the wish to see the work of the successful competitor drew him to Antwerp, and what was his surprise, on entering the hall, to hear his own name proclaimed as the victor's!

His mother supported herself and him by a little business in soap. To increase her delight he had changed the gold paid to him into shining five franc pieces. His pockets almost burst under the weight, but there was no end to the rejoicing when he flung one handful of silver coins after another on the little counter and told how he had obtained them.

No one who heard him relate this story could help liking him.

Another distinguished visitor at Hirsau was Prince Puckler Muskau. He had heard that his young Kottbus acquaintance had begun to devote himself to Egyptology. This interested the old man, who, as a special favourite of Mohammed Ali, had spent delightful days on the Nile and made all sorts of plans for Egypt. Besides, he was personally acquainted with the great founders of my science, Thomas Young and Francois Champollion, and had obtained an insight into deciphering the hieroglyphics. He knew all the results of the investigations, and expressed an opinion concerning them. Without having entered deeply into details he often hit the nail on the head. I doubt whether he had ever held in his hand a book on these subjects, but he had listened to the answers given by others to his skilful questions with the same keen attention that he bestowed on mine, and the gift of comprehension peculiar to him enabled him to rapidly shape what he heard into a distinctly outlined picture. Therefore he must have seemed to laymen a very compendium of science, yet he never used this faculty to dazzle others or give himself the appearance of erudition.

"Man cannot be God," he wrote—I am quoting from a letter received the day after his visit—"yet 'to be like unto God' need not remain a mere theological phrase to the aspirant. Omniscience is certainly one of the noblest attributes of the Most High, and the nearer man approaches it the more surely he gains at least the shadow of a quality to which he cannot aspire."

Finally he discussed his gardening work in the park at Branitz, and I regret having noted only the main outlines of what he said, for it was as interesting as it was admirable. I can only cite the following sentence from a letter addressed to Blasewitz: "What was I to do? A prince without a country, like myself, wishes at least to be ruler in one domain, and that I am, as creator of a park. The subjects over whom I reign obey me better than the Russians, who still retain a trace of free will, submit to their Czar. My trees and bushes obey only me and the eternal laws implanted in their nature, and which I know. Should they swerve from them even a finger's breadth they would no longer be themselves. It is pleasant to reign over such subjects, and I would rather be a despot over vegetable organisms than a constitutional king and executor of the will of the 'images of God,' as men call the sovereign people."

He talked most delightfully of the Viceroy of Egypt, Mohammed Ali, and described the plan which he had laid before this brilliant ruler of arranging a park around the temple on the island of Philae, and creating on the eastern bank of the hill beneath shady trees, opposite to the beautiful island of Isis, a sanitarium especially for consumptives; and whoever has seen this lovely spot will feel tempted to predict great prosperity for such an enterprise. My mother had heard the prince indulge in paradoxical assertions in gay society, and the earnestness which he now showed led her to remark that she had never seen two natures so radically unlike united in one individual. Had she been able to follow his career in life she would have recovered a third, fourth, and fifth.

These visits brought life and change into our quiet existence, and when four weeks later my brother Ludo joined us he was delighted with the improvement in my appearance, and I myself felt the benefit which my paralyzed muscles had received from the baths and the seclusion.

The second season at Wildbad, thanks to the increased intimacy with the friends whose acquaintance we had made there, was even more enjoyable than the first.

Frau Hallberger was a very beautiful young woman. Her husband, who was to become my dearest friend, was detained in Stuttgart by business. She was unfortunately obliged to use the waters of the springs medicinally, and many an hour was clouded by mental and physical discomfort.

Yet the vivacity of her intellect, her rare familiarity with all the newest literature, and her unusually keen appreciation of everything which was beautiful in nature stimulated and charmed us. I have never seen any one seek flowers in the field and forest so eagerly, and she made them into beautiful bouquets, which Louis Gallait called "bewitching flower madrigals."

Moritz Hartmann had not fully recovered from the severe illness which nearly caused his death while he was a reporter in the Crimean War. His father-in-law, Herr Rodiger, accompanied him and watched him with the most touching solicitude. My mother soon became sincerely attached to the author, who possessed every quality to win a woman's heart. He had been considered the handsomest member of the Frankfort Parliament, and no one could have helped gazing with pleasure at the faultless symmetry of his features. He also possessed an unusually musical voice. Gallait said that he first thought German a language pleasing to the ear when he heard it from Hartmann's lips.

These qualities soon won the heart of Frau Puricelli, who had at first been very averse to making his acquaintance. The devout, conservative lady had heard enough of his religious and political views to consider him detestable. But after Hartmann had talked and read aloud to her and her daughter in his charming way, she said to me, "What vexes me is that in my old age I can't help liking such a red Democrat."

During that summer was formed the bond of friendship which, to his life's premature end, united me to Moritz Hartmann, and led to a correspondence which afforded me the greater pleasure the more certain I became that he understood me. We met again in Wildbad the second and third summers, and with what pleasure I remember our conversations in the stillness of the shady woods! But we also shared a noisy amusement, that of pistol practice, to which we daily devoted an hour. I was obliged to fire from a wheel-chair, yet, like Hartmann, I could boast of many a good shot; but the skill of Herr Rodiger, the author's father-in-law, was really wonderful. Though his hand trembled constantly from an attack of palsy, I don't know now how many times he pierced the centre of the ace of hearts.

It was Hartmann, too, who constantly urged me to write. With all due regard for science, he said he could not admit its right to prison poesy when the latter showed so strong an impulse towards expression. I secretly admitted the truth of his remark, but whenever I yielded to the impulse to write I felt as if I were being disloyal to the mistress to whom I had devoted all my physical and mental powers.

The conflict which for a long time stirred my whole soul began. I could say much more of the first years I spent at Wildbad, but up to the fifth season they bore too much resemblance to one another to be described in detail.

A more brilliant summer than that of 1860 the quiet valley of the Enz will hardly witness again, for during that season the invalid widow of the Czar Nicholas of Russia came to the springs with a numerous suite, and her presence attracted many other crowned heads—the King of Prussia, afterwards the Emperor William I, her royal brother; her beautiful daughter, Queen Olga of Wurtemberg, who, when she walked through the grounds with her greyhound, called to mind the haughty Artemis; the Queen of Bavaria—But I will not enumerate all the royal personages who visited the Czarina, and whose presence gave the little town in the Black Forest an atmosphere of life and brilliancy. Not a day passed without affording some special feast for the eyes.

The Czarina admired beauty, and therefore among her attendants were many, ladies who possessed unusual attractions. When they were seated in a group on the steps of the hotel the picture was one never to be forgotten. A still more striking spectacle was afforded by a voyage made on the Enz by the ladies of the Czarina's court, attired in airy summer dresses and adorned with a lavish abundance of flowers. From the shore gentlemen flung them blossoms as they were borne swiftly down the mountain stream. I, too, had obtained some roses, intended especially for Princess Marie von Leuchtenberg, of whom the Czarina's physician, Dr. Karel, whose acquaintance we made at the Burckhardts, had told so many charming anecdotes that we could not help admiring her.

We also met a very beautiful Countess Keller, one of the Czarina's attendants, and I can still see distinctly the brilliant scene of her departure.

Wildbad was not then connected with the rest of the world by the railroad. The countess sat in an open victoria amid the countless gifts of flowers which had been lavished upon her as farewell presents. Count Wilhorsky, in the name of the Czarina, offered an exquisitely beautiful bouquet. As she received it, she exclaimed, "Think of me at nine o'clock," and the latter, with his hand on his heart, answered with a low bow, "Why, Countess, we shall think of you all day long."

At the same instant the postillion raised his long whip, the four bays started, a group of ladies and gentlemen, headed by the master of ceremonies, waved their handkerchiefs, and it seemed as if Flora herself was setting forth to bless the earth with flowers.

For a long time I imagined that during the first summer spent there I lived only for my health, my scientific studies, and from 1861 my novel An Egyptian Princess, to which I devoted several hours each day; but how much I learned from intercourse with so great a variety of persons, among whom were some whom a modest scholar is rarely permitted to know, I first realized afterwards. I allude here merely to the leaders of the aristocracy of the second empire, whose acquaintance I made through the son of my distinguished Parisian instructor, Vicomte de Rouge.

CHAPTER XXVI.
CONTINUANCE OF CONVALESCENCE AND THE FIRST NOVEL.

The remainder of the summer I spent half with my mother, half with my aunt, and pursued the same course during the subsequent years, until from 1862 I remained longer in Berlin, engaged in study, and began my scientific journeys.

There were few important events either in the family circle or in politics, except the accession to the throne of King William of Prussia and the Franco-Austrian war of 1859. In Berlin the "new era" awakened many fair and justifiable hopes; a fresher current stirred the dull, placid waters of political life.

The battles of Magenta and Solferino (June 4 and 24, 1859) had caused great excitement in the household of my aunt, who loved me as if I were her own son, and whose husband was also warmly attached to me. They felt the utmost displeasure in regard to the course of Prussia, and it was hard for me to approve of it, since Austria seemed a part of Germany, and I was very fond of my uncle's three nearest relatives, who were all in the Austrian service.

The future was to show the disadvantage of listening to the voice of the heart in political affairs. Should we have a German empire, and would there be a united Italy, if Austria in alliance with Prussia had fought in 1859 at Solferino and Magenta and conquered the French?

At Hosterwitz I became more intimately acquainted with the lyric poet, Julius Hammer. The Kammergerichtrath-Gottheiner, a highly educated man, lived there with his daughter Marie, whose exquisite singing at the villa of her hospitable sister-in-law so charmed my heart. Through them I met many distinguished men-President von Kirchmann, the architect Nikolai, the author of Psyche, Privy Councillor Carus, the writer Charles Duboc (Waldmuller) with his beautiful gifted wife, and many others.

Many a Berlin acquaintance, too, I met again at Hosterwitz, among them the preacher Sydow and Lothar Bucher.

To the friendship of this remarkable man, whom I knew just at the time he was associated with Bismarck, I owe many hours of enjoyment. Many will find it hardly compatible with the reserved, quiet manner of the astute, cool politician, that during a slight illness of my mother he read Fritz Reuter's novels aloud to her—he spoke Plattdeutsch admirably—as dutifully as a son.

So there was no lack of entertainment during leisure hours, but the lion's share of my time was devoted to work.

The same state of affairs existed during my stay with my aunt, who occupied a summer residence on the estate of Privy-Councillor von Adelsson, which was divided into building lots long ago, but at that time was the scene of the gayest social life in both residences.

The owner and his wife were on the most intimate terms with my relatives, and their daughter Lina seemed to me the fairest of all the flowers in the Adelsson garden. If ever a girl could be compared to a violet it was she. I knew her from childhood to maidenhood, and rejoiced when I saw her wed in young Count Uexkyll-Guldenbrand a life companion worthy of her.

There were many other charming girls, too, and my aunt, besides old friends, entertained the leaders of literary life in Dresden.

Gutzkow surpassed them all in acuteness and subtlety of intellect, but the bluntness of his manner repelled me.

On the other hand, I sincerely enjoyed the thoughtful eloquence of Berthold Auerbach, who understood how to invest with poetic charm not only great and noble subjects, but trivial ones gathered from the dust. If I am permitted to record the memories of my later life, I shall have more to say of him. It was he who induced me to give to my first romance, which I had intended to call Nitetis, the title An Egyptian Princess.

The stars of the admirable Dresden stage also found their way to my aunt's.

One day I was permitted to listen to the singing of Emmy La Gruas, and the next to the peerless Schroder-Devrient. Every conversation with the cultured physician Geheimerath von Ammon was instructive and fascinating; while Rudolf von Reibisch, the most intimate friend of the family, whose great talents would have rendered him capable of really grand achievements in various departments of art, examined our skulls as a phrenologist or read aloud his last drama. Here, too, I met Major Serre, the bold projector of the great lottery whose brilliant success called into being and insured the prosperity of the Schiller Institute, the source of so much good.

This simple-hearted yet energetic man taught me how genuine enthusiasm and the devotion of a whole personality to a cause can win victory under the most difficult circumstances. True, his clever wife shared her husband's enthusiasm, and both understood how to attract the right advisers. I afterwards met at their beautiful estate, Maxen, among many distinguished people, the Danish author Andersen, a man of insignificant personal appearance, but one who, if he considered it worth while and was interested in the subject, could carry his listeners resistlessly with him. Then his talk sparkled with clever, vivid, striking, peculiar metaphors, and when one brilliant description of remarkable experiences and scenes followed another he swiftly won the hearts of the women who had overlooked him, and it seemed to the men as if some fiend were aiding him.

During the first years of my convalescence I could enjoy nothing save what came or was brought to me. But the cheerful patience with which I appeared to bear my sufferings, perhaps also the gratitude and eagerness with which I received everything, attracted most of the men and women for whom I really cared.

If there was an entertaining conversation, arrangements were always made that I should enjoy it, at least as a listener. The affection of these kind people never wearied in lightening the burden which had been laid upon me. So, during this whole sad period I was rarely utterly wretched, often joyous and happy, though sometimes the victim to the keenest spiritual anguish.

During the hours of rest which must follow labour, and when tortured at night by the various painful feelings and conditions connected even with convalescence from disease, my restrictions rose before me as a specially heavy misfortune. My whole being rebelled against my sufferings, and—why should I conceal it?—burning tears drenched my pillows after many a happy day. At the time I was obliged to part from Nenny this often happened. Goethe's "He who never mournful nights" I learned to understand in the years when the beaker of life foams most impetuously for others. But I had learned from my mother to bear my sorest griefs alone, and my natural cheerfulness aided me to win the victory in the strife against the powers of melancholy. I found it most easy to master every painful emotion by recalling the many things for which I had cause to be grateful, and sometimes an hour of the fiercest struggle and deepest grief closed with the conviction that I was more blessed than many thousands of my fellow-mortals, and still a "favourite of Fortune." The same feeling steeled my patience and helped to keep hope green and sustain my pleasure in existence when, long after, a return of the same disease, accompanied with severe suffering, which I had been spared in youth, snatched me from earnest, beloved, and, I may assume, successful labour.

The younger generation may be told once more how effective a consolation man possesses—no matter what troubles may oppress him—in gratitude. The search for everything which might be worthy of thankfulness undoubtedly leads to that connection with God which is religion.

When I went to Berlin in winter, harder work, many friends, and especially my Polish fellow-student, Mieczyslaw helped me bear my burden patiently.

He was well, free, highly gifted, keenly interested in science, and made rapid progress. Though secure from all external cares, a worm was gnawing at his heart which gave him no rest night or day—the misery of his native land and his family, and the passionate longing to avenge it on the oppressor of the nation. His father had sacrificed the larger portion of his great fortune to the cause of Poland, and, succumbing to the most cruel persecutions, urged his sons, in their turn, to sacrifice everything for their native land. They were ready except one brother, who wielded his sword in the service of the oppressor, and thus became to the others a dreaded and despised enemy.

Mieczyslaw remained in Berlin raging against himself because, an intellectual epicurean, he was enjoying Oriental studies instead of following in the footsteps of his father, his brothers, and most of his relatives at home.

My ideas of the heroes of Polish liberty had been formed from Heinrich Heine's Noble Pole, and I met my companion with a certain feeling of distrust. Far from pressing upon me the thoughts which moved him so deeply, it was long ere he permitted the first glimpse into his soul. But when the ice was once broken, the flood of emotion poured forth with elementary power, and his sincerity was sealed by his blood. He fell armed on the soil of his home at the time when I was most gratefully rejoicing in the signs of returning health—the year 1863. I was his only friend in Berlin, but I was warmly attached to him, and shall remember him to my life's end.

The last winter of imprisonment also saw me industriously at work. I had already, with Mieczyslaw, devoted myself eagerly to the history of the ancient East, and Lepsius especially approved these studies. The list of the kings which I compiled at that time, from the most remote sources to the Sassanida, won the commendation of A. von Gutschmid, the most able investigator in this department. These researches led me also to Persia and the other Asiatic countries. Egypt, of course, remained the principal province of my work. The study of the kings from the twenty-sixth dynasty—that is, the one with which the independence of the Pharaohs ended and the rule of the Persians under Cambyses began in the valley of the Nile—occupied me a long time. I used the material thus acquired afterward for my habilitation essay, but the impulse natural to me of imparting my intellectual gains to others had induced me to utilize it in a special way. The material I had collected appeared in my judgment exactly suited for a history of the time that Egypt fell into the power of Persia. Jacob Burckhardt's Constantine the Great was to serve for my model. I intended to lay most stress upon the state of civilization, the intellectual and religious life, art, and science in Egypt, Greece, Persia, Phoenicia, etc., and after most carefully planning the arrangement I began to write with the utmost zeal.

> [I still have the unfinished manuscript; but the farther I advanced
>
> the stronger became the conviction, now refuted by Eduard Meyer,
>
> that it would not yet be possible to write a final history of that
>
> period which would stand the test of criticism.]

While thus engaged, the land of the Pharaohs, the Persian court, Greece in the time of the Pisistratidae and Polycrates grew more and more distinct before my mental vision. Herodotus's narrative of the false princess sent by Pharaoh Amasis to Cambyses as a wife, and who became the innocent cause of the war through which the kingdom of the Pharaohs lost its independence, would not bear criticism, but it was certainly usable material for a dramatic or epic poem. And this material gave me no peace.

Yes, something might certainly be done with it. I soon mastered it completely, but gradually the relation changed and it mastered me, gave me no rest, and forced me to try upon it the poetic power so long condemned to rest.

When I set to work I was not permitted to leave the house in the evening. Was it disloyal to science if I dedicated to poesy the hours which others called leisure time? The question was put to the inner judge in such a way that he could not fail to say "No." I also tried successfully to convince myself that I merely essayed to write this tale to make the material I had gathered "live," and bring the persons and conditions of the period whose history I wished to write as near to me as if I were conversing with them and dwelling in their midst. How often I repeated to myself this well-founded apology, but in truth every instinct of my nature impelled me to write, and at this very time Moritz Hartmann was also urging me in his letters, while Mieczyslaw and others, even my mother, encouraged me.

I began because I could not help it, and probably scarcely any work ever stood more clearly arranged, down to the smallest detail, in its creator's imagination, than the Egyptian Princess in mine when I took up my pen. Only the first volume originally contained much more Egyptian material, and the third I lengthened beyond my primary intention. Many notes of that time I was unwilling to leave unused and, though the details are not uninteresting, their abundance certainly impairs the effect of the whole.

As for the characters, most of them were familiar.

How many of my mother's traits the beautiful, dignified Rhodopis possessed! King Amasis was Frederick William IV, the Greek Phanes resembled President Seiffart. Nitetis, too, I knew. I had often jested with Atossa, and Sappho was a combination of my charming Frankfort cousin Betsy, with whom I spent such delightful days in Rippoldsau, and lovely Lina von Adelsson. Like the characters in the works of the greatest of writers—I mean Goethe—not one of mine was wholly invented, but neither was any an accurate portrait of the model.

I by no means concealed from myself the difficulties with which I had to contend or the doubts the critics would express, but this troubled me very little. I was writing the book only for myself and my mother, who liked to hear every chapter read as it was finished. I often thought that this novel might perhaps share the fate of my Poem of the World, and find its way into the fire.

No matter. The greatest success could afford me no higher pleasure than the creative labour. Those were happy evenings when, wholly lifted out of myself, I lived in a totally different world, and, like a god, directed the destinies of the persons who were my creatures. The love scenes between Bartja and Sappho I did not invent; they came to me. When, with brow damp with perspiration, I committed the first one to paper in a single evening, I found the next morning, to my surprise, that only a few touches were needed to convert it into a poem in iambics.

This was scarcely permissible in a novel. But the scene pleased my mother, and when I again brought the lovers together in the warm stillness of the Egyptian night, and perceived that the flood of iambics was once more sweeping me along, I gave free course to the creative spirit and the pen, and the next morning the result was the same.

I then took Julius Hammer into my confidence, and he thought that I had given expression to the overflowing emotion of two loving young hearts in a very felicitous and charming way.

While my friends were enjoying themselves in ball-rooms or exciting society, Fate still condemned me to careful seclusion in my mother's house. But when I was devoting myself to the creation of my Nitetis, I envied no man, scarcely even a god.

So this novel approached completion. It had not deprived me of an hour of actual working time, yet the doubt whether I had done right to venture on this side flight into fairer and better lands during my journey through the department of serious study was rarely silent.

At the beginning of the third volume I ventured to move more freely.

Yet when I went to Lepsius, the most earnest of my teachers, to show him the finished manuscript, I felt very anxious. I had not said even a word in allusion to what I was doing in the evening hours, and the three volumes of my large manuscript were received by him in a way that warranted the worst fears. He even asked how I, whom he had believed to be a serious worker, had been tempted into such "side issues."

This was easy to explain, and when he had heard me to the end he said: "I might have thought of that. You sometimes need a cup of Lethe water. But now let such things alone, and don't compromise your reputation as a scientist by such extravagances."

Yet he kept the manuscript and promised to look at the curiosity.

He did more. He read it through to the last letter, and when, a fortnight later; he asked me at his house to remain after the others had left, he looked pleased, and confessed that he had found something entirely different from what he expected. The book was a scholarly work, and also a fascinating romance.

Then he expressed some doubts concerning the space I had devoted to the Egyptians in my first arrangement. Their nature was too reserved and typical to hold the interest of the unscientific reader. According to his view, I should do well to limit to Egyptian soil what I had gained by investigation, and to make Grecian life, which was familiar to us moderns as the foundation of our aesthetic perceptions, more prominent. The advice was good, and, keeping it in view, I began to subject the whole romance to a thorough revision.

Before going to Wildbad in the summer of 1863 I had a serious conversation with my teacher and friend. Hitherto, he said, he had avoided any discussion of my future; but now that I was so decidedly convalescing, he must tell me that even the most industrious work as a "private scholar," as people termed it, would not satisfy me. I was fitted for an academic career, and he advised me to keep it in view. As I had already thought of this myself, I eagerly assented, and my mother was delighted with my resolution.

How we met in Wildbad my never-to-be-forgotten friend the Stuttgart publisher, Eduard von Hallberger; how he laid hands upon my Egyptian Princess; and how the fate of this book and its author led through joy and sorrow, pleasure and pain, I hope, ere my last hour strikes, to communicate to my family and the friends my life and writings have gained.

When I left Berlin, so far recovered that I could again move freely, I was a mature man. The period of development lay behind me. Though the education of an aspiring man ends only with his last breath, the commencement of my labours as a teacher outwardly closed mine, and an important goal in life lay before me. A cruel period of probation, rich in suffering and deprivations, had made the once careless youth familiar with the serious side of existence, and taught him to control himself.

After once recognizing that progress in the department of investigation in which I intended to guide others demanded the devotion of all my powers, I succeeded in silencing the ceaseless longing for fresh creations of romance. The completion of a second long novel would have imperilled the unity with myself which I was striving to attain, and which had been represented to me by the noblest of my instructors as my highest goal in life. So I remained steadfast, although the great success of my first work rendered it very difficult. Temptations of every kind, even in the form of brilliant offers from the most prominent German publishers, assailed me, but I resisted, until at the end of half a lifetime I could venture to say that I was approaching my goal, and that it was now time to grant the muse what I had so long denied. Thus, that portion of my nature which was probably originally the stronger was permitted to have its life. During long days of suffering romance was again a kind and powerful comforter.

Severe suffering had not succeeded in stifling the cheerful spirit of the boy and the youth; it did not desert me in manhood. When the sky of my life was darkened by the blackest clouds it appeared amid the gloom like a radiant star announcing brighter days; and if I were to name the powers by whose aid I have again and again dispelled even the heaviest clouds which threatened to overshadow my happiness in existence, they must be called gratitude, earnest work, and the motto of blind old Langethal, "Love united with the strife for truth."

THE END.